SHADOWS OF DISSENT

Unveiling Contentious Events that Shaped the Formative Years of the Muslim Community

WRITTEN BY
Āyatullāh Nāṣir Makārim Shīrāzī

TRANSLATED BY
Saleem Bhimji and a Group of Translators

EDITED BY
Arifa Hudda

ISBN: 978-1-927930-61-8
Written by Āyatullāh Nāṣir Makārim Shīrāzī
Translated by Saleem Bhimji and a Group of Translators
Edited by Arifa Hudda

Cover Design and Layout by Saleem Bhimji

Published by Islamic Publishing House

www.iph.ca · iph@iph.ca

DEDICATION

بسم الله الرحمن الرحيم

In the Name of Allah,
the All-Compassionate,
the All-Merciful

The publication of this work has been possible due to the support of generous donors, and has been kindly donated for the *Isaale Thawaab* (Eternal Reward) of the *Marhumeen* of the Karim, Khimji, Manji Walli, Namdar, Nanji, Pirbhai, Premji, and Rattansi Families; as well as other donors who wished to remain anonymous, and for the *Shuhadā'* (Martyrs) and all *Marhumeen* (Deceased Ones).

Please recite Sūrah al-Fātiḥa once, followed by Sūrah al-Ikhlāṣ three times for their reward.

DEDICATIONS CONTINUED ON NEXT PAGE

Please also keep the following *Marhumeen* in your intention when reciting the Sūrah al-Fātiḥa and Sūrah al-Ikhlāṣ:

Marhuma Afifa Tarbhai
Marhuma Raziabai Pirbhai
Marhum Mohammad Rasul
Marhuma Alina Tarbhai
Marhuma Fatmabai Sharif Jiwa
Marhuma Bai Bai Amir

The *Marhumeen* in the Families of:

Anwar
Asaria
Bhimji
Datoo
Frahmand
Haji Ismail
Hudda
Jaffer Dhanji
Jamal
Jessa
Lakhani
Lalji Rawji
Manji-Daya
Rahim
Sajan
Tarbhai

All the *Marhumeen* in the Families of the Donors

Transliteration Table

The method of transliteration of Islamic terminology from the ʿArabic language has been carried out according to the standard transliteration table mentioned below.

ء	ʾ	س	s	م	m
ا	a	ش	sh	ن	n
ب	b	ص	ṣ	و	w
ت	t	ض	ḍ	ه	h
ث	th	ط	ṭ	ي	y
ج	j	ظ	ḍ		
ح	ḥ	ع	ʿ		
خ	kh	غ	gh		
د	d	ف	f		
ذ	dh	ق	q		
ر	r	ك	k		
ز	z	ل	l		

Short Vowels		Long Vowels	
ـَ	a	ا	ā
ـِ	i	ي	ī
ـُ	u	و	ū

Honourific Symbols

The following icons are used extensively in this book when referencing notable personalities.

ﷻ	*ʿAzza wa Jalla* *Mighty and Majestic* Used for Allah ﷻ
ﷺ	*Ṣallallahu ʿalayhi wa ālihi wa sallam* *May Allah bless him and his family and grant them peace* Used for Prophet Muḥammad ﷺ
عليه السلام	*ʿAlayhis Salām* *Peace be upon him* (singular) Used for a Prophet or Divinely-Appointed Imam
عليها السلام	*ʿAlayhas Salām* *Peace be upon her* (singular) Used for one noble woman
عليهما السلام	*ʿAlayhimas Salām* *Peace be upon them* (dual) Used for two male Prophets or Divinely-Appointed Imams or respected female personalities
عليهم السلام	*ʿAlayhimus Salām* *Peace be upon them* (plural) Used for three or more Prophets or Divinely-Appointed Imams or respected female personalities
عجل الله تعالى فرجه الشريف	*ʿAjjallāhu Taʿalā Farajahul Sharīf* *May Allah, the Exalted, hasten his noble relief (reappearance)* Used specifically for Imam al-Mahdī عجل الله تعالى فرجه الشريف

Shadows of Dissent is a translation of six books that cover the following historical topics:

The Event of the Pen and Paper

The Legitimacy of the Event at Saqīfah

Fire in the House of Revelation

An Analysis of the Life of ʿUmar ibn al-Khaṭṭāb

The Marriage of Umm Kulthūm binte ʿAlī

The Six-Person Shūrā Devised to Select a Caliph

Table of Contents

Publisher's Introduction i
Introduction to this Work xi

Chapter One: The Event of the Pen and Paper 13

Isnād of the Ḥadīth of "The Pen and Paper" 15
Examples of Opposition to the Prophet ﷺ 23
Disputes in the Presence of the Prophet ﷺ 26
Reaction of Prophet Muḥammad ﷺ 27
Cause of Sadness of Ibn ʿAbbās 29
Were the Actions of the Companions Justifiable? 30
A More Important Issue 33
Bibliography 35

Chapter Two: The Legitimacy of the Event at Saqīfah 37

Introduction 39
How did the Saqīfah Banū Sāʿida Episode Unfold? 40
The First Report 46
Second Report: ʿUmar's Recollection of Saqīfah 53
Other Notable Points 56
Reactions 58
Allegiance 59
Position of Some Companions 61
The Position of the Ahlul Bayt ᵃ 64
Attack, Assault, and Threats of Arson 71
The Role of ʿUmar in Solidifying the Caliphate of Abū Bakr 81
Conclusion 84
Bibliography 89

Chapter Three: Fire in the House of Revelation 93

Myth Or Reality: An Introduction 95
Fāṭima al-Zahrāʾ ᵃ in the Words of the Prophet ﷺ 95
Respecting the House of Fāṭima al-Zahrāʾ ᵃ 97
Desecration of the House of Fāṭima ᵃ 98
Opinion of Ibn Abī Shaybah 99
Opinion of Al-Balādhurī 100

Opinion of Ibn Qutaybah 100
Opinion of Ṭabarī 102
Opinion of Ibn ʿAbd Rabbih 103
Opinion of Abū ʿUbayd 104
Opinion of Ṭabarānī 105
Opinion of Ibn ʿAbd Rabbih 106
Opinion of Naẓẓām 106
Opinion of Mubarrad 107
Opinion of Maṣʿūdī 107
Opinion of Dhahabī 108
Opinion of ʿAbdul Fattāḥ ʿAbdul Maqṣūd 108
Conclusion 109

Chapter Four: An Analysis of the Life of ʿUmar ibn al-Khaṭṭāb ..111

An Analysis of the Life of ʿUmar ibn al-Khaṭṭāb 113
The Character of the Second Caliph 115
During the Lifetime of Prophet Muḥammad ﷺ 116
Assaulting his Female Muslim Servant 116
Physically Attacking his Own Sister 117
Attacking Abū Hurayrah and Directly Objecting to the Prophet ﷺ118
Direct Onslaught Against the Messenger of Allah ﷺ 121
Unduly Accusations Against the Prophet ﷺ 124
The Event at Ṣaqīfah 126
Harsh Attitude During His Caliphate 130
Brutal Whippings 133
Humiliating Children by Striking Them 134
Striking Mourning Women 135
Out of Fear, a Woman 138
A Woman Miscarries her Child 139
Afraid to Speak One's Mind 140
Imprisoning Companions 145
The Authority of Allah ﷻ on Earth 145
Taking Pleasure in Always Looking Stern 146
Waited for One Year... 146
An Attack against Abū Maṭar 147
Attack with the Whip - Even at Prayer Time 148

Forced Marriages 149
Splitting Open the Head of ʿUthmān ibn Ḥunayf 150
Get Away from Me, Ibn ʿAbbās! 151
You Speak to the Caliph! 153
Do Not be the Reason for the Persecution 155
Anger with his Family 156
Constant Harsh Nature 157
An Outcry 157
Physically Assaulting his Wife 159
Marriage on the Condition of No Abuse 160
Anger and Snapping at Others 161
Etiquette of the Noble Prophet ﷺ 162
Bibliography 165

Chapter Five: The Marriage of Umm Kulthūm binte ʿAlī 169

Introduction 171
Who is Umm Kulthūm? 173
What Scholars Say about this Marriage 175
Reflections about this Marriage 177
Ethical Questions Surrounding Some Narrations 177
Umm Kulthūm's Age at the Time of Marriage 179
Quick Tempered 179
Motives behind such a Marriage 181
Examining the Chain of Narrators 183
Threats 189
Conclusion 200
Bibliography 203

Chapter Six: The Six-Person Shūrā Devised to Elect a Caliph 209

Introduction 211
The Edict of ʿUmar ibn al-Khaṭṭāb 212
Other Points to Consider 215
The Method of Choosing a Caliph 218
Foresight of Imam ʿAlī ؑ 219
Death of ʿUmar and the Shūrā 220
Reactions and Responses 225

Imam ʿAlī's ﷺ Account of the Shūrā 228
Prioritizing the Interests of the Muslims 229
Ṭalḥa's Position 232
Analysis and Examination 233
Conclusion 250
Bibliography 253

Conclusion by the Publisher 257

The Last Word 259
The Event of the Pen and Paper 260
The Legitimacy of the Event at Ṣaqīfah 260
Fire in the House of Revelation 261
An Analysis of the Life of ʿUmar ibn al-Khaṭṭāb 261
The Marriage of Umm Kulthūm binte ʿAlī to ʿUmar 262
The Six-Person Shūrā of ʿUmar Devised to Select a Caliph 262
Final Thoughts 262

Our Other Publications 265

Other Publications Available 267
Other Translations 270
Upcoming Publications by the IPH 272
Supporting Our Projects 275

In the Name of Allah,
the All-Compassionate,
the All-Merciful.

Publisher's Introduction

What is the philosophy of history? Why study what happened in the past that seems to have no bearing or impact on our present or future? Why do some people devote their entire lives to recording and preserving events, and later publish them – as seemingly, such things have absolutely no merit?

According to the Stanford Encyclopedia of Philosophy, the philosophy of history is explained as such: "The concept of history plays a fundamental role in human thought. It invokes notions of human agency, change, the role of material circumstances in human affairs, and the putative meaning of historical events. It raises the possibility of "learning from history;" and it suggests the possibility of better understanding ourselves in the present, by understanding the forces, choices, and circumstances that brought us to our current situation. It is therefore unsurprising that philosophers have sometimes turned their attention and efforts to examine history itself and the nature of historical knowledge. These reflections can be grouped together into a body of work called "philosophy of history.""[1]

The importance of history is further elaborated upon in the article referenced, and the following foundational points are mentioned to create a conceptual map of the nature of historical knowing:

1. First, historians are interested in providing conceptualizations and factual descriptions of events and circumstances in the past.
2. Second, historians often want to answer "why" questions: "Why did this event occur? What were the conditions and forces that brought it about?"
3. Third, and related to the previous point, historians are sometimes interested in answering a "how" question: "How did this outcome happen? What were the processes through which the outcome occurred?"
4. Fourth, often historians are interested in piecing together the human meanings and intentions that underlie a given complex series of historical actions. They want to help the reader make sense of the historical events and actions in terms of the thoughts, motives, and states of mind of the participants.
5. Finally, historians face an even more basic intellectual task: that of discovering and making sense of the archival information that exists about a given event or time in the past. Historical data do not speak for themselves; archives are incomplete, ambiguous, contradictory, and confusing. A historian needs to interpret individual pieces of evidence; and he or she needs to be able to somehow fit the mass of evidence into a coherent and truthful story.

---

[1] Referenced from: plato.stanford.edu/entries/history/ – Last accessed on July 16, 2025.

In short, historians conceptualize, describe, contextualize, explain, and interpret events and circumstances of the past. In essence, they carry out three important tasks:

1. They sketch out ways of representing the complex activities and events of the past.
2. They explain and interpret significant outcomes.
3. They base their findings on evidence in the present that bears upon facts about the past.

Their accounts need to be grounded on the evidence that is available from historical records; and their explanations and interpretations require that the historian arrives at hypotheses about social causes and cultural meanings. Historians can turn to the best available theories in social and behavioural sciences to arrive at inferences on causal mechanisms and human behaviour, so that historical statements depend upon factual inquiry and theoretical reasoning. The historian's task is to shed light on the: what, why, and how of the past – based on inferences from the evidence of the present.[2]

Today, in our seemingly 'advanced age,' some Muslims argue against the relevance of history – usually regarding specific events and individuals, feeling that there is no benefit in reviewing the history of Islam as it pertains to certain individuals, and their often-destructive actions. They say that whatever happened in the past should remain in the past, and that we should not review the actions and reactions that took place not only 1,400 years ago, but even in our contemporary history of various families and their dynasties over Muslim lands.

These people argue that delving into the depths of the history of Islam will do nothing but open wounds that have taken 14 centuries to heal – and may further polarize the already weak Muslim

---

[2] Referenced from: plato.stanford.edu/entries/history/ – Last accessed on July 16, 2025.

community.

However, to disregard Islamic history – and more specifically from the time shortly before the death of Prophet Muḥammad ﷺ, immediately after his passing away, and the first few centuries thereafter – is to do a great disservice to religion and humanity. In essence, those who willfully turn a blind eye to the early history of Islam are acting with treachery against Allah ﷻ, the Quran and the legacy of Prophet Muḥammad ﷺ.

As Muslims, our dedication must be to Allah ﷻ, and the religion of Islam – even if this means that our analysis into early Islamic history may open a "can of worms" that will make us uneasy or uncomfortable.

Muslims of all sects must realize that other than the Prophets عليهم السلام that Allah ﷻ sent, and **some** of their select family members, as well as a handful of others whom Allah ﷻ has chosen to protect from blemishes, rendering them immaculate *(maʿṣūm)*, everyone else's lives, choices, and actions are open for scrutiny. If done using academic rigour, and through maintaining fairness, balance, and impartiality, then this is one of the greatest endeavours that we can engage in, and it is an act of devotion to Allah ﷻ: in fact, it is to engage in what Allah ﷻ does throughout His Book in which He peels back the layers of the lives of the righteous men and women, as well as the lives of the criminals – men and women alike – even if they be the wife of a Prophet of Allah ﷻ.

Although not a book of history per se, the Quran is vividly clear when it comes to discussing history, and as such, we see that in its 114 chapters, Allah ﷻ narrates countless stories of past generations. If history was of no use, or if we were not permitted to critically analyze historical figures, then why would Allah ﷻ dedicate so much of the Quran – a Book of guidance, self-building, and spiritual growth – to speaking about personalities like Prophet Ādam عليه السلام, and the crimes of his son, Qābīl against his own brother, Ḥābīl; Prophet

Nūḥ عليه السلام and his nemeses – his own family members such as his wife and son; Prophet Lūṭ عليه السلام and his wife who aided and abetted the perverse people of the region; Prophet Mūsā عليه السلام and the challenges he had to go through with people of his own tribe, the Banī Isrāʾīl; or Prophet Muḥammad ﷺ, and some of the people around him such as two of his wives and others who are regarded as his companions but who openly challenged him, and in some cases, were ready to physically attack him?

If analyzing and discussing these individuals was taboo and off limits, then we need to question why Allah ﷻ would reveal certain chapters of the Quran such as Sūrah al-Munāfiqūn (Chapter 63) in which He very clearly and openly criticizes "companions" of the Prophet ﷺ who were more attracted to this transient world than they were to Islam.

We must ask Allah ﷻ why He revealed clear condemnation of a group of the companions of Prophet Muḥammad ﷺ contained in Sūrah al-Jumuʿah (Chapter 62) in which they were reprimanded for leaving him 'standing alone' in the Friday prayers while they ran after the goods of this temporary world.

We must ask the question why Sūrah al-Taḥrīm (Chapter 66) was revealed in which the Prophet ﷺ was given Knowledge of the Unseen *(ʿIlm al-Ghayb)* about two of his wives who were guilty of insulting him and plotting against him, then were called out by Allah ﷻ as being women who, seemingly, did not believe or understand that the Prophet ﷺ had direct communication with Allah ﷻ and received news from the hidden realms. In fact, in this chapter, Allah ﷻ even told the Prophet ﷺ that if they, meaning ʿĀyesha binte Abū Bakr and Ḥafṣa binte ʿUmar, were to plan and plot against him, then Allah ﷻ, Angel Jibrāʾīl عليه السلام, the righteous believers, and other angels would be there to back him up and support him against these two![3] How critical must a situation become for Allah ﷻ to prepare for Jibrāʾīl ؑ and His Army of Angels to go to war against certain wives of the Prophet ﷺ!?

With this said, we need to be open-minded and free-thinking Muslims and review Islamic history and its personalities if we wish to be honest and truthful to the Quranic ethos. We need to remove any biases we have about ALL personalities in Islamic history – regardless of if they are directly or indirectly mentioned in the Quran, and regardless of their relationship to Prophet Muḥammad ﷺ. We must realize that they were mere mortals – prone to errors, lapses of judgement, and in some cases, outright contempt for Islam, Muslims, and the Noble Prophet of Islam ﷺ. Other than Prophet Muḥammad ﷺ, and those select individuals who have been kept away from all impurities – meaning the Ahlul Bayt ؑ – everyone else in Islamic history can have their lives scrutinized.

The goal of such an analysis is nothing other than to recognize who the true and sincere believers are, so that we can seek to emulate their characteristics, and distance ourselves from those who disguised themselves in the clothing of Islam while entertaining doubts about Islam and the status of Prophet Muḥammad ﷺ.

---

[3] Quran, Sūrah al-Taḥrīm (66), Verse 4:

﴿إِن تَتُوبَآ إِلَى ٱللَّهِ فَقَدْ صَغَتْ قُلُوبُكُمَا ۖ وَإِن تَظَٰهَرَا عَلَيْهِ فَإِنَّ ٱللَّهَ هُوَ مَوْلَىٰهُ وَجِبْرِيلُ وَصَٰلِحُ ٱلْمُؤْمِنِينَ ۖ وَٱلْمَلَٰٓئِكَةُ بَعْدَ ذَٰلِكَ ظَهِيرٌ ٤﴾

"If you two [wives of the Prophet – referring to ʿĀyesha binte Abū Bakr and Ḥafṣa binte ʿUmar] turn to Allah in repentance, [then that is indeed what you should do] for the hearts of both of you swerved from what is right. But if you back each other up against him [Prophet Muḥammad ﷺ], then be mindful that indeed Allah Himself is His Guardian, and [the Archangel] Jibrāʾīl, and the righteous ones among the believers, and the angels moreover, (are his) helpers."

It is in this light that we present this anthology of six unique books written by one of the senior scholars, His Eminence, Āyatullāh Nāṣir Makārim Shīrāzī.

The goal of this work is to ensure that a fair and unbiased review of the early history of Islam which has shaped the faith today and has been used, misused, and abused by "Muslims" throughout the ages, including the likes of the Taliban, ISIS, and many other groups, is carried out free from all pre-conceived notions. As Muslims, we must make every effort to better understand Islam – not only its present, but more importantly, our troubled past, and how it has shaped the current climate, and what awaits us in the future.

Such works must not be seen as attacks against the sentiments, nor against personalities revered by other Muslims. Rather, this compilation has been translated and published to honestly and sincerely foster dialogue, discussion, and greater research into certain Islamic personalities and their actions. Our goal in releasing this work is in no way to antagonize any individuals or groups within the fold of Islam.

In closing, we hope that this publication in the field of Islamic history will serve as a stepping-stone for other scholars and researchers to conduct similar reviews into the lives of other influential individuals who make up the early history of Islam. Through such works, we can better understand where we, as a faith tradition, came from, and where we are headed. We can also build bridges of understanding amongst the English-speaking Muslim community.

This collection of six books that you hold in your hands has been rendered into English by myself, as well as a group of Translators selected specifically for this work. All the translations in this anthology have been thoroughly reviewed and edited to ensure accuracy and continuity in the reading. As you will notice, some of the books in this anthology do not have a Conclusion and/or a

Bibliography – as these were not present in the original works – despite having checked multiple editions of the original series. Thus, this is why they are not included in this book.

As much as possible, we have relied on the Arabic text and English translations of all the sources from their original books – specifically those found online and have quoted them verbatim with no alterations other than paragraph formatting. Any grammatical or spelling errors HAVE NOT been corrected to ensure faithfulness to the original text.

First and foremost, I would like to thank Allah ﷻ for allowing us to translate and publish this important historical work. This is a project that has been running for close to 10 years, and without His support and guidance along the way, we would not have been able to complete it.

We would also like to appreciate the group of Translators – who requested to remain anonymous – and were gracious enough to take on the task of translating some of the six books in this series. May Allah ﷻ bless them and reward them for their efforts and grant them even more blessings in their lives.

Next, we extend our heartfelt thanks to our editor and my wife, Sr. Arifa Hudda, whose tireless dedication and expertise have been instrumental in bringing this project to fruition. For over 25 years, Sr. Arifa has been a cornerstone of the Islamic Publishing House, guiding our publications with her keen insight and unwavering commitment to excellence. Her contribution to this work, as well as all our publications has been invaluable. We ask Allah ﷻ to continue to bless her and keep her under His protection.

We would also like to thank the donors who financially contributed towards the publishing of this book, and we ask you to recite a Sūrah al-Fātiḥa for their rewards and their dearly departed loved ones *(marhumeen)*.

May Allah ﷻ accept this humble act from us and allow the beauty of Islam to shine from its ‘sometimes troublesome past’ and debatable personalities – none of whom are above reproach.

جَاءَ الْحَقُّ وَزَهَقَ الْبَاطِلُ
إِنَّ الْبَاطِلَ كَانَ زَهُوقًا

“The truth has come, and falsehood has vanished. Indeed, falsehood (by nature) is ever bound to vanish.”

Quran, Sūrah al-Isrāʾ (17), Verse 81

Saleem Bhimji
7th of Safar, 1446 AH
2nd August, 2025 CE

Martyrdom Anniversary of the second Imam, Ḥasan ibn ʿAlī al-Mujtabā (ʿa)

Kitchener, Ontario, Canada

Introduction to this Work

The history of Islam has, embedded within itself, an abundance of indications of the religion's grandeur and the truthfulness of Prophet Muḥammad ﷺ.

The religion of Islam is laden with themes that are very effective to draw those near who are far from this religion, and how great it would be if the scholars of Islam spared no effort in demonstrating these truths; among them being the conduct and kindness of Prophet Muḥammad ﷺ that contributed towards the rapid development of Islam, putting up a strong stand against the powerful and stubborn foes, and eventually giving rise to a society built on knowledge and sophistication.

Nonetheless, there are some aspects of Islamic history that religious scholars are obliged to clarify without prejudice. They must give compelling explanations when reviewing the controversial historical matters that shaped this religion, especially to the truth-seeking youth, so that they do not turn their backs to the pure Islam.

Our aim in this series of research articles[1] is to highlight some of the contentious issues in Islamic history, and to provide comprehensive and thought-provoking responses to these points of dispute within the Muslim nation.

Since the historical events reviewed in this series are inexplicably tied to one another, we have presented each one of them in chronological order. Thus, we first refer to the inexplicable Event of "The Pen and Paper." This will be a brief discussion, but in the future, if Allah ﷻ permits, we will further expand on this topic.

---

[1] The original work that this book is based on was initially published as six independent booklets which we have published as one book. (Tr.)

Chapter One

The Event of the Pen and Paper

Isnād[1] of the Ḥadīth of "The Pen and Paper"

In the last days of the life of Prophet Muḥammad ﷺ, a group of his companions went to visit him, and he said to them, as has been famously reported by Muslim historians and narrators of *Ḥadīth*: "Bring me a pen and paper so that I may write a document for you that if you follow it, you will never go astray." However, some of the companions present in that gathering objected and stopped him

---

[1] *Isnād* is an Arabic term used in the study of *Ḥadīth* – and in Shīʿa Islam, it refers to the recorded sayings and traditions of Prophet Muḥammad, his daughter Fāṭima al-Zahrāʾ ؑ, and the 12 Imams ؑ. It is the chain of narrators through which a particular *ḥadīth* has been transmitted from its source to the final compiler of a collection of *Ḥadīth* or the scholar that is narrating the *ḥadīth*.

The *isnād* is a crucial aspect of *Ḥadīth* evaluation, as it serves to establish the authenticity and reliability of a *ḥadīth* by tracing its chain of narration back to the original source. Each link in the *isnād* represents a narrator who heard the *ḥadīth* from the previous narrator and then transmitted it to the next.

The structure of an *isnād* typically follows this format: "Person A narrated to us, from Person B, from Person C, ..., from Prophet Muḥammad (or his daughter Fāṭima al-Zahrāʾ ؑ, or one of the 12 Imams ؑ)."

The *isnād* allows scholars to analyze the trustworthiness and credibility of each narrator in the chain, ensuring that the *ḥadīth* has been accurately preserved and transmitted. Factors such as the narrators' memory, piety, and reliability are considered when evaluating the strength of an *isnād*.

A strong and unbroken *isnād*, with reliable and trustworthy narrators, is an important factor in determining the authenticity and acceptance of a *ḥadīth*. Conversely, a weak or broken *isnād* may raise doubts about the reliability of a *ḥadīth* and may lead to its rejection.

The study of *isnād* is a critical component of *Ḥadīth* Sciences *(ʿUlūm al-Ḥadīth)*, as it provides the means to verify the authenticity and preservation of the teachings of Prophet Muḥammad ﷺ, his immaculate daughter, Fāṭima al-Zahrāʾ ؑ, and the 12 Imams ؑ throughout the centuries.

from doing this.

This *ḥadīth* is recorded six times in *Ṣaḥīḥ al-Bukhārī*.[2]

[2] Bukhārī, Muḥammad ibn Ismā'īl al-, *Ṣaḥīḥ al-Bukhārī, Kitāb al-'Ilm,* Chapter 39, Tradition 4; *Kitāb al-Jihād wa al-Sīr,* Chapter 175, Tradition 1; *Kitāb al-Jizya,* Chapter 6, Tradition 2; *Kitāb al-Maghāzī,* Chapter 84 (Chapter on the Sickness and Death of the Prophet), Tradition 4 and 5; *Kitāb al-Marīdh,* Chapter 17 (Chapter of the saying of the patient: "Get up from me"), Tradition 1. The below text has been extracted from *Ṣaḥīḥ al-Bukhārī, Kitāb al-'Ilm,* Chapter 39, Tradition 4, from www.sunnah.com:

حَدَّثَنَا يَحْيَى بْنُ سُلَيْمَانَ قَالَ حَدَّثَنِي ابْنُ وَهْبٍ قَالَ أَخْبَرَنِي يُونُسُ عَنِ ابْنِ شِهَابٍ عَنْ عُبَيْدِ اللَّهِ بْنِ عَبْدِ اللَّهِ عَنِ ابْنِ عَبَّاسٍ قَالَ لَمَّا اشْتَدَّ بِالنَّبِيِّ صَلَّى اللَّهُ عَلَيْهِ وَسَلَّمَ وَجَعُهُ قَالَ: ائْتُونِي بِكِتَابٍ أَكْتُبْ لَكُمْ كِتَابًا لَا تَضِلُّوا بَعْدَهُ. قَالَ عُمَرُ إِنَّ النَّبِيَّ صَلَّى اللَّهُ عَلَيْهِ وَسَلَّمَ غَلَبَهُ الْوَجَعُ وَعِنْدَنَا كِتَابُ اللَّهِ حَسْبُنَا فَاخْتَلَفُوا وَكَثُرَ اللَّغَطُ. قَالَ: قُومُوا عَنِّي وَلَا يَنْبَغِي عِنْدِي التَّنَازُعُ. فَخَرَجَ ابْنُ عَبَّاسٍ يَقُولُ إِنَّ الرَّزِيَّةَ كُلَّ الرَّزِيَّةِ مَا حَالَ بَيْنَ رَسُولِ اللَّهِ صَلَّى اللَّهُ عَلَيْهِ وَسَلَّمَ وَبَيْنَ كِتَابِهِ.

Ibn 'Abbās said: "When the ailment of the Prophet ﷺ became worse, he said: 'Bring for me (writing) paper and I will write for you a statement after which you will not go astray.' But 'Umar said: 'The Prophet is seriously ill, and we have got Allah's Book with us and that is sufficient for us.' But the companions of the Prophet ﷺ differed about this and there were a hue and cry. On that, the Prophet ﷺ said to them: 'Go away (and leave me alone). It is not right that you should quarrel in front of me." Ibn 'Abbās came out saying: "It was most unfortunate (a great disaster) that Allah's Messenger ﷺ was prevented from writing that statement for them because of their disagreement and noise. (Note: It is apparent from this tradition that Ibn 'Abbās had witnessed the event and came out saying this statement. The truth is not so, for Ibn 'Abbās used to say this statement on narrating the tradition, and he had not witnessed the event personally. See *Fatḥ al-Bārī fī Sharḥ Ṣaḥīḥ al-Bukhārī*, Aḥmad ibn Muḥammad al-'Askalānī, Vol. 1, Pg. 220 - See Tradition No. 228, Vol. 4).

It is also mentioned three times in *Ṣaḥīḥ Muslim*[3] – both books being the most credible works of the Ahlul Sunnah.

According to the Sunnī scholar and compiler of *Ḥadīth*, Imam al-

---

[3] Naysābūrī, Muslim ibn al-Ḥajjāj al-, *Ṣaḥīḥ Muslim*, *Kitāb al-Waṣīyyah*, Chapter 6, Traditions 6, 7, and 8. The Arabic text of this is as follows:

حَدَّثَنِي مُحَمَّدُ بْنُ رَافِعٍ وَعَبْدُ بْنُ حُمَيْدٍ قَالَ عَبْدٌ أَخْبَرَنَا وَقَالَ ابْنُ رَافِعٍ حَدَّثَنَا عَبْدُ الرَّزَّاقِ أَخْبَرَنَا مَعْمَرٌ عَنِ الزُّهْرِيِّ عَنْ عُبَيْدِ اللَّهِ بْنِ عَبْدِ اللَّهِ بْنِ عُتْبَةَ عَنِ ابْنِ عَبَّاسٍ قَالَ لَمَّا حُضِرَ رَسُولُ اللَّهِ صَلَّى اللَّهُ عَلَيْهِ وَسَلَّمَ وَفِي الْبَيْتِ رِجَالٌ فِيهِمْ عُمَرُ بْنُ الْخَطَّابِ فَقَالَ النَّبِيُّ صَلَّى اللَّهُ عَلَيْهِ وَسَلَّمَ: هَلُمَّ أَكْتُبْ لَكُمْ كِتَابًا لَا تَضِلُّونَ بَعْدَهُ. فَقَالَ عُمَرُ إِنَّ رَسُولَ اللَّهِ صَلَّى اللَّهُ عَلَيْهِ وَسَلَّمَ قَدْ غَلَبَ عَلَيْهِ الْوَجَعُ وَعِنْدَكُمُ الْقُرْآنُ حَسْبُنَا كِتَابُ اللَّهِ. فَاخْتَلَفَ أَهْلُ الْبَيْتِ فَاخْتَصَمُوا فَمِنْهُمْ مَنْ يَقُولُ قَرِّبُوا يَكْتُبْ لَكُمْ رَسُولُ اللَّهِ صَلَّى اللَّهُ عَلَيْهِ وَسَلَّمَ كِتَابًا لَنْ تَضِلُّوا بَعْدَهُ. وَمِنْهُمْ مَنْ يَقُولُ مَا قَالَ عُمَرُ. فَلَمَّا أَكْثَرُوا اللَّغْوَ وَالْإِخْتِلَافَ عِنْدَ رَسُولِ اللَّهِ صَلَّى اللَّهُ عَلَيْهِ وَسَلَّمَ قَالَ رَسُولُ اللَّهِ صَلَّى اللَّهُ عَلَيْهِ وَسَلَّمَ: قُومُوا. قَالَ عُبَيْدُ اللَّهِ: فَكَانَ ابْنُ عَبَّاسٍ يَقُولُ: إِنَّ الرَّزِيَّةَ كُلَّ الرَّزِيَّةِ مَا حَالَ بَيْنَ رَسُولِ اللَّهِ صَلَّى اللَّهُ عَلَيْهِ وَسَلَّمَ وَبَيْنَ أَنْ يَكْتُبَ لَهُمْ ذٰلِكَ الْكِتَابَ مِنِ اخْتِلَافِهِمْ وَلَغَطِهِمْ.

When Allah's Messenger ﷺ was about to leave this world, there were persons (around him) in his house, 'Umar ibn al-Khaṭṭāb being one of them. Allah's Apostle ﷺ said: Come, I may write for you a document; you would not go astray after that. Thereupon Umar said: Verily, Allah's Messenger ﷺ is deeply afflicted with pain. You have the Quran with you. The Book of Allah is sufficient for us. Those who were present in the house differed. Some of them said: Bring him (the writing material) so that Allah's Messenger ﷺ may write a document for you and you would never go astray after him, and some among them said what 'Umar had (already) said. When they indulged in nonsense and began to dispute in the presence of Allah's Messenger ﷺ, he said: Get up (and go away). 'Ubaidullah said: Ibn 'Abbās used to say: There was a heavy loss, indeed a heavy loss, that due to their dispute and noise. Allah's Messenger ﷺ could not write (or dictate) the document for them.

Muslim, the first part of this incident in his book, *Ṣaḥīḥ Muslim,* is recorded as follows: "Saʿīd ibn Jubayr reported that Ibn ʿAbbās said: 'Oh, Thursday! What a day that was.'[4]

At that point, Ibn ʿAbbās cried, and I saw tears which looked like pearls running down his cheeks.

He (Ibn ʿAbbās) said: 'The Messenger of Allah said: 'Bring me a bone and a pen – or a tablet and a pen – so that I may write for you a document that you may never go astray after me…'''"[5]

One would assume that after hearing this request of the Messenger of Allah ﷺ, the companions who were present would have quickly prepared a pen and paper with great enthusiasm and interest in recording the final words of their Prophet ﷺ – being that he was wanting to write his final will.

In addition, the Quran mentions how it is an obligation to obey the orders of Prophet Muḥammad ﷺ; and further, as the Prophet ﷺ himself noted, the document was tied to their perpetual guidance and would have ensured that they never deviated after he left this world. Also, the Prophet ﷺ was sick, lying on his death bed, so

---

[4] This incident happened on Thursday, and according to the narration from Ṭabarī, the Prophet ﷺ died on Monday – four days later. Ṭabarī writes in the events of the 11th year of the migration: "All historians unanimously agree that the day the Messenger of Allah passed away was on Monday." In *Fatḥ al-Bārī fī Sharḥ Ṣaḥīḥ al-Bukhārī,* Ibn Ḥajr al-ʿAsqalānī also writes in Volume 7, Pg. 739: "The Prophet fell ill on Thursday and passed away on Monday."

[5] *Ṣaḥīḥ Muslim, Kitāb al-Waṣīyyah,* Chapter 6, Tradition 7. The Arabic text of this is as follows:

يَوْمُ الخَمِيسِ، وَمَا يَوْمُ الْخَمِيسِ ثُمَّ جَعَلَ تَسِيلُ دُمُوعُهُ حتَّى رَأَيْتُ عَلَىٰ خَدَّيْهِ كَأَنَّهَا نِظَامُ اللُّؤْلُؤِ، قَالَ: قَالَ رَسُولُ اللهِ صَلَّى اللهُ عَلَيْهِ وَسَلَّمَ: ائْتُونِي بالْكَتِفِ وَالدَّوَاةِ، أَوِ اللَّوْحِ وَالدَّوَاةِ، أَكْتُبْ لَكُمْ كِتَابًا لَنْ تَضِلُّوا بَعْدَهُ أَبَدًا...

obviously he wanted to express his final remarks. That is why the companions of Prophet Muḥammad ﷺ were expected to swiftly provide a pen and paper to write down the final words of their leader without any delay. Surprisingly, however, several companions stood against him in non-compliance.

Their reactions are unbelievable, yet their actions are authentically established and recorded in authentic books *(Ṣiḥāḥ)*,[6] and other well-known pieces of historical literature.

According to these narrations, a dispute arose in the presence of the Prophet ﷺ. Some tried to provide him with a pen and paper, while others retorted that there was no need to do as he asked. In some of the narrations, the names of those who objected to the request of Prophet Muḥammad ﷺ seems to be whitewashed.[7] However, in other narrations, it has been clearly mentioned that ʿUmar ibn al-Khaṭṭāb stood chiefly in defiance of the request of the final Messenger, Prophet Muḥammad ﷺ.

For instance, it has been mentioned in *Ṣaḥīḥ al-Bukhārī* that after the request from Prophet Muḥammad ﷺ for a pen and paper, ʿUmar ibn al-Khaṭṭāb turned to the companions present in the room and said: "The Prophet has been overwhelmed by sickness (hence, why he is speaking like this). You have the Quran with you. The Book of

---

[6] Plural of *ṣaḥīḥ*: authentic/correct books of *Ḥadīth*. This is a term which the Sunnī scholars attribute to their six major books of *Ḥadīth* literature.

[7] *Ṣaḥīḥ al-Bukhārī, Kitāb al-Jihād wa al-Sīr,* Chapter 175, Tradition 1; *Kitāb al-Jizya,* Chapter 6, Tradition 2; *Kitāb al-Maghāzī,* Chapter 84 (Chapter on the sickness and death of the Prophet), Traditions 4 and 5; *Ṣaḥīḥ Muslim, Kitāb al-Waṣīyyah,* Chapter 6, Traditions 6 and 7. The Arabic text of this is as follows:

إِنَّ النَّبِيَّ غَلَبَ عَلَيْهِ الْوَجَعُ، وَعِنْدَكُمُ الْقُرْآنُ، حَسْبُنَا كِتَابُ اللهِ.

Allah is sufficient for us."[8]

With a slight difference in the text, Bukhārī quotes the same words from ʿUmar ibn al-Khaṭṭāb in another section of his book. In that narration, he details it such that Ibn ʿAbbās said: "When the sickness of the Prophet grew worse, he said: 'Bring me a paper, so that I may write something for you after which you will never go astray.' ʿUmar said: 'The Prophet has been overwhelmed by sickness. We have the Book of Allah which is sufficient.'"[9]

In addition, in one of the three reports found in *Ṣaḥīḥ Muslim*, the name of ʿUmar ibn al-Khaṭṭāb is also mentioned as the objector.[10]

---

[8] *Ṣaḥīḥ al-Bukhārī, Kitāb al-Jihād wa al-Sīr,* Chapter 175, Tradition 1; *Kitāb al-Jizya,* Chapter 6, Tradition 2; *Kitāb al-Maghāzī,* Chapter 84 (Chapter on the Sickness and Death of the Prophet), Traditions 4 and 5; *Ṣaḥīḥ Muslim, Kitāb al-Waṣīyyah,* Chapter 6, Traditions 6 and 7. The Arabic text of this is as follows:

إِنَّ النَّبِيَّ غَلَبَ عَلَيْهِ الْوَجَعُ، وَعِنْدَكُمُ الْقُرآنَ، حَسْبُنَا كِتَابَ اللهِ.

[9] *Ṣaḥīḥ al-Bukhārī, Kitāb al-Marīḍ,* Chapter17 (Chapter of the Saying of the Patient: "Get up from me"), Tradition 1. The Arabic text of this is as follows:
أُئْتُونِي بِكَتِفٍ أَكْتُبْ لَكُمْ كِتَابًا لَنْ تَضِلُّوا بَعْدَهُ. قَالَ عُمَرُ: إِنَّ النَّبِيَّ غَلَبَهُ الْوَجَعُ، وَعِنْدَنَا كِتَابَ اللهِ حَسْبُنَا.

[10] *Ṣaḥīḥ Muslim, Kitāb al-Waṣīyyah,* Chapter 6, Traditions 6 and 7 [Arabic and English translation taken from www.sunnah.com]:
حَدَّثَنِي مُحَمَّدُ بْنُ رَافِعٍ، وَعَبْدُ بْنُ حُمَيْدٍ قَالَ عَبْدٌ أَخْبَرَنَا وَقَالَ ابْنُ رَافِعٍ حَدَّثَنَا عَبْدُ الرَّزَّاقِ أَخْبَرَنَا مَعْمَرٌ عَنِ الزُّهْرِيِّ عَنْ عُبَيْدِ اللهِ بْنِ عَبْدِ اللهِ بْنِ عُتْبَةَ عَنِ ابْنِ عَبَّاسٍ قَالَ: لَمَّا حُضِرَ رَسُولُ اللهِ صَلَّى اللهُ عَلَيْهِ وَسَلَّمَ وَفِي الْبَيْتِ رِجَالٌ فِيهِمْ عُمَرُ بْنُ الْخَطَّابِ فَقَالَ النَّبِيُّ صَلَّى اللهُ عَلَيْهِ وَسَلَّمَ: هَلُمَّ أَكْتُبْ لَكُمْ كِتَابًا لَا تَضِلُّونَ بَعْدَهُ. فَقَالَ عُمَرُ إِنَّ رَسُولَ اللهِ صَلَّى اللهُ عَلَيْهِ وَسَلَّمَ قَدْ غَلَبَ

Considering the similarities of the statements when compared to one another, there is no doubt about the objection of ʿUmar ibn al-Khaṭṭāb to the words of Prophet Muḥammad ﷺ.

Furthermore, in some narrations, the word: "They said"[11] or

---

عَلَيْهِ الْوَجَعُ وَعِنْدَكُمُ الْقُرْآنُ حَسْبُنَا كِتَابُ اللَّهِ. فَاخْتَلَفَ أَهْلُ الْبَيْتِ فَاخْتَصَمُوا فَمِنْهُمْ مَنْ يَقُولُ قَرِّبُوا يَكْتُبْ لَكُمْ رَسُولُ اللَّهِ صَلَّى اللَّهُ عَلَيْهِ وَسَلَّمَ كِتَابًا لَنْ تَضِلُّوا بَعْدَهُ. وَمِنْهُمْ مَنْ يَقُولُ مَا قَالَ عُمَرُ. فَلَمَّا أَكْثَرُوا اللَّغْوَ وَالْإِخْتِلَافَ عِنْدَ رَسُولِ اللَّهِ صَلَّى اللَّهُ عَلَيْهِ وَسَلَّمَ قَالَ رَسُولُ اللَّهِ صَلَّى اللَّهُ عَلَيْهِ وَسَلَّمَ: قُومُوا. قَالَ عُبَيْدُ اللَّهِ فَكَانَ ابْنُ عَبَّاسٍ يَقُولُ إِنَّ الرَّزِيَّةَ كُلَّ الرَّزِيَّةِ مَا حَالَ بَيْنَ رَسُولِ اللَّهِ صَلَّى اللَّهُ عَلَيْهِ وَسَلَّمَ وَبَيْنَ أَنْ يَكْتُبَ لَهُمْ ذٰلِكَ الْكِتَابَ مِنِ اخْتِلَافِهِمْ وَلَغَطِهِمْ.

When Allah's Messenger ﷺ was about to leave this world, there were persons (around him) in his house, ʿUmar ibn al-Khaṭṭāb being one of them. Allah's Apostle ﷺ said: "Come, I may write for you a document; you would not go astray after that." Thereupon Umar said: "Verily Allah's Messenger ﷺ is deeply afflicted with pain. You have the Quran with you. The Book of Allah is sufficient for us." Those who were present in the house differed. Some of them said: "Bring him (the writing material) so that Allah's Messenger ﷺ may write a document for you, and you would never go astray after him; and some among them said what ʿUmar had (already) said. When they indulged in nonsense and began to dispute in the presence of Allah's Messenger ﷺ, he said: 'Get up (and go away).' ʿUbaydullāh said: 'Ibn ʿAbbās used to say: 'There was a heavy loss, indeed a heavy loss, that, due to their dispute and noise. Allah's Messenger ﷺ could not write (or dictate) the document for them.'"

11 *Ṣaḥīḥ al-Bukhārī*, *Kitāb al-ʿIlm*, Chapter 39, Tradition 4 [Arabic and English translation taken from www.sunnah.com]:

حَدَّثَنَا يَحْيَى بْنُ سُلَيْمَانَ قَالَ حَدَّثَنِي ابْنُ وَهْبٍ قَالَ أَخْبَرَنِي يُونُسُ عَنِ ابْنِ شِهَابٍ عَنْ عُبَيْدِ اللَّهِ بْنِ عَبْدِ اللَّهِ عَنِ ابْنِ عَبَّاسٍ قَالَ لَمَّا اشْتَدَّ بِالنَّبِيِّ صَلَّى اللَّهُ عَلَيْهِ وَسَلَّمَ وَجَعُهُ قَالَ: ائْتُونِي بِكِتَابٍ

"Some of them said"[12] has been used, and from the review of the texts, ʿUmar ibn al-Khaṭṭāb was, at the least, one of the people present who opposed Prophet Muḥammad ﷺ in writing his last will.

As stated previously, this event has been mentioned six times by Bukhārī, and three times by Muslim. Given these reports, one can conclude that after the objection of ʿUmar ibn al-Khaṭṭāb, some of the companions present supported him, while others opposed him.

Although many other scholars of the Ahlul Sunnah have reported this event in their books,[13] we will only consider reports from *Ṣaḥīḥ*

أَكْتُبُ لَكُمْ كِتَابًا لَا تَضِلُّوا بَعْدَهُ. قَالَ عُمَرُ: إِنَّ النَّبِيَّ صَلَّى اللّٰهُ عَلَيْهِ وَسَلَّمَ غَلَبَهُ الْوَجَعُ وَعِنْدَنَا كِتَابُ اللّٰهِ حَسْبُنَا فَاخْتَلَفُوا وَكَثُرَ اللَّغطُ. قَالَ: قُومُوا عَنِّي وَلَا يَنْبَغِي عِنْدِي التَّنَازُعُ. فَخَرَجَ ابْنُ عَبَّاسٍ يَقُولُ إِنَّ الرَّزِيَّةَ كُلَّ الرَّزِيَّةِ مَا حَالَ بَيْنَ رَسُولِ اللّٰهِ صَلَّى اللّٰهُ عَلَيْهِ وَسَلَّمَ وَبَيْنَ كِتَابِهِ.

Ibn ʿAbbās said: "When the ailment of the Prophet ﷺ became worse, he said: 'Bring for me (writing) paper and I will write for you a statement after which you will not go astray.' But ʿUmar said: 'The Prophet is seriously ill, and we have got Allah's Book with us and that is sufficient for us.' But the companions of the Prophet ﷺ differed about this and there was a hue and cry. On that, the Prophet ﷺ said to them: 'Go away (and leave me alone). It is not right that you should quarrel in front of me.'" Ibn ʿAbbās came out saying: "It was most unfortunate (a great disaster) that Allah's Messenger ﷺ was prevented from writing that statement for them because of their disagreement and noise." (Note: It is apparent from this tradition that Ibn ʿAbbās had witnessed the event and came out saying this statement. The truth is not so, for Ibn ʿAbbās used to say this statement on narrating the tradition and he had not witnessed the event personally.)

[12] *Ṣaḥīḥ Muslim, Kitāb al-Waṣīyyah,* Chapter 6, Traditions 6 and 7.

[13] Shaybānī, Aḥmad ibn Muḥammad ibn Ḥanbal al-, *Musnad Aḥmad,* Vol. 1, Pp. 222, 293, 324, 325 and 355; Vol. 3, Pg. 346; Aḥmad ibn ʿAlī ibn Muthanna, *Musnad Abū Yaʿlā,* Vol. 3, Pg. 395; Muḥammad ibn Ḥibbān al-Bustī, *Ṣaḥīḥ Ibn Ḥibbān,* Vol. 8, Pg. 201; Muḥammad ibn Jarīr al-Ṭabarī,

al-Bukhārī and *Ṣaḥīḥ Muslim,* which are the most authentic books of the Ahlul Sunnah.

Examples of Opposition to the Prophet ﷺ

We now wish to discuss the comments made in opposition to Prophet Muḥammad ﷺ. Once again, it is noteworthy to emphasize that all the following expressions are found in the most authentic books of the Ahlul Sunnah – namely *Ṣaḥīḥ al-Bukhārī* and *Ṣaḥīḥ Muslim.*

In one instance, it has been mentioned: "Some of them said: 'Indeed, illness has taken over the Messenger of Allah, and you have the Quran, so the Book of Allah is sufficient for us.'"[14]

In another tradition, it is stated: "ʿUmar (ibn al-Khaṭṭāb) said: 'Indeed, illness has taken over the Messenger of Allah, and you have the Quran, so the Book of Allah is sufficient for us.'"[15]

In yet another similar narration: "ʿUmar (ibn al-Khaṭṭāb) said: 'Indeed, illness has taken over the Prophet, and you have the Quran, so the Book of Allah is sufficient for us.'"[16]

Tārīkh al-Rusul wa al-Mulūk, Vol. 3, Pg. 193; ʿAlī ibn Muḥammad al-Shaybānī, *Al-Kāmil fī al-Tārīkh,* Vol. 2, Pg. 185; and other books.

14 *Ṣaḥīḥ al-Bukhārī, Kitāb al-Maghāzī,* Chapter 84, Tradition 5. The Arabic text of this is as follows:

فَقَالَ بَعْضُهُمْ: إِنَّ رَسُولَ اللّٰهِ قَدْ غَلَبَهُ الْوَجْعُ، وَعِنْدَكُمُ الْقُرْآنُ، حَسْبُنَا كِتَابُ اللّٰهِ.

15 *Ṣaḥīḥ Muslim, Kitāb al-Waṣīyyah,* Chapter 6, Tradition 8. The Arabic text of this is as follows:

فَقَالَ عُمَرُ: إِنَّ رَسُولَ اللّٰهِ قَدْ غَلَبَ عَلَيْهِ الْوَجْعُ، وَعِنْدَكُمُ الْقُرْآنُ، حَسْبُنَا كِتَابُ اللّٰهِ.

16 *Ṣaḥīḥ al-Bukhārī, Kitāb al-Marīḍ,* Chapter 17, Tradition 1. The Arabic text of this is as follows:

فَقَالَ عُمَرُ: إِنَّ النَّبِيَّ قَدْ غَلَبَ عَلَيْهِ الْوَجْعُ، وَعِنْدَكُمُ الْقُرْآنُ، حَسْبُنَا كِتَابُ اللّٰهِ.

In another place, the event has been quoted as follows: "'Umar (ibn al-Khaṭṭāb) said: 'Indeed, the illness has taken over the Prophet and we have the Book of Allah, it is sufficient for us.'"[17]

As per the above statements, to prevent Prophet Muḥammad ﷺ from writing the document, 'Umar ibn al-Khaṭṭāb justified himself by saying: "The Prophet is overwhelmed by sickness [thus, he does not know what he is saying], and we have the Quran which is enough for our guidance."

Among the five instances, the word *Hajra* has been used twice in the interrogative mode, and once in the indicative mode.

In one instance in the traditions, the phrase which has been mentioned is: "They said: 'Is the Messenger of Allah well?'"[18] While twice, the phrase mentioned is: "They said: 'What is wrong with him? Is he well? Let us ask him.'"[19]

So, what is the meaning of *Hajra* (as was used by 'Umar ibn al-Khaṭṭāb)? Linguists define *Hajr* as 'delirium' when it is used for sick people.

Fayyūmī, in his book, *Al-Miṣbāḥ al-Munīr,* has written the following regarding the meaning of *Hajra*: "When a sick person speaks deliriously: it means that they are talking improperly and

---

[17] *Ṣaḥīḥ al-Bukhārī, Kitāb al-'Ilm,* Chapter 49, Tradition 4. The Arabic text of this is as follows:

قَالَ عُمَرُ: إِنَّ النَّبِيَّ غَلَبَهُ الْوَجَعُ، وَعِنْدَنَا كِتَابُ اللَّهِ، حَسْبُنَا.

[18] Ibid., *Kitāb al-Jihād wa al-Sīr,* Chapter 175, Tradition 1. The Arabic text of this is as follows:

فَقَالُوا: أَهْجَرَ رَسُولُ اللَّهِ.

[19] Ibid., *Kitāb al-Maghāzī,* Chapter 84, Tradition 4; *Ṣaḥīḥ Muslim, Kitāb al-Waṣīyyah,* Chapter 6, Tradition 6. The Arabic text of this is as follows:

فَقَالُوا: مَا شَأْنُهُ؟ أَهَجَرَ؟ إِسْتَفْهِمُوهُ.

nonsensically."[20]

In addition, it has been mentioned in the famous lexicon, *Lisān al-ʿArab,* that: "*Hajra* means talking nonsense, and *hujr* is a gerund[21] and means 'obscene speech.' When this word is attributed to a sleeping or sick person, then it means that 'one is delirious and says inappropriate words in one's sleep or in their state of sickness.'"[22]

How can anyone say such words about Prophet Muḥammad ﷺ, the final Messenger of Allah ﷻ, and the link between Allah ﷻ and humanity?

How can this degrading quality be attributed to him, while the Quran says about him that: "Nor does he speak from [his own] inclination."[23]

Furthermore, the Noble Quran in another verse says: "And whatever the Messenger gives you, take it, and whatever he has

---

[20] Fayyūmī, Aḥmad ibn Muḥammad al-, *Miṣbāḥ al-Munīr,* under the word *hajara.* The Arabic text of this is as follows:

هَجَرَ الْمَرِيضَ فِي كَلَامِهِ هَجَرًا أَيْضًا خَلَطَ وَهَذَي.

[21] A gerund is a verb that in its present participle form (root verb + "ing") that acts as a noun in a sentence. It is a form that is derived from a verb, but that functions as a noun, in English, it would end in -ing. For example: *asking* in the phrase: *Do you mind my asking you?*

[22] Khazrajī, Muḥammad ibn Mukarram al-, *Lisān al-ʿArab,* under the word *hajara*:

الهَجْر: الهذيان والهُجْر بالضم: الإسم من الأهجار وهو الأفحاش وهَجَر في نومه ومرضه يهجُر هجرًا: هذي; هَجر.

[23] Quran, Sūrah al-Najm (53), Verse 3:

﴿وَمَا يَنطِقُ عَنِ ٱلْهَوَىٰٓ ٣﴾

forbidden you, refrain from (that)."[24]

In addition, the Quran further says: "So let those beware who dissent from his [the Prophet's] order, lest *fitnah* (trials, afflictions dissension, strife, etc.) strikes them or a painful punishment."[25]

Disputes in the Presence of the Prophet ﷺ

In addition to the profane words that we previously mentioned, some companions began to quarrel in the presence of the Messenger of Allah ﷺ. A group of them supported ʿUmar ibn al-Khaṭṭāb, while another group opposed him saying: "Let the Messenger of Allah write his will!"

According to some narrations mentioned in *Ṣaḥīḥ al-Bukhārī,* it is stated that: "They (the companions) disputed with each other and raised their voices (while in the presence of Prophet Muḥammad ﷺ)."[26]

---

[24] Quran, Sūrah al-Ḥashr (59), Verse 7:

﴿...وَمَآ ءَاتَىٰكُمُ ٱلرَّسُولُ فَخُذُوهُ وَمَا نَهَىٰكُمْ عَنْهُ فَٱنتَهُوا۟...﴾

[25] Quran, Sūrah al-Nūr (24), Verse 63:

﴿...فَلْيَحْذَرِ ٱلَّذِينَ يُخَالِفُونَ عَنْ أَمْرِهِۦٓ أَن تُصِيبَهُمْ فِتْنَةٌ أَوْ يُصِيبَهُمْ عَذَابٌ أَلِيمٌ ﴿٦٣﴾﴾

Ibn Kathīr, the famous Sunnī scholar, writes: "The pronoun ***'hi'*** in *amrihi* refers to the Messenger of Allah" He further writes:

أن تصيبهم فتنة.

"That is, opposing him (the Messenger of Allah ﷺ) causes sedition;" and:

أي في قلوبهم من كفر أو نفاق أو بدعة.

"That is, the hearts of such people fall into disbelief, hypocrisy, or heresy." (*Tafsīr al-Quran al-ʿAẓīm* of Ibn Kathīr, Vol. 5, Pg. 131)

[26] *Ṣaḥīḥ al-Bukhārī, Kitāb al-ʿIlm,* Chapter 39, Tradition 4. The Arabic text of this is as follows:

In four narrations from *Ṣaḥīḥ al-Bukhārī* and *Ṣaḥīḥ Muslim*, it has been stated that: "They disputed, and it is not appropriate to dispute in the presence of the Prophet."[27]

In three other narrations from *Ṣaḥīḥ al-Bukhārī* and *Ṣaḥīḥ Muslim*, it has been mentioned, with a slight difference in words, that: "Those who were present in the house differed. Some of them said: 'Bring him (the writing material) so that Allah's Messenger may write a document for you, so that you never go astray after him.' While some among them said what 'Umar had (already) said."[28]

These contents fully indicate that the companions were arguing in the presence of the Prophet ﷺ, and these comments were exchanged between them.

Reaction of Prophet Muḥammad ﷺ

The reaction that the Messenger of Allah ﷺ showed against such inappropriate behaviour and quarreling is also noteworthy. According to what is mentioned in *Ṣaḥīḥ al-Bukhārī* and *Ṣaḥīḥ Muslim*, two types of reactions have been narrated regarding the

---

فَاخْتَلَفُوا وَكَثُرَ اللَّغَطُ.

[27] *Ṣaḥīḥ al-Bukhārī, Kitāb al-Jihād wa al-Sīr,* Chapter 175, Tradition 1; *Kitāb al-Jizya,* Chapter 6, Tradition 2; *Kitāb al-Maghāzī,* Chapter 84, Tradition 4 and 5; *Ṣaḥīḥ Muslim, Kitāb al-Waṣīyyah,* Chapter 6, Tradition 6. The Arabic text of this is as follows:

فَتَنَازَعُوا وَلَا يَنْبَغِي عِنْدَ نَبِيٍّ تَنَازُعٌ.

[28] *Ṣaḥīḥ al-Bukhārī, Kitāb al-Mariḍ,* Chapter 17, Tradition 1; *Kitāb al-Maghāzī,* Chapter 84, Tradition 5; *Ṣaḥīḥ Muslim, Kitāb al-Waṣīyyah,* Chapter 6, Tradition 8. The Arabic text of this is as follows:

فَاخْتَلَفَ أَهْلُ الْبَيْتِ فَاخْتَصَمُوا، فَكَانَ مِنْهُمْ مَنْ يَقُولُ: قَرِّبُوا يَكْتُبْ لَكُمُ النَّبِيُّ صَلَّى اللهُ عَلَيْهِ وَسَلَّمَ كِتَابًا لَنْ تَضِلُّوا بَعْدَهُ، وَمِنْهُمْ مَنْ يَقُولُ مَا قَالَ عُمَرُ.

Prophet ﷺ.

In one report, it is noted that Prophet Muḥammad ﷺ addressed the people present and said: "Stay away from me because dispute in my presence is not proper."[29] In this remark, the anger of the final Messenger ﷺ, as well as his displeasure with their profane words and misbehaviour is obvious.

When the conflict intensified and the Prophet ﷺ was insulted by such inappropriate words, he is quoted to have said: "Leave me alone! The state that I am currently in is much better than what you are provoking me into."[30] This is most likely referring to the state of spiritual content and bliss that Prophet Muḥammad ﷺ was entering as he proceeded to leave this world and meet his Creator, being blessed with having the special attention of Allah ﷻ in the last

---

[29] *Ṣaḥīḥ al-Bukhārī, Kitāb al-ʿIlm,* Chapter 39, Tradition 4. In some narrations, only the word *qūmū* (get up!) is mentioned. *Ṣaḥīḥ al-Bukhārī, Kitāb al-Marīḍ,* Chapter 17, Tradition 1; *Kitāb al-Maghāzī,* Chapter 84, Tradition 5; *Ṣaḥīḥ Muslim, Kitāb al-Waṣīyyah,* Chapter 6, Tradition 8. The Arabic text of this is as follows:

قُومُوا عَنِّي وَلَا يَنْبَغِي عِنْدِي التَّنَازُعُ.

[30] *Ṣaḥīḥ al-Bukhārī, Kitāb al-Jizya,* Chapter 6, Tradition 2; *Kitāb al-Maghāzī,* Chapter 84, Tradition 4; *Kitāb al-Jihād wa al-Sīr,* Chapter 175, Tradition 1; In this tradition, the word "دعوني" is used instead of "ذروني." In general, the first word is considered more polite and appropriate for formal situations or when making requests, while the second word is more informal and can be seen as more assertive or even slightly impolite depending on the context and tone. The Arabic text of this is as follows:

ذَرُونِي، فَالَّذِي أَنَا فِيهِ خَيْرٌ مِمَّا تَدْعُونِي إِلَيْهِ.

Also, in *Ṣaḥīḥ Muslim, Kitāb al-Waṣīyyah,* Chapter 6, Tradition 6, what is documented is:

قَالَ: دَعَوْنِي فَالَّذِي أَنَا فِيهِ خَيرٌ.

moments of his life.

Cause of Sadness of Ibn ʿAbbās

According to five narrations from the six *Ṣiḥāḥ* books of the Ahlul Sunnah, when Ibn ʿAbbās wanted to report this incident, he first mentioned it with great emotion and sadness, then narrated the incident.

For example, Saʿīd ibn Jubayr, according to the citation in *Ṣaḥīḥ al-Bukhārī* says Ibn ʿAbbās said: "It was Thursday, and what a dreadful Thursday it was!"[31]

Then Saʿīd ibn Jubayr adds: "Ibn ʿAbbās cried so much that tears rolled down his cheek, falling onto the ground."[32]

The regret of Ibn ʿAbbās and his incessant tears were due to the insult that was directed to the Messenger of Allah ﷺ, and because the final Prophet ﷺ was prevented from writing the document that, if it was permitted to have been written, would have prevented the entire nation from going astray.

In four other quotations from *Ṣaḥīḥ al-Bukhārī* and *Ṣaḥīḥ Muslim* about this incident, after explaining the event, Ibn ʿAbbās felt extremely sorry about the Prophet ﷺ being prevented from writing what he wished to dictate.

For example, a narration from ʿUbaydullāh ibn ʿAbdullāh quotes

---

[31] The Arabic text of this is as follows:

يَوْمَ الْخَمِيسِ وَمَا يَوْمَ الْخَمِيسِ.

[32] *Ṣaḥīḥ al-Bukhārī, Kitāb al-Jizya,* Chapter 6, Tradition 2. A similar theme is mentioned in several other quotes. *Ṣaḥīḥ al-Bukhārī, Kitāb al-Jihād wa al-Sīr,* Chapter 175, Tradition 1; *Kitāb al-Maghāzī,* Chapter 84, Tradition 4 (Without quoting Ibn ʿAbbās); *Ṣaḥīḥ Muslim, Kitāb al-Waṣīyyah,* Chapter 6, Traditions 6 and 7. The Arabic text of this is as follows:

ثمّ بكى حتّي بلّ دمعه الحصي.

Ibn ʿAbbās as follows (after explaining the prevention of the writing): "ʿUbaydullāh said: 'Ibn ʿAbbās used to say: 'It was a great disaster that their dispute and noise prevented the Messenger of Allah from writing that document for them.''"[33]

Were the Actions of the Companions Justifiable?

When explaining these *aḥādīth*, commentators of the reports found in the *Ṣiḥāḥ* books of the Ahlul Sunnah reiterated that the Prophet ﷺ was immaculate – both in times of sickness and good health - and that his statements were always completely truthful.

The famous Sunnī scholar, Ibn Ḥajr al-ʿAsqalānī quotes from Al-Qurṭubī that: "The word *hajr* in this *ḥadīth* refers to 'a sick person who is not speaking properly, hence he is ignored.'" Then he adds: "The occurrence of that from the Prophet is impossible because he is immaculate when healthy and sick, due to His saying: 'He does not speak out of (his own) desire,' and according to his saying: 'In anger and contentment, I only say what is true.'"[34]

Additionally, the Sunnī scholar, Badr al-Dīn al-ʿAynī states similar words in *ʿUmdat al-Qārī*, another commentary of *Ṣaḥīḥ al-*

---

[33] *Ṣaḥīḥ al-Bukhārī, Kitāb al-Marīḍ,* Chapter 17, Tradition 1; *Kitāb al-ʿIlm,* Chapter 39, Tradition 4; *Kitāb al-Maghāzī,* Chapter 84, Tradition 5; *Ṣaḥīḥ Muslim, Kitāb al-Waṣīyyah,* Chapter 6, Tradition 8. The Arabic text of this is as follows:

قَالَ عُبَيْدُ اللّٰهِ، فَكَانَ ابنُ عَبَّاسٍ يَقُولُ: إِنَّ الرَّزِيَّةَ كُلَّ الرَّزِيَّةِ مَا حَالَ بَيْنَ رَسُولِ اللّٰهِ صَلَّى اللّٰهُ عَلَيْهِ وَسَلَّمَ وَبَيْنَ أَنْ يَكْتُبَ لَهُمْ ذٰلِكَ الْكِتَابَ مِنَ اخْتِلَافِهِمْ وَلَغَطِهِمْ.

[34] ʿAsqalānī, Abūl Faḍl Aḥmad al-, *Fatḥ al-Bārī fī Sharḥ Ṣaḥīḥ al-Bukhārī,* Vol. 7, Pp. 739-740. The Arabic text of this is as follows:

ووقوع ذٰلك من النبي صلى اللّٰه عليه وسلّم مستحيل لأنّه معصوم في صحّته ومرضه لقوله تعالى ﴿وَمَا يَنْطِقُ عَنِ الْهَوَي﴾ وَلقوله صلّى اللّٰه عليه وسلّم إِنِّي لَا أَقُولُ فِي الْغَضَبِ وَالرِّضَا إِلَّا حَقًّا.

Bukhārī.[35]

Another famous Sunnī scholar named al-Nawawī, in his commentary of *Ṣaḥīḥ Muslim* writes: "Know that the Prophet was immaculate *(maʿṣūm)* from lying, and from altering any of the legal rulings – whether he was in good health or illness."[36]

In addition to the verses of the Noble Quran mentioned earlier, these comments indicate that the status of the Prophet ﷺ is beyond any belief that a false word could have ever been spoken by him throughout his entire life.

However, several Sunnī scholars have tried to whitewash this undeniable historical issue, which is quite startling.

There is no defense for such an incident to have ever taken place, and rather than providing illogical justifications, would it not be better for those Sunnī scholars to put aside their prejudices and admit that a terrible mistake was made by that one individual – namely ʿUmar ibn al-Khaṭṭāb – or to submit that a group of individuals – meaning a certain group of companions who were present at that fateful event – said and did things that were not in line with the teachings of the Quran and the utterances of Prophet Muḥammad ﷺ?

For instance, in the book, *Fatḥ al-Bārī fī Sharḥ Ṣaḥīḥ al-Bukhārī* which is one of the most important books of the Sunnī brethren, it is stated that: "The scholars are unanimous that ʿUmar's saying: 'The

---

35 ʿAynī, Maḥmūd ibn Aḥmad al-, *ʿUmdat al-Qārī*, Vol. 12, Pg. 388.

36 Nawawī, Yaḥyā ibn Sharaf al-, *Sharḥ Ṣaḥīḥ Muslim*, Vol. 4, Pg. 257. The Arabic text of this is as follows:

إِعْلَمْ أَنَّ النَّبِيَّ مَعْصُومٌ مِنَ الْكَذِبِ وَمِنْ تَغْيِيرِ شَيْءٍ مِنَ الْأَحْكَامِ الشَّرْعِيَّةِ فِي حَالِ صِحَّتِهِ وَحَالِ مَرَضِهِ.

Quran is sufficient for us'[37] is a sign of ʿUmar's deep knowledge of the Islamic Sciences and the precision of his opinion."

One should ask: Is the earlier statement which ʿUmar ibn al-Khaṭṭāb has been quoted as saying that: "The Prophet has been overwhelmed by sickness (and he does not know what he is saying)," also a sign of his deep insight into the Islamic Sciences and his precision with respect to the religion of Islam?

Moreover, is the Book of Allah ﷻ, the Quran, enough without the *Sunnah* and guidance of Prophet Muḥammad ﷺ?

For example, the number of *rakaʿāt* in the mandatory prayers, the minimum amount *(nisāb)* of alms *(zakāt)*, the number of rounds in the circumambulation *(ṭawāf)* of the Kaʿbah during the *Ḥajj* or *ʿUmrah*, the number of times to perform the walk between the two mountains of Ṣafā and Marwah *(saʿī)*, the throwing of the small pebbles during the *Ḥajj* pilgrimage *(rāmī al-jamarāt)*, and other Laws of Islam *(Aḥkām)* are only mentioned in the *Sunnah* of Prophet Muḥammad ﷺ, and are not found at all in the Quran [so how is the Quran 'sufficient']!

Is the negation of such matters a sign of the "deep insight and knowledge" of ʿUmar ibn al-Khaṭṭāb and his accuracy in understanding this religion?

Please reflect on this point and reanalyze this entire discussion with an open mind.

Would it not be better to admit that the companions made a major mistake, and that ʿUmar ibn al-Khaṭṭāb is guilty of the crimes which he perpetrated against Prophet Muḥammad ﷺ and the religion of Islam, rather than trying to justify and misrepresent the events that really transpired?

---

[37] The Arabic text of this is as follows:

حَسْبُنَا كِتَابُ اللّٰهِ.

A More Important Issue

While these remarks mentioned in six instances in *Ṣaḥīḥ al-Bukhārī*, as well as the three instances in *Ṣaḥīḥ Muslim*, are inappropriate and shameful, a more important question must be asked: What exactly did the Noble Prophet ﷺ want to write, or order to be written, that it was faced with such strong opposition?

Firstly, we know that the matter was certainly related to the last days of the life of Prophet Muḥammad ﷺ.

Secondly, it must have been an extremely important issue such that if it was acted upon, then any confusion or disagreement arising after his passing away would have been resolved.

Thirdly, the issue was not pleasant to some of the attendees, and they must have had a solid idea as to what the Prophet ﷺ wanted to dictate to the Muslim nation, thus they opposed it.

Given the history of Islam up to that point and the statement of Prophet Muḥammad ﷺ that he wanted to ensure that the Muslim community would not differ after his death, it stands to reason that the respected readers can deduce that the issue was nothing other than the matter of Successorship *(Khilāfah)* and Guardianship *(Wilāyah)* of none other than ʿAlī ibn Abī Ṭālib ؑ.

We believe that the Prophet of Islam ﷺ sought to, for one last time, confirm the Leadership *(Imāmah)* and Caliphate *(Khilāfah)* of Imam ʿAlī ؑ after having made various statements introducing Imam ʿAlī ؑ to the nation *(ummah)* over the twenty-three years of his Prophetic mission, especially during the occasion of Ghadīr Khumm. Indeed, this assumption is further supported by the numerous statements from Prophet Muḥammad ﷺ about his Ahlul Bayt ؑ, especially those contained in the famous and well-known traditions, one being that of the *Ḥadīth* of *Thaqalayn*.

If Allah ﷻ wills, we will discuss the *Ḥadīth* of *Ghadīr* and the *Ḥadīth* of *Thaqalayn* in subsequent books.

In conclusion, we urge the esteemed readers to read this chapter once more. Let it soak into your mind. Reflect on what you have read, and then in the end, we leave it to you to make your own judgement.

Bibliography

The Noble Quran.

ʿAsqalānī, Shihāb al-Dīn Abūl Faḍl Aḥmad ibn Nūr al-Dīn ʿAlī ibn Muḥammad ibn Ḥajr al-, *Fatḥ al-Bārī fī Sharḥ Ṣaḥīḥ al-Bukhārī* (Riyadh: Maktabah al-Ubaykān, 1421 AH).

ʿAynī, Abū Muḥammad Maḥmūd ibn Aḥmad ibn Mūsā Badr al-Dīn al-, *ʿUmdat al-Qārī* (Beirut: Dār al-Fikr, 1st Edition, 2005 CE).

Bukhārī, Abū ʿAbdillāh Muḥammad ibn Ismāʿīl al-, *Ṣaḥīḥ al-Bukhārī* (Beirut: Dār al-Fikr, 1st Edition, 2005 CE - Researched by Ṣiddīqī Jamīl al-Aṭṭār).

Bustī, Muḥammad ibn Ḥibbān al-, *Ṣaḥīḥ Ibn Ḥibbān* (Muʾassasah al-Risālah: 2nd Edition, 1414 AH - Annotated by Shuʿayb al-Arʿnāut).

Dhuhlī, Abū ʿAbdillāh Aḥmad ibn Muḥammad ibn Ḥanbal al-, *Musnad Aḥmad* (Beirut: Dār al-Sādir, n.d.).

Dimashqī, Abūl Fiḍāʾ ʿImād al-Dīn Ismāʿīl ibn ʿUmar ibn Kathīr al-Qurayshī al-, *Tafsīr al-Quran al-ʿAẓīm* (Beirut, 1996 CE).

Fayyūmī, Aḥmad ibn Muḥammad, *Al-Miṣbāḥ al-Munīr* (Annotated by Muḥammad ʿAbdul Ḥamīd, 1347 AH).

Jazarī, ʿAlī ʿIzz al-Dīn ibn al-Athīr al-, *Al-Kāmil fī al-Tārīkh* (Beirut: Dār al-Kutub al-ʿIlmīyyah, 3rd Edition, 1418 AH - Annotated by Abūl Fiḍā ʿAbdullāh al-Qāḍī).

Khazrajī, Muḥammad ibn Mukarram ibn ʿAlī ibn Aḥmad ibn Manẓūr al-Anṣārī al-Ifrīqī al-Miṣrī al-, *Lisān al-ʿArab* (Beirut: Dār al-Sādir, 1st Edition, 1997 CE).

Mawṣilī, Abū Yaʿlā al-, *Musnad Abū Yaʿlā* (Beirut: Dār al-Amoun li Turāth, 2nd Edition, n.d.).

Nawawī, Abū Zakariyyā Yaḥyā ibn Sharaf al-, *Ṣaḥīḥ Muslim bi Sharh al-Nawawī* (Beirut: Ibn Sharīf al-Anṣārī, 2007 CE).

Naysābūrī, Abūl Ḥusayn ʿAsākir al-Dīn Muslim ibn al-Ḥajjāj al-, *Ṣaḥīḥ Muslim* (Beirut: Dār al-Fikr, 1st Edition, 2004 - Annotated by Ṣiddīqī Jamīl al-Aṭṭār).

Ṭabarī, Abū Jaʿfar Muḥammad ibn Jarīr ibn Yazīd al-, *Tārīkh al-Rusul wa al-Mulūk* (Beirut: Al-Aʿlam Institute, 4th Edition, n.d.).

Chapter Two

The Legitimacy of the Event at Saqīfah

Introduction

One of the scandalous issues that took place in the history of Islam is the event that unfolded at Saqīfah[1] Banū Sāʿida, and the subsequent selection of a caliph.

Inquiring minds should ask themselves as to the nature of the Islamic caliphate.

Should the selection of a caliph for the Muslims be based on a clear and specific method or not?

Should the selection of a caliph after the Messenger of Allah ﷺ be based on nomination or recommendation, or should it be a choice made by the people, as is the case in a democracy?

If it is the democracy model that Muslims accept, then is it based on the consensus of Muslims in general, or the consensus of the Muslim scholars?

If it is the consensus of the scholars, then what are the criteria that they must employ to select the caliph?

Finally, can any of these models be enforced through threats or coercion?

Each of the above questions requires detailed discussions that need to be addressed separately. However, what is of interest in this present work is an examination of the method of selecting the first caliph and evaluating its legitimacy.

Did the gathering at the Saqīfah of Banū Sāʿida truly have the mandate or legitimacy to choose a caliph? Was the Saqīfah a place like today's consultative assemblies where the elites of the

---

[1] Saqīfah: Refers to a roofed place with pillars, and it is attributed to the clan of Banū Sāʿida, descendants of Sāʿida ibn ʿUbādah, who belonged to the Khazraj tribe. (*Muʿjam al-Buldān*, Vol. 3, Pp. 228-229.)

This place served as a meeting point for the *Anṣār*, and a venue for their consultations. (*ʿUmdat al-Qārī*, Vol. 16, Pg. 185.)

Right after the demise of the Messenger of Allah ﷺ, some of the companions gathered there to choose Abū Bakr as the successor to the Prophet ﷺ.

community gather, consult, and then elect an executive authority through voting? Or was it a sudden, exceptional incident?

In other words, was this incident a democratic choice in the political culture of Islam, or was it a power struggle between vying tribes resulting in the victory of one group over another?

Can the method of selecting the first caliph be considered applicable to Muslims today in their selection of rulers?

Can it be presented as a clear and prominent point in Islamic history for the world to take pride in and use as a rational framework to understand leadership in Islam?

These are some of the numerous questions that revolve around the gathering at the Saqīfah of Banū Sāʿida.

We believe that examining and discussing this important event in Islamic history will open new horizons for impartial researchers, making the path to truth easier to traverse.

In this light, we will divide our discussion surrounding the Saqīfah of Banū Sāʿida into the following categories:

1. First, how did the incident at Saqīfah Banū Sāʿida unfold?

We will then delve into the reactions in the following sections:

1. Formal pledges of allegiance.
2. Positions held by some of the companions.
3. Response of the Ahlul Bayt ﷺ.
4. The role of ʿUmar ibn al-Khaṭṭāb in solidifying the caliphate of Abū Bakr.

We will then provide a conclusion.

We endeavour to rely on sources that are accepted by the Sunnī Muslims in these discussions, and to examine historical facts in a clear and transparent manner, leaving no room for doubt.

How did the Saqīfah Banū Sāʿida Episode Unfold?

This incident has been extensively documented in the historical and *Ḥadīth* literature of the Ahlul Sunnah. Although there are some varying differences in the details, the essence remains consistent.

Before narrating the incident, it is necessary to mention a few points.

This incident occurred on the day of the death of Prophet Muḥammad ﷺ. According to the Ahlul Sunnah historians, the Prophet ﷺ passed away on Monday, the twelfth day of Rabīʿ al-Awwal.[2]

Ṭabarī writes under the heading, *The Events of the Eleventh Year of the Hijrah*: "There is no disagreement among scholars that the Prophet passed away on a Monday during the month of Rabīʿ al-Awwal in the eleventh year of the Hijrah. However, there is a difference of opinion regarding which specific Monday it was. Some say it was the second day of Rabīʿ al-Awwal, while others say it was the twelfth day."[3]

He also states: "The incident of Saqīfah and the pledge of allegiance to Abū Bakr took place while the body of the Prophet was being prepared for burial. This occurred on the same day, Monday, and the next day, Tuesday, was the day when the Prophet's burial took place. Some have also said that the Prophet was buried three days after his demise, as people came in groups to offer prayers on his blessed body.[4] ʿĀyesha narrated that the Prophet was buried on the night of Wednesday."[5]

Ṭabarī goes on to state that: "During the initial hours after the

---

[2] *Tārīkh al-Rusul wa al-Mulūk*, Vol. 3, Pg. 199.

[3] Ibid., Pg. 200; *Al-Kamil fī al-Tārīkh*, Vol. 2, Pg. 323. This opinion of Ṭabarī does not seem plausible as it is impossible for the 2nd of a month to be a Monday and for the 12th of the same month to also be a Monday – it must be a Wednesday. The Shīʿa opinion with respect to the passing away of Prophet Muḥammad ﷺ is that he left this world on the 28th of Ṣafar. (Tr.)

[4] *Tārīkh al-Rusul wa al-Mulūk*, Vol. 3, Pg. 211; *Al-Kāmil fī al-Tārīkh*, Vol. 2, Pg. 332.

[5] *Tārīkh al-Rusul wa al-Mulūk*, Vol. 3, Pg. 217.

demise of the Messenger of Allah, ʿUmar denied the reports of his death. Saʿīd ibn Musayyib narrates from Abū Hurayrah that when the Messenger of Allah passed away, ʿUmar ibn al-Khaṭṭāb stood up and said: 'Some hypocrites think that the Messenger of Allah has passed away. By Allah, the Messenger of Allah has not died. Just as Mūsā was absent from his people for forty days to receive the Tawrāh, the Messenger of Allah has also gone to his Lord and is absent, and he will return after some time.' He proceeded to threaten the people and said: 'By Allah, if anyone claims that the Messenger of Allah has died, I will cut off their hands and feet!'"[6]

According to another narration, Abū Bakr was not present in Madina at the time of the Prophet's ﷺ demise, and when he arrived in Madina, he saw ʿUmar standing and frightening the people, saying: "The Messenger of Allah is alive, he has not passed away!"[7]

According to yet another narration, ʿUmar ibn al-Khaṭṭāb threatened to kill people, however, when Abū Bakr heard ʿUmar's words, he recited the following verse to him: "Indeed, you (O Muḥammad) will die, and indeed, they (too) will die."[8]

He also recited the verse which states: "Muḥammad is only a Messenger. [Other] Messengers have passed away before him. So, if

---

[6] *Tārīkh al-Rusul wa al-Mulūk,* Vol. 3, Pg. 200; Abdul Malik ibn Hishām, *Al-Sīrah al-Nabawiyyah,* Vol. 2, Pg. 655, completed by Ibn Athīr, Vol. 2, Pg. 323. The Arabic text of this is as follows:

والله ليرجعنّ رسول الله فليقطعنّ ايدي رجال وأرجلهم يزعمون أن رسول الله مات.

[7] *Tārīkh al-Rusul wa al-Mulūk,* Vol. 3, Pg. 202. The Arabic text of this is as follows:

إن رسول اللهِ حيٌّ لم يمت.

[8] Quran, Sūrah al-Zumar (39), Verse 30:

﴿إِنَّكَ مَيِّتٌ وَإِنَّهُم مَّيِّتُونَ ٣٠﴾

he was to die or be killed, would you turn back on your heels [to disbelief]?"[9] Upon hearing these verses and Abū Bakr's words, ʿUmar calmed down and refrained from further speech.[10]

According to yet another narration, ʿUmar ibn al-Khaṭṭāb drew his sword and shouted: "With this sword, I will strike anyone who claims that the Messenger of Allah has died!"[11]

What may have motivated ʿUmar ibn al-Khaṭṭāb to deny the death of the Messenger of Allah ﷺ and label those who believed that the Prophet ﷺ had died as hypocrites, while the death of previous Prophets and in fact, all human beings – was a commonly accepted reality?

Moreover, the Quranic verses that Muslims had always recited and heard clearly testified to the fact that the Messenger of Allah ﷺ would also experience his inevitable demise.

It is farfetched to believe that ʿUmar ibn al-Khaṭṭāb had not heard these verses or was ignorant of this reality, especially since he took a firm stance against the Prophet ﷺ being permitted to write his will during the final moments of his life, stating: "Sufficient for us is the

---

[9] Quran, Sūrah Āle ʿImrān (3), Verse 144:

﴿وَمَا مُحَمَّدٌ إِلَّا رَسُولٌ قَدْ خَلَتْ مِن قَبْلِهِ ٱلرُّسُلُ ۚ أَفَإِين مَّاتَ أَوْ قُتِلَ ٱنقَلَبْتُمْ عَلَىٰٓ أَعْقَٰبِكُمْ...﴾

[10] *Tārīkh al-Rusul wa al-Mulūk,* Vol. 3, Pg. 202.

[11] ʿUmar's denial and response to those who claimed that the Messenger of Allah ﷺ had passed away is also mentioned in reputable books apart from the mentioned sources. Examples include *Ṣaḥīḥ al-Bukhārī,* Vol. 4, Pg. 194; *Musnad Aḥmad,* Vol. 6, Pp. 219-220; Aḥmad ibn Yaḥyā ibn Jābir al-Balādhurī, *Ansāb al-Ashrāf,* Vol. 1, Pp. 563 and 566; Ibn Kathīr al-Qurayshī al-Dimashqī, *Al-Bidāyah wa al-Nihāyah,* Vol. 5, Pp. 241-243, ʿAbdul Raḥmān ibn Muḥammad ibn Khaldūn, *Tārīkh Ibn Khaldūn,* Vol. 2, Pp. 486-487; Shams al-Dīn al-Dhahabī, *Tārīkh al-Islam,* Vol. 1, Pp. 563-565; Aḥmad ibn Abī Yaʿqūbī, *Tārīkh Yaʿqūbī,* Vol. 2, Pg. 114; *Ṭabaqāt al-Kubrā,* Vol. 2, Pp. 205-206.

Book of Allah."[12]

If ʿUmar ibn al-Khaṭṭāb considered the Book of Allah ﷻ to be sufficient as guidance, it naturally follows that he should have been well-versed with the Quran and the reality of death of Prophet Muḥammad ﷺ.

Furthermore, the Messenger of Allah ﷺ hinted at his own impending demise in the Farewell Pilgrimage and informed his companions about his passing away one month before it occurred in Madina![13]

ʿAbdullāh ibn Masʿūd says: "The Prophet informed us about his impending death one month before his passing. He gathered us at the house of ʿĀyesha, gave us instructions, and said: 'The time of separation has approached, and I am returning to Allah and the Lote Tree of the Utmost Boundary.'"[14]

---

[12] *Ṣaḥīḥ Bukhārī*, Vol. 57, Pg. 138, Vol. 7, Pg. 9, the explanation of this story was given in the previous Chapter on *The Event of the Pen and Paper*. The Arabic text of this is as follows:

حَسْبُنَا كِتَابُ اللّٰهِ.

[13] See: *Musnad Aḥmad,* Vol. 5, Pg. 262; *Al-Bidāyah wa al-Nihāyah*, Vol. 5, Pg. 215. Interestingly, Ibn Kathīr narrates that Umar ibn al-Khaṭṭāb cried after hearing the verse of the completion of Islam (Quran, 5:3): "Today, I have perfected your religion for you, and I have completed My blessings upon you, and I have approved Islam as your religion." Those present who heard him cry asked him: "Why are you crying?" To this, ʿUmar replied: "There is nothing after perfection but imperfection. Surely, perfection will be flawed later, and some kind of flaw and deficiency is waiting for us." After quoting this sentence from ʿUmar, Ibn Kathīr says: "It is as if ʿUmar had understood the (imminent) death of the Prophet of Allah from this verse."

[14] The Arabic text of this is as follows:

قَدْ دَنَا الْفِرَاقُ وَالْمُنْقَلَبُ إِلَى اللهِ إِلَى سِدْرَةِ الْمُنْتَهَى.

Ibn Masʿūd added: "In that gathering, we also asked about bathing the body of the Prophet, how to shroud him, and even about performing the prayers over him *(Ṣalāt al-Mayyit)*. The Prophet provided answers and spoke about who should enter his grave."

Ṭabarī narrates this incident in detail in his book of history.[15]

Nevertheless, it was clear to every Muslim that the Messenger of Allah ﷺ would depart from this world. However, ʿUmar ibn al-Khaṭṭāb denied his departure and threatened the people. The motivation behind the denial of ʿUmar ibn al-Khaṭṭāb about the death of Prophet Muḥammad ﷺ and his intimidation of the people remains an unanswered question.

One possibility for his denial is that Abū Bakr was not present in Madina at the time of the Prophet's ﷺ departure, and there was a fear that during this period, someone not approved by ʿUmar ibn al-Khaṭṭāb would be chosen for the caliphate of the Muslims. Therefore, by raising doubts and threatening the Muslims, he was able to divert their attention from the caliphate after the death of the Messenger of Allah ﷺ.

As historians note, after Abū Bakr arrived and recited those verses, ʿUmar ibn al-Khaṭṭāb then accepted that Prophet Muḥammad ﷺ had indeed passed away.

Bukhārī writes in his *Ṣaḥīḥ* that: "The Messenger of Allah passed away, and Abū Bakr was in Sunḥ (a place outside Madina)."[16]

According to a narration from Ibn Kathīr, Sālim ibn ʿUbayd – who

---

[15] *Tārīkh al-Rusul wa al-Mulūk,* Vol. 3, Pg. 192; *Al-Ṭabaqāt al-Kubrā,* Vol. 2, Pg. 197; *Al-Kāmil fī al-Tārīkh,* Vol. 2, Pg. 319; ʿAbdul Raḥmān ibn ʿAlī al-Jawzī, *Al-Muntaẓam,* Vol. 4, Pg. 34, have also narrated this event.

[16] *Ṣaḥīḥ al-Bukhārī,* Vol. 4, Pg. 193. Yaʿqūbī mentions Sunḥ as a place outside Madina in his *Tārīkh,* Yaʿqūbī, Vol. 2, Pg. 127. The Arabic text of this is as follows:

إِنَّ رَسُولَ اللّٰهِ مَاتَ وأَبُو بَكْرٍ بِالسُّنْحِ.

was a freed slave of Ḥudhayfah, went to Abū Bakr in Sunḥ and informed him about the death of the Messenger of Allah ﷺ.[17]

Bearing in mind all these preliminary points, we now turn to the incident of Saqīfah and what transpired there.

The First Report

Ṭabarī narrates from ʿAbdullāh ibn ʿAbdul Raḥmān ibn Abī ʿUmrah al-Anṣārī that: "When the Messenger of Allah passed away, the *Anṣār* gathered in the Saqīfah of Banū Sāʿida and said: 'After Muḥammad, the chosen successor should be Saʿd ibn ʿUbādah.'

They went to Saʿd ibn ʿUbādah, a prominent individual from the tribe of Khazraj, and brought him there while he was ill. Saʿd said to one of his sons or nephews: 'Since I am sick and unable to address this gathering, listen to my words, then convey them loudly to this gathering.'

After praising and thanking Allah, Saʿd said: 'O group of *Anṣār*, you have a distinguished position and virtue in Islam that no other Arab tribe possesses. Know that Muḥammad lived among his people (in Mecca) for more than ten years, inviting them to worship the Merciful Allah, to abstain from idolatry and polytheism. However, few people believed in him, and they were unable to defend the Messenger of Allah, support his religion, and protect themselves from injustice until Allah desired to grant you virtue and honour, and made you the recipients of His special blessings. Thus, He bestowed upon you the faith in Allah and His Messenger and granted

---

[17] Dimashqī, Ismāʿīl ibn ʿUmar ibn Kathīr al-, *Al-Bidāyah wa al-Nihāyah*, Vol. 5, Pg. 244. It is worth noting that Sālim was the person whom ʿUmar mentioned at the time of his death, stating that if Sālim were alive, he would not have transferred the caliphate through consultation, rather he would have appointed him as his successor. Refer to ʿIzz al-Dīn ibn al-Athīr, *Usd al-Ghābah fī Maʿrifah al-Ṣaḥābah* Vol. 2, Pg. 156; *Tārīkh al-Rusul wa al-Mulūk*, Vol. 4, Pg. 227.

you the ability to defend the Messenger of Allah and his companions, and to strengthen him and his religion, and engage in *jihād* against his enemies, to the extent that the Arabs became obedient to the command of Allah and the religion of Islam. The Messenger of Allah departed from this world while he was pleased with you, and you were the light of his eyes. Now, make the matter of caliphate your own, as it belongs to you and not to others.'

They all replied to Saʿd: 'Your opinion is correct, and your words are true. We will not overlook you, and we will appoint you as the leader of this matter, for you are a competent individual among us and a source of satisfaction for the righteous believers.'

They exchanged words among themselves, then said: 'If the Quraysh migrants do not accept our decision and say: 'We are the migrants and the first companions of the Messenger of Allah, and we are from his own people. So why do you dispute with us over the caliphate after the Messenger of Allah?' What should we answer?'

Some of those present said: 'We will say: 'We are leaders, and you are leaders, and we will not accept anything without this matter.''

When Saʿd ibn ʿUbādah heard this response, he said: 'This is the beginning of weakness and (our) defeat.'[18]

When ʿUmar ibn al-Khaṭṭāb heard about this incident, he went to the house of the Prophet and sent someone to Abū Bakr, who was in his own house. At that time, ʿAlī was busy preparing the shroud and burial of the Messenger of Allah.

ʿUmar ibn al-Khaṭṭāb dispatched someone to Abū Bakr, but Abū Bakr replied: 'I am currently occupied.'

ʿUmar ibn al-Khaṭṭāb sent him again, stating that there was an urgent matter requiring his presence.

---

[18] The Arabic text of this is as follows:

هٰذَا أَوَّلُ الْوَهْنِ.

Eventually, Abū Bakr arrived and ʿUmar ibn al-Khaṭṭāb inquired if he was aware of the *Anṣār's* gathering at Saqīfah, and their intention to appoint Saʿd ibn ʿUbādah as the caliph. The noteworthy statement made during the gathering being: 'We are leaders, and you are leaders.'

Without delay, they hastened towards Saqīfah, encountering Abū ʿUbādah al-Jarrah on their way, and together, they proceeded towards the *Anṣār*.

Reflecting on the event, ʿUmar ibn al-Khaṭṭāb shares his thoughts: 'Upon our arrival, I had the intention to speak, but Abū Bakr advised me to remain calm and allow him to speak first, assuring me that I could express my thoughts afterwards. To my surprise, Abū Bakr not only conveyed my intended message, but also articulated it more eloquently.'"

ʿAbdullāh ibn ʿAbdul Raḥmān al-Anṣārī narrates this incident as follows: "Abū Bakr initiated his discourse by offering gratitude and praising Allah. He acknowledged that Allah had appointed Muḥammad as His Messenger, entrusting him with the task of guiding people towards worshipping Allah alone, and forsaking the worship of multiple deities, which was difficult for the Arab polytheists to abandon as it was an ancestral religion. In this context, Allah favoured the early migrants *(Muhājirūn)* from the tribe of the Prophet, who wholeheartedly affirmed the message of the Prophet, believed in him, and supported him.

They endured severe persecution and rejection from their own people with steadfastness. This was even though most of the people opposed and criticized them. However, the group of early migrants remained undeterred by their small numbers and the animosity of their adversaries. They were pioneers in worshipping Allah and believing in Him and His Messenger. They were loyal companions and close associates of the Prophet. Consequently, after the Prophet, they are the most deserving of assuming the caliphate. They did not engage in conflict with the unjust and tyrants over this matter.

As for the group of *Anṣār*, no one denies your excellence in faith and your illustrious history in Islam. Allah has appointed you as the helpers and supporters of His religion and the Divine Message of our Prophet. The migration of the Prophet was towards you, and his esteemed wives and trusted companions emerged from among your ranks. After the early *Muhājirūn*, no one holds a position comparable to yours. Hence, we are the leaders, and you are the ministers.[19] We consult with you, and no decision is made without your input."

Ḥabāb ibn Mundhīr from the tribe of Khazraj spoke up, addressing the *Anṣār* saying: "O group of *Anṣār*! Take matters into your own hands, for they are present in your city under your protection. They will never dare to oppose you, and the people only acknowledge your opinions and views. You possess honour, wealth, and a strong community. Therefore, never allow disagreements to arise among yourselves, as it will undermine your unity and compromise your strength. If this group *(Muhājirūn)* does not accept your proposal, then let us share the leadership. We will remove them from our city and assume control ourselves."

ʿUmar ibn al-Khaṭṭāb replied: "Two swords cannot fit into one sheath. By Allah, the Arabs will never be satisfied to have you as their leader while the Prophet was not from among you. However, they would accept a leader from a tribe that the Prophet belonged to. We have clear evidence and undeniable reasons against those who oppose our caliphate. Anyone who challenges us in governing and ruling according to the teachings of Muḥammad has deviated from the right path, acted disobediently, and exposed themselves to destruction."

---

[19] The Arabic text of this is as follows:

نَحْنُ الْأُمَرَاءُ وَأَنْتُمُ الْوُزَرَاءُ.

Ḥabāb rose again and said: "O group of *Anṣār*! Take matters into your own hands and pay no attention to the words of this man (ʿUmar ibn al-Khaṭṭāb) and his companions, for they seek to seize your rightful position. If they do not accept your proposal, then expel them from your city and take charge. By Allah, you deserve more of the caliphate than them, for it is through your swords that others have embraced this religion. I speak as an experienced man who has witnessed the ups and downs of life. Listen to my words..."

ʿUmar ibn al-Khaṭṭāb said: "In that case, may Allah kill you!"[20]

Ḥabāb replied: "Rather, may you be killed!"[21]

Abū ʿUbādah said: "O group of *Anṣār*, you were the first to support and assist the religion and have not deviated from it as others have."

Bashīr ibn Saʿd al-Anṣārī from the tribe of Aws stood up and said: "O group of *Anṣār*! By Allah, if we are involved in *jihād* against the polytheists and have a great history in the religion, it is not our intention to seek superiority in this matter. Our actions were not driven by worldly desires, for Allah has shown His favour upon us in these efforts. Know that Muḥammad is from the tribe of Quraysh, and his people are more deserving than us in this matter. By Allah, there will never come a day when I engage in conflict with them regarding this matter. Fear Allah, and do not oppose them or engage in strife and conflict."

At that moment, Abū Bakr said: "These two men, ʿUmar and Abū ʿUbādah, are present. Pledge allegiance to whomever you desire."

The two men responded: "By Allah, with you present, we will

---

[20] The Arabic text of this is as follows:

إِذًا يَقْتُلُكَ اللهُ.

[21] The Arabic text of this is as follows:

بَلْ إِيَّاكَ يُقْتَلُ.

never become the leaders. For you are the foremost among the *Muhājirūn*, the one who stood alongside the Prophet in the cave, and the successor to the Messenger of Allah in prayer.[22] We know that prayer is the greatest act of worship for Muslims. So, who is more deserving than you to be prioritized or entrusted with the caliphate? Open your hand, and we will pledge allegiance to you."

When ʿUmar ibn al-Khaṭṭāb and Abū ʿUbādah intended to pledge allegiance to Abū Bakr, Bashīr ibn Saʿd intervened and pledged allegiance to Abū Bakr first.

Then, ʿUmar ibn al-Khaṭṭāb and Abū ʿUbādah stepped forward and pledged their allegiance to Abū Bakr.

At that moment, Ḥabāb ibn Mundhir exclaimed: "O Bashīr ibn Saʿd, you have acted wrongfully without any necessity. Are you harbouring jealousy towards your cousin Saʿd ibn ʿUbādah in the matter of caliphate?"

Bashīr responded: "By Allah, no! I did not intend to engage in conflict over a matter that Allah had decreed for us."

When the Aws and Khazraj witnessed Bashīr ibn Saʿd's position and the invitation extended to Quraysh on one hand, and the desire of the Khazraj to appoint Saʿd ibn ʿUbādah as the leader on the other hand, some among them, including Usayd ibn Ḥuḍayr, who held a prominent position among the Aws, said: "If the Khazraj were to become the leaders even once, they would forever surpass you in this

---

[22] This is a reference to the popularly held Sunnī belief (which the Shīʿa scholars do not accept) that in the days leading to the sickness and eventual death of Prophet Muḥammad ﷺ, since he was unable to lead the Congregational Prayers *(Ṣalāt al-Jamāʿah)*, Abū Bakr was appointed to lead the Muslim community in Madina in the congregational prayers. Based on their flawed logic, the Sunnī opinion is that just as Abū Bakr was qualified to lead the community in Congregational Prayers, this indicates that he was also qualified to lead the community as the caliph of the final Messenger ﷺ. (Tr.)

virtue, and you will never have a share in leadership, therefore, let us rise and pledge allegiance to Abū Bakr."

Upon hearing these words, members of the tribe of Aws stood up and pledged allegiance to Abū Bakr, thwarting the plans of Saʿd ibn ʿUbādah and the Khazraj for leadership.

ʿAbdullāh ibn ʿAbdul Raḥmān further recounts that the people in that gathering eagerly rushed to pledge allegiance to Abū Bakr, while some of Saʿd ibn ʿUbādah supporters cautioned: "Be careful with Saʿd, do not harm him!"

Hearing this, ʿUmar ibn al-Khaṭṭāb declared: "Kill him! May Allah kill him!"[23]

Saʿd then stood up and declared: "I wanted to strike you so hard that it would shatter your arms!"

Saʿd grasped ʿUmar's beard and ʿUmar warned: "If even a single hair is removed, I will break your teeth."

Abū Bakr intervened, saying: "O ʿUmar, remain calm, for in this situation, kindness and compassion are more effective."

Hearing this, ʿUmar ibn al-Khaṭṭāb released his grip on Saʿd.

Saʿd stated firmly: "By Allah, if I were not ill, I would raise such a cry in the streets and alleyways of Madina that you, ʿUmar, and your companions would seek shelter in your homes. By Allah, I will send you to a people who have always been obeyed and followed, and not people that do as they please." He then said: "Take me away from this place," so they assisted him and escorted him to his home.[24]

Keep in mind that everything we are mentioning with respect to

---

[23] The Arabic text of this is as follows:

أُقْتُلُوا قَتَلَهُ اللّٰهُ.

[24] *Tārīkh al-Rusul wa al-Mulūk*, Vol. 3, Pp. 222-218; summarized with some differences as seen in the narration of ʿAbdullāh ibn Muslim ibn Qutayba al-Dīnawarī, *Al-Imāmah wa al-Siyāsah*, Vol. 1, Pp. 21-28; and Ibn Athīr, Vol. 2, Pp. 328-331.

the Event at Saqīfah is coming straight from the books of the Ahlul Sunnah – we are **not** adding anything from the books of the Shīʿa in this regard.

Second Report: ʿUmar's Recollection of Saqīfah

According to a narration found in *Ṣaḥīḥ al-Bukhārī*, there is statement from Ibn ʿAbbās that during *Ḥajj*, ʿUmar ibn al-Khaṭṭāb overheard some individuals saying: "If ʿUmar passes away, we will pledge allegiance to so-and-so."[25]

These words greatly unsettled ʿUmar, prompting him to address the matter during an evening gathering in Minā. However, ʿAbdul Raḥmān ibn ʿAwf advised him against it, pointing out the diverse nature of the audience and the potential for misinterpretation. He suggested waiting until they reached Madina, where *Dār al-Hijrah* stood, and the esteemed leaders of the community resided. ʿUmar accepted this advice.

Ibn ʿAbbās stated that: "Upon their arrival in Madina, on a Friday, ʿUmar ibn al-Khaṭṭāb ascended the pulpit and delivered a speech, expressing his concerns. He remarked: 'I have heard people saying that if I were to pass away, then they will pledge allegiance to someone else.'

He went on to say: 'No one has the right to say that the pledge to Abū Bakr was a hasty, thoughtless act that was completed.'[26]

---

[25] In the introduction of *Fatḥ al-Bārī* (Pg. 337), it is quoted from *Ansāb al-Ashrāf* of Balādhurī that the original news was that Zubayr said: "If ʿUmar dies, we will pledge allegiance to ʿAlī." See also Aḥmad ibn Yaḥyā ibn Jābir al-Balādhurī, *Ansāb al-Ashrāf*, Vol. 1, Pg. 581. The Arabic text of this is as follows:

لَوْ قَدْ مَاتَ عُمَرُ بَايَعْنَا عَلِيًّا.

[26] The Arabic text of this is as follows:

ʿUmar said: ʻKnow that the oath of allegiance (to Abū Bakr) was indeed a hastily made decision without careful reflection, however, Allah protected the Muslims from the potential harm that could have arisen.'"[27]

Through this event, ʿUmar ibn al-Khaṭṭāb emphasized the importance of avoiding such hasty actions, and the necessity of consulting the Muslim community before pledging allegiance to anyone [although he noted that Allah ﷻ protected the Muslims even though they made such a hasty decision].

Subsequently, ʿUmar recounted the events that unfolded at Saqīfah, saying: "After the passing away of the Messenger of Allah, a group of *Anṣār* opposed us and gathered at Saqīfah Banū Sāʿida. ʿAlī, Zubayr, and their supporters also voiced their opposition.

In response, the *Muhājirūn* approached Abū Bakr. I suggested to Abū Bakr that we should meet our *Anṣārī* brothers. As we drew closer to them, two righteous *Anṣārī* men confronted us, inquiring about our destination. We explained that we were going to meet our *Anṣārī* brethren. They cautioned us, advising us to stay away and attend to our own affairs. However, we disregarded their advice and proceeded to gather with them at Saqīfah Banū Sāʿida. There, I noticed a man wrapped in a garment, and upon inquiring, I learned it was Saʿd ibn ʿUbādah, who was unwell. Shortly after, a speaker from the *Anṣār* arose and delivered a sermon."

ʿUmar shared that he had intended to convey his own eloquent words, but Abū Bakr intervened, commencing his own speech with composure and dignity. Abū Bakr expressed the idea that while the

---

إِنَّـمَا كَانَتْ بَيْعَةُ أَبِي بَكْرٍ فَلْتَةً وَتَـمَّتْ.

[27] The Arabic text of this is as follows:

أَلَا وَإِنَّـمَا قَدْ كَانَتْ كَذٰلِكَ وَلٰكِنْ وَقَى اللّٰهُ شَرَّهَا.

Anṣār possessed the virtues they mentioned, the caliphate should rightfully reside among the Quraysh, who excelled in lineage and status among the Arab tribes.

ʿUmar ibn al-Khaṭṭāb continued: "Then he (Abū Bakr) added: 'I prefer one of these two men,' pointing to me and Abū ʿUbādah, 'So pledge allegiance to whoever you choose.' Then he held my hand and Abū ʿUbādah's hand. But it was burdensome for me to assume leadership over a group in which Abū Bakr was present!

Amidst this, a man from the *Anṣār*, named Ḥabāb ibn Mundhir, suggested having one leader from among us and one leader from among them, the Quraysh. The news spread, and there was an outcry, causing me to fear discord and division among the people. Therefore, I said to Abū Bakr: 'Open your hand, so that I may pledge allegiance to you.' He opened his hand, and I pledged allegiance to him. The *Muhājirūn* present there and the *Anṣār* also pledged allegiance to him; and in the process, we turned Saʿd ibn ʿUbādah into a humbled state. Someone then shouted: 'You killed Saʿd!' I replied: 'May Allah kill Saʿd ibn ʿUbādah!'"[28]

ʿUmar ibn al-Khaṭṭāb continued: "By Allah, we could not have found a better course of action than pledging allegiance to Abū Bakr. We were concerned that if we separated from the *Anṣār* in this manner and no pledge took place, then they may have pledged allegiance to one of their own. Then, we would have faced the dilemma of either pledging allegiance to someone we were not content with, or engaging in opposition and conflict, which would have led to corruption. Therefore, I reiterated once again that no one should pledge allegiance to anyone without consulting the Muslims. Neither the one pledging allegiance, nor the one receiving it should

---

[28] The Arabic text of this is as follows:

قَتَلَ اللّٰهُ سَعْدَ بْنُ عُبَادَةَ.

follow through, lest both meet their demise!"

It appears that ʿUmar issued the permission for killing the two[29] with this statement.[30]

Other Notable Points

In other narrations concerning the incident of Saqīfah, additional noteworthy points have been mentioned, some of which we mention below.

According to an account of Ṭabarī, on the day of Saqīfah after the discussions concluded, ʿUmar ibn al-Khaṭṭāb said to Abū Bakr: "Open your hand so that I may pledge allegiance to you."

Abū Bakr responded to ʿUmar, saying: "You open your hand so that I may pledge allegiance to you."

Each of them tried to open their companion's hand to pledge allegiance,[31] and in this struggle, ʿUmar got the upper hand (as he was physically the stronger of the two),[32] so ʿUmar opened Abū Bakr's hand, and the pledge was made. Thus, ʿUmar [forcefully]

---

29 Presumably what is meant by 'killing the two' is Saʿd ibn ʿUbādah and Ḥabāb ibn Mundhir. (Tr.)

30 *Ṣaḥīḥ al-Bukhārī*, Vol. 8, Pp. 25-28, Book of Combatting Disbelievers and Apostates (with some summarization). The above incident has been narrated with variations in numerous other books, including *Musnad Aḥmad*, Vol. 1, Pp. 55-56; *Al-Muṣannaf of ʿAbdul Razzāq*, Vol. 5, Pp. 439-445, Tradition 9758; *Ṣaḥīḥ of Ibn Ḥibbān*, Vol. 2, Pp. 146-151.

31 The Arabic text of this is as follows:

كُلٌّ مِنْهُمَا يُرِيدُ صَاحِبِهِ يَفْتَحُ يَدِهِ يُضْرِبُ عَلَيْهَا.

32 The Arabic text of this is as follows:

وَكَانَ عُمَرُ أَشَدُّ الرَّجُلَيْنِ.

opened Abū Bakr's hand...[33]

According to Ṭabarī and Ibn Athīr's accounts, at Saqīfah, when ʿUmar and others pledged allegiance to Abū Bakr, all the *Anṣār,* or according to some narrations, a group of the *Anṣār* said: "We will only pledge allegiance to ʿAlī."[34]

According to another narration, when Saʿd was confined, someone shouted: "You killed Saʿd," ʿUmar said: "May Allah kill him! He is a hypocrite."[35] This was probably due to the opposition of Saʿd regarding what was going on at Saqīfah.

After the death of the Messenger of Allah ﷺ, ʿAbbās, the uncle of the Prophet ﷺ, said to Imam ʿAlī ﵇: "Come, let us go among the people so that I can pledge allegiance to you in front of them, and as a result, two people will not dispute about you."

However, Imam ʿAlī ﵇ was busy preparing the burial of the Messenger of Allah ﷺ, so he did not accept and said: "Are there men amongst them who deny our rights and usurp our position?"[36]

ʿAbbās replied: "You shall soon see how it will be!" After Abū Bakr

---

[33] *Tārīkh al-Rusul wa al-Mulūk*, Vol. 3, Pg. 203. The Arabic text of this is as follows:

فَفَتَحَ عُمَرُ يَدِ أَبِي بَكْرٍ...

[34] Ibid., Pg. 202; *Al-Kāmil fī al-Tārīkh*, Vol. 2, Pg. 325. The Arabic text of this is as follows:

فَقَالَتِ الْأَنْصَارُ أَوْ بَعْضَ الْأَنْصَارُ: لَا نُبَايِعُ إِلَّا عَلِيًّا.

[35] *Tārīkh al-Rusul wa al-Mulūk*, Vol. 3, Pg. 223. The Arabic text of this is as follows:

قَتَلَهُ اللهُ إِنَّهُ مُنَافِقٌ.

[36] The Arabic text of this is as follows:

أَوْ مِنْهُمْ مَنْ يُنْكِرُ حَقَّنَا وَيَسْتَبِدُّ عَلَيْنَا.

was pledged allegiance to, ʿAbbās said to Imam ʿAlī ﷺ: "O ʿAlī! Did I not tell you that if you delay, others will take the caliphate away?"[37]

It has been narrated from Ibrāhīm al-Taymī that after the departure of the Messenger of Allah ﷺ, ʿUmar went to Abū ʿUbādah and said: "Open your hand so that I can pledge allegiance to you."[38] Then he added: "This is because you were called the trustworthy one by the tongue of the Messenger of Allah for this nation!" Abū ʿUbādah replied to ʿUmar: "How can you make such a suggestion and want to pledge allegiance to me, while the caliph and the companion of the Prophet are among you?"[39]

According to a narration from Ibn Abī Shaybah, Abū Bakr, and ʿUmar were so occupied with taking the pledge of allegiance (from people) that they did not even attend the burial of the Messenger of Allah (indeed, Abū Bakr and ʿUmar did not witness the burial of the Prophet).[40]

Was this gathering at Saqīfah, and these actions for the benefit of the Muslims, or for the advancement of seizing the caliphate?!

Reactions

In the previous section, we discussed the Event of Saqīfah, and the

---

[37] *Ansāb al-Ashrāf*, Vol. 1, Pg. 583, Vol. 1180; Like this narration, there are also other ones found in *Al-Imāmah wa al-Siyāsah*, Vol. 1, Pg. 21; and *Al-Ṭabaqāt al-Kubrā*, Vol. 2, Pg. 190.

[38] The Arabic text of this is as follows:

أَبْسُطْ يَدَكَ لِأُبَايِعَكَ.

[39] Dhahabī, Muḥammad ibn Aḥmad ibn ʿUthmān al-, *Tārīkh al-Islam*, Vol. 3, Pg. 9.

[40] Kūfī, ʿAbdullāh ibn Muḥammad ibn Abī Shaybah al-, *Al-Muṣannaf*, Vol. 8, Pg. 572, Vol. 5. The Arabic text of this is as follows:

إِنَّ أَبَا بَكْرٍ وعُمَرَ لَا يَشْهَدَا دَفْنَ النَّبِيِّ (صَلَّى اللَّهُ عَلَيْهِ وَسَلَّمَ).

appointment of Abū Bakr as the caliph, which happened suddenly and through a series of events and confrontations. After Bashīr ibn Sa'd, 'Umar ibn al-Khaṭṭāb and Abū 'Ubādah quickly pledged allegiance to Abū Bakr, and a group of *Anṣār* also pledged allegiance to him.

This was the beginning of the incident, but the continuation of events and reactions has its own separate narrative, which we will now examine.

Allegiance

Bura' ibn 'Āzib[41] said the following: "I was always attached to the Banū Hāshim, and when the Messenger of Allah passed away, I was concerned that the Quraysh would exclude them from leadership. Thus, I was in a state of restlessness and rushed to the Banū Hāshim who were in the room of the Messenger of Allah beside his noble body. I would go and come back, while also keeping an eye on the leaders of Quraysh. Amid this commotion, I noticed that Abū Bakr and 'Umar disappeared; and after a while, I heard someone say: 'Abū Bakr has been given the pledge of allegiance!' Without hesitation, I headed towards them and saw Abū Bakr coming with 'Umar, Abū 'Ubādah, and a group of the companions of Saqīfah. Whoever reached them, would place his hand in Abū Bakr's hand as a sign of allegiance, whether he liked it or not.[42] Upon witnessing this scene,

---

[41] Bura' ibn 'Āzib ibn Ḥārith al-Khazrajī al-Anṣārī was one of the companions of the Messenger of Allah ﷺ. He accompanied Imam 'Alī ؑ in the Battles of Jamal, Ṣiffīn, and Nahrawān. After the passing away of Imam 'Alī ؑ, he settled in Kūfa and remained there until he left this world during the time of Mā'idah ibn Zubayr. Reference: Yūsuf ibn 'Abdullāh ibn Muḥammad ibn 'Abdul Barr, *Al-Istī'āb fī Ma'rifah al-Aṣḥāb*, Vol. 1, Pp. 157-158.

[42] The Arabic text of this is as follows:

I became upset and quickly proceeded towards the Banū Hāshim. I saw that the door [to their house] was closed, so I knocked on it forcefully, and said: 'A group of people have pledged allegiance to Abū Bakr.'

ʿAbbās, the uncle of the Prophet said: 'May your hands remain soiled with dust (a derogatory statement). Sit on the soil of humiliation until the end of time.'

Then he (ʿAbbās) turned towards ʿAlī and the Banū Hāshim, and said: 'I gave you an order, but you did not listen' (referring to ʿAbbās's request to Imam ʿAlī ﷺ to come so they could pledge allegiance to him, but ʿAlī ﷺ did not accept it due to being occupied with the preparations for the burial of the Messenger of Allah ﷺ)."

Buraʾ ibn ʿĀzib added: "I was in great grief until the evening when I saw Miqdād, Salmān, Abū Dharr, ʿUbādah ibn al-Ṣāmit, Abū al-Haytham ibn Tayyhān, Ḥudhayfah, and ʿAmmār. They intended to consult among the *Muhājirūn* regarding the caliphate matter."

This news reached Abū Bakr and ʿUmar, who sent Abū ʿUbādah, and Mughīra ibn Shuʿbah to meet with them and seek their opinion to counter this news. Mughīra said: "Meet with ʿAbbās and give him and his sons a share in the leadership so that this will separate them from ʿAlī." [A tactic commonly used by politicians even today – referred to as divide and conquer.]

Abū Bakr, ʿUmar, Abū ʿUbādah, and Mughīra went to ʿAbbās (this incident took place on the second night after the passing away of the Messenger of Allah ﷺ). Abū Bakr, after praising and glorifying Allah, honoured ʿAbbās and said: "Some people have appointed me as their guardian and ruler, and I have accepted it. However, it is observed that those who object to this allegiance come to you, seeking your support, and they may consider you as their refuge. Nevertheless, we

---

فمدّوا يده فمسحوها على يد أبي بكر يبايعه شاء ذلك أو أبى.

have come here to secure a share for you and your descendants in this leadership, both during your lifetime and afterwards."[43]

ʿUmar, in a threatening tone, added: "We do not want you to oppose what Muslims have unanimously agreed upon, and cause trouble for yourself or the Muslims."

ʿAbbās did not accept this proposal and said: "If the caliphate is your right, then hold it firmly without showing favouritism or generosity; and if it is the right of the believers to have a say, then you have no right to interfere, and they should be free to decide. If it is our right, then we are not satisfied with some of it – we want all of it to be given to us."[44]

Position of Some Companions

According to the accounts of the historians, some companions refrained from giving their allegiance to Abū Bakr.

Ibn ʿAbdul Barr narrates that Saʿd ibn ʿUbādah and a group from the tribe of Khazraj, as well as some individuals from the Quraysh, did not pledge allegiance to Abū Bakr initially. However, after some time, apart from Saʿd ibn ʿUbādah, the others pledged their allegiance.

Similarly, on the day of the general allegiance, Imam ʿAlī ﷺ, Zubayr, Ṭalḥa, and Khālid ibn Saʿīd from the Quraysh did not pledge their allegiance to Abū Bakr.[45] However, after a certain period, it is reported that some of them also pledged their allegiance, as narrated by Ibn Athīr. However, Imam ʿAlī ﷺ, members of the Banū Hāshim,

---

[43] The Arabic text of this is as follows:

... وَنَحْنُ نُرِيدُ أَنْ نَجْعَلَ لَكَ فِي هٰذَا الْأَمْرِ نَصِيبًا وَلِمَنْ بَعْدَكَ مِنْ عَقِبِكَ...

[44] Madā'inī, Abū Ḥamīd ibn Abī al-Ḥadīd al-Muʿtazilī al-, *Sharḥ Nahj al-Balāgha*, Vol. 1, Pg. 29 (summarized).

[45] *Al-Istīʿāb fī Maʿrifah al-Aṣḥāb*, Vol. 3, Pg. 973.

Zubayr, Khālid ibn Saʿīd, and Saʿd ibn ʿUbādah did not pledge their allegiance until after the passing away of Lady Fāṭima al-Zahrāʾ ‎ﷺ, which some historians report took place around six months after the departure of the Messenger of Allah ﷺ.[46]

In some other books of history, the names of several other companions who did not initially give their allegiance to Abū Bakr are mentioned, and these include ʿAbbās ibn ʿAbdul Muṭṭalib, Faḍl ibn ʿAbbās, Salmān al-Fārsī, ʿAmmār ibn Yāsir, Buraʾ ibn ʿĀzib, and Abī ibn Kaʿb.[47]

It is also narrated from Salmān al-Fārsī that when the allegiance was taken for Abū Bakr, he said: "Some of you pledged allegiance, while others did not. If they had pledged allegiance to ʿAlī, blessings from the heavens and the earth would have been showered upon them, and they would have benefited from that which is above them and that which is beneath them."[48]

Additionally, it has been stated that Abū Dharr was not present in the city of Madina when the Messenger of Allah ﷺ passed away. He arrived in Madina after Abū Bakr had become the caliph, and he is quoted to have said: "You have settled for something trivial and left aside the family of your Prophet. If you had entrusted this matter to the family of your Prophet, then there never would have been any disagreement among you."[49]

Ibn Athīr also mentions that Abān ibn Saʿīd, the brother of Khālid ibn Saʿīd, did not pledge allegiance to Abū Bakr, along with his

---

[46] *Usd al-Ghābah fī Maʿrifah al-Ṣaḥābah*, Vol. 3, Pg. 228.

[47] *Tārīkh al-Yaʿqūbī*, Vol. 2, Pg. 124.

[48] *Ansāb al-Ashrāf*, Vol. 1, Pg. 591. The Arabic text of this is as follows:

كرداذ وناكاكرذاد أي عملتم وَمَا عملتم لَوْ بَايَعُوا عَلِيًّا لَأَكَلُو مِنْ فَوْقِهِمْ وَمِنْ تَحْتِ أَرْجُلِهِمْ.

[49] *Sharḥ Nahj al-Balāgha*, Vol. 6, Pg. 13. The Arabic text of this is as follows:

أصبتم قناعة وتركتهم قرابة لو جعلتم هذا الأمر في أهل بيت نبيّكم لما اختلف عليكم إثنان.

brother. Khālid is quoted as having said the following to the Banū Hāshim: “You are tall trees bearing good fruit, and we are the ones who follow you.” Therefore, when the Banū Hāshim pledged allegiance, then he pledged allegiance.[50]

According to Ibn Abī al-Ḥadīd, we also know that ʿUbādah ibn Ṣāmit, Abū al-Haytham ibn Tayyihān, and Ḥudhayfah were among those who opposed giving the oath of allegiance to Abū Bakr.

As for Saʿd ibn ʿUbādah, he never pledged allegiance until the end of his life. Ṭabarī writes: “He (Saʿd ibn ʿUbādah) did not participate in their prayers, was absent from their gatherings, did not accompany them in *Ḥajj*, and was not seen with them.”[51]

With respect to Saʿd ibn ʿUbādah, it is also written that he did not pledge allegiance to Abū Bakr and left Madina, but later he returned. He settled in the region of Ḥawrān in Syria and passed away in the year 14 AH or 15 AH during the caliphate of ʿUmar ibn al-Khaṭṭāb, and ended up being killed in Ḥawrān. Strangely, his murder was attributed to the *jinn*. Even more than this, it is reported that some people composed poems about his killing in the dialect of the *jinn*.[52]

According to the account of Balādhurī, ʿUmar sent someone to him to take his allegiance, or otherwise, he would have him killed. He went, and since Saʿd ibn ʿUbādah did not pledge allegiance, the

---

[50] *Usd al-Ghābah fī Maʿrifah al-Ṣaḥābah*, Vol. 1, Pp. 47 and 575. The Arabic text of this is as follows:

إنّكم لطوال الشجر طيّبوا الثمر ونحن تبع لكم.

[51] *Tārīkh al-Rusul wa al-Mulūk*, Vol. 3, Pg. 223; *Al-Muntaẓam*, Vol. 4, Pg. 68 adds: “He did not observe fasting based on their declaration of the fasting day, and he did not accept their declaration of the first day of the month.”

[52] *Al-Istīʿāb fī Maʿrifah al-Aṣḥāb*, Vol. 2, Pg. 599; *Usd al-Ghābah fī Maʿrifah al-Ṣaḥābah*, Vol. 2, Pg. 205.

person killed him with an arrow and attributed it to the *jinn*.[53]

The Position of the Ahlul Bayt ﷺ

The position of the Ahlul Bayt ﷺ is significant and influential in accordance with the narration of *Thaqalayn*,[54] which has been

---

[53] *Ansāb al-Ashrāf*, Vol. 1, Pg. 589. Ibn Abī al-Ḥadīd writes: "Some say that the Amīr of Sham (Syria) killed him because he disobeyed the *imam* (the caliph)." *Sharḥ Nahj al-Balāgha*, Vol. 10, Pg. 111. Ibn ʿAbd Rabbīh al-Andalūsī writes: "ʿUmar sent someone to Sham and said that if he does not pledge allegiance, then he should be killed. Despite all efforts, Saʿd ibn ʿUbādah did not pledge allegiance, so he was killed with an arrow." *Al-ʿIqd al-Farīd*, Vol. 4, Pg. 260.

[54] The *Tradition of Thaqalayn (Ḥadīth al-Thaqalayn)* is mentioned in *Ṣaḥīḥ Muslim*, Book of Virtues of the Companions, under the Chapter of the Virtues of ʿAlī ibn Abī Ṭālib ﷺ, Tradition 9:

حَدَّثَنِي زُهَيْرُ بْنُ حَرْبٍ وَشُجَاعُ بْنُ مَخْلَدٍ جَمِيعًا عَنِ ابْنِ عُلَيَّةَ قَالَ زُهَيْرٌ حَدَّثَنَا إِسْمَاعِيلُ بْنُ إِبْرَاهِيمَ حَدَّثَنِي أَبُو حَيَّانَ حَدَّثَنِي يَزِيدُ بْنُ حَيَّانَ قَالَ انْطَلَقْتُ أَنَا وَحُصَيْنُ بْنُ سَبْرَةَ وَعُمَرُ بْنُ مُسْلِمٍ إِلَى زَيْدِ بْنِ أَرْقَمَ فَلَمَّا جَلَسْنَا إِلَيْهِ قَالَ لَهُ حُصَيْنٌ لَقَدْ لَقِيتَ يَا زَيْدُ خَيْرًا كَثِيرًا رَأَيْتَ رَسُولَ اللَّهِ صَلَّى اللَّهُ عَلَيْهِ وَسَلَّمَ وَسَمِعْتَ حَدِيثَهُ وَغَزَوْتَ مَعَهُ وَصَلَّيْتَ خَلْفَهُ لَقَدْ لَقِيتَ يَا زَيْدُ خَيْرًا كَثِيرًا حَدِّثْنَا يَا زَيْدُ مَا سَمِعْتَ مِنْ رَسُولِ اللَّهِ صَلَّى اللَّهُ عَلَيْهِ وَسَلَّمَ قَالَ يَا ابْنَ أَخِي وَاللَّهِ لَقَدْ كَبِرَتْ سِنِّي وَقَدُمَ عَهْدِي وَنَسِيتُ بَعْضَ الَّذِي كُنْتُ أَعِي مِنْ رَسُولِ اللَّهِ صَلَّى اللَّهُ عَلَيْهِ وَسَلَّمَ فَمَا حَدَّثْتُكُمْ فَاقْبَلُوا وَمَا لَا فَلَا تُكَلِّفُونِيهِ. ثُمَّ قَالَ قَامَ رَسُولُ اللَّهِ صَلَّى اللَّهُ عَلَيْهِ وَسَلَّمَ يَوْمًا فِينَا خَطِيبًا بِـمَاءٍ يُدْعَى خُمًّا بَيْنَ مَكَّةَ وَالْمَدِينَةِ فَحَمِدَ اللَّهَ وَأَثْنَى عَلَيْهِ وَوَعَظَ وَذَكَّرَ ثُمَّ قَالَ: أَمَّا بَعْدُ أَلَا أَيُّهَا النَّاسُ فَإِنَّمَا أَنَا بَشَرٌ يُوشِكُ أَنْ يَأْتِيَ رَسُولُ رَبِّي فَأُجِيبَ وَأَنَا تَارِكٌ فِيكُمْ ثَقَلَيْنِ أَوَّلُهُمَا كِتَابُ اللَّهِ فِيهِ الْهُدَى وَالنُّورُ فَخُذُوا بِكِتَابِ اللَّهِ وَاسْتَمْسِكُوا بِهِ. فَحَثَّ عَلَى كِتَابِ اللَّهِ وَرَغَّبَ فِيهِ ثُمَّ قَالَ: وَأَهْلُ بَيْتِي أُذَكِّرُكُمُ اللَّهَ فِي أَهْلِ بَيْتِي أُذَكِّرُكُمُ اللَّهَ فِي أَهْلِ بَيْتِي أُذَكِّرُكُمُ اللَّهَ فِي أَهْلِ بَيْتِي. فَقَالَ لَهُ حُصَيْنٌ وَمَنْ أَهْلُ بَيْتِهِ يَا زَيْدُ

أَلَيْسَ نِسَاؤُهُ مِنْ أَهْلِ بَيْتِهِ قَالَ نِسَاؤُهُ مِنْ أَهْلِ بَيْتِهِ وَلَكِنْ أَهْلُ بَيْتِهِ مَنْ حُرِمَ الصَّدَقَةَ بَعْدَهُ. قَالَ
وَمَنْ هُمْ قَالَ هُمْ آلُ عَلِيٍّ وَآلُ عَقِيلٍ وَآلُ جَعْفَرٍ وَآلُ عَبَّاسٍ. قَالَ كُلُّ هَؤُلاَءِ حُرِمَ الصَّدَقَةَ قَالَ نَعَمْ.

Narrated to me Zuhayr ibn Ḥarb and Shujāʿ ibn Makhlad, both from Ibn ʿUlayyah. Zuhayr said: Ismāʿīl ibn Ibrāhīm narrated to us, Abū Ḥayyān narrated to me, Yazīd ibn Ḥayyān reported: "I went along with Ḥusain ibn Sabra and ʿUmar ibn Muslim to Zayd ibn Arqam, and as we sat by his side, Ḥuṣain said to him: 'Zayd, you have been able to acquire a great virtue that you saw Allah's Messenger ﷺ, listened to his talk, fought by his side in (different) battles, and offered prayer behind me. Zayd, you have in fact earned a great virtue. Zayd, narrate to us what you heard from Allah's Messenger ﷺ. He said: 'I have grown old and have almost spent my age, and I have forgotten some of the things which I remembered in connection with Allah's Messenger ﷺ, so accept whatever I narrate to you, and which I do not narrate do not compel me to do that.' He then said: 'One day, Allah's Messenger ﷺ stood up to deliver a sermon at a watering place known as Khumm situated between Mecca and Madina. He praised Allah, extolled Him and delivered the sermon and exhorted (us) and said: 'Now to our purpose. O people, I am a human being. I am about to receive a messenger (the angel of death) from my Lord, and I, in response to Allah's call, (bid good-bye to you), but I am leaving among you two weighty things: the one being the Book of Allah in which there is right guidance and light, so hold fast to the Book of Allah and adhere to it. He exhorted (us) (to hold fast) to the Book of Allah, then said: The second are the members of my household I remind you (of your duties) to the members of my family.' He (Ḥuṣain) said to Zayd: 'Who are the members of his household? Aren't his wives the members of his family?' Thereupon he said: 'His wives are the members of his family, (but here) the members of his family are those for whom acceptance of *zakāt* is forbidden.' And he said: 'Who are they?' Thereupon he said: ʿAli and the offspring of ʿAli, ʿAqīl and the offspring of ʿAqil, and the offspring of Jaʿfar and the offspring of ʿAbbās. Ḥuṣain said:

transmitted through both the Shīʿa and Sunnī sources. It states that the Ahlul Bayt, alongside the Noble Quran, are the only sources of guidance for the Muslim community, and Muslims are obligated to hold onto BOTH and not separate from either one of them. Therefore, knowing their position in this matter is crucial.

Of course, we know that the Ahlul Bayt refers to Imam ʿAlī, Lady Fāṭima al-Zahrāʾ, Imam Ḥasan, and Imam Ḥusayn.[55] Thus, based on the *Ḥadīth of Thaqalayn*, what matters after the passing away of Prophet Muḥammad was the stance of Imam ʿAlī

'These are those for whom the acceptance of *zakāt* is forbidden.' Zayd said: 'Yes.'"

Additionally, numerous other books of *Ṣiḥāḥ* of the Sunnī *aḥādīth* have also cited this tradition through various narrations, including *Musnad Aḥmad*, Vol. 3, Pp. 14, 26, 39, Vol. 4, Pg. 367, Vol. 5, Pp. 182, 189; *Sunan Dārimī*, Vol. 2, Pg. 432; *Sunan Tirmidhī*, Vol. 5, Pg. 329, *Tradition* 3876; *Sunan al-Kubrā* by Bayhaqī, Vol. 2, Pg. 148, Vol. 7, Pg. 30; *Muʿjam al-Zawāʾid* by Haythamī, Vol. 9, Pp. 162-163; *Sunan al-Kubrā* by Nasāʾī, Vol. 5, Pg. 51; *Ṣaḥīḥ* Ibn Khuzaymah, Vol. 4, Pg. 162; *Kanz al-ʿUmmāl*, Vol. 1, Pp. 172, 870-872, Pp. 173, 1873, Tradition 898, Pg. 185, Traditions 943-946; *Ṣawāʾiq al-Muḥriqah*, Pg. 148 (for references from the Imāmī sources, refer to *Biḥār al-Anwār*, Vol. 23, Pp. 106-147).

[55] Regarding the meaning of Ahlul Bayt in Verse 33 of Sūrah al-Aḥzāb (33) – "Indeed, Allah desires to repel impurity from you, O people of the Household, and purify you with thorough purification" – it refers to Fāṭima, Ḥasan, and Ḥusayn – refer to *Ṣaḥīḥ Muslim*, Book of Virtues of the Companions, under the Chapter on the Virtues of the Prophet's Household, Tradition 1; *Sunan Tirmidhī*, Vol. 5, Pg. 141, Tradition 3216, Pg. 142, Tradition 3217. In *Al-Durr al-Manthūr*, it explicitly mentions in more than ten narrations that Ahlul Bayt refers to ʿAlī, Fāṭima, Ḥasan, and Ḥusayn – *Al-Durr al-Manthūr*, Vol. 6, Pp. 603-607, under the explanation of Verse 33 of Sūrah al-Aḥzāb. *Musnad Aḥmad*, Vol. 1, Pg. 331, Vol. 3, Pg. 259, Vol. 4, Pg. 107, Vol. 6, Pp. 292, 298, 304; *Al-Mustadrak ʿalā al-Ṣaḥīḥhayn*, Vol. 2, Pg. 416.

🕊 and Lady Fāṭima al-Zahrā' 🕊, and not necessarily who the companions took to be the caliph.

Did Imam ʿAlī 🕊 give his allegiance to Abū Bakr?

Did Lady Fāṭima al-Zahrā' 🕊 approve of the caliph who was selected at Saqīfah?

According to historical accounts, Imam ʿAlī 🕊, Zubayr, and the Banū Hāshim did **not** pledge allegiance to Abū Bakr.

ʿUmar went to them, as narrated by Ṭabarī, and Zubayr unsheathed his sword against ʿUmar and said: "As long as the pledge of allegiance to ʿAlī is not taken, I will not unsheathe my sword [to fight in any wars or battles that are orchestrated by Abū Bakr or others as I find them to be illegitimate]." To this, ʿUmar responded: "Take Zubayr's sword and strike it against the ground." ʿUmar then ordered some individuals to forcibly bring Imam ʿAlī 🕊 and Zubayr to him, and when they came, he said to them: "You must pledge allegiance – whether willingly or unwillingly."[56]

According to another narration, someone asked Zuhrī:[57] "Did ʿAlī not pledge allegiance after six months?"

He replied: "Yes, indeed, ʿAlī had not pledged allegiance during

---

[56] *Tārīkh al-Rusul wa al-Mulūk*, Vol. 3, Pg. 203. The Arabic text of this is as follows:

لتباعيان وأنتما طائعان أو لتبايعان وأنتما كارهان.

[57] Muḥammad ibn Muslim ibn ʿUbaydullāh al-Zuhrī (d. 124 AH/741-2 CE), also referred to as Ibn Shihāb or simply al-Zuhrī, was a *tabiʾī* – coming after the first generation of the companions of Prophet Muḥammad 🌹. He was an Arab jurist, and narrator of *aḥādīth* credited with pioneering the development of *Sīrah-Maghāzī* – meaning accounts of the battles of Islam, as well as *Ḥadīth* literature. Raised in Madina, he studied *Ḥadīth* and *Maghāzī* under the scholars of Madina before rising to prominence in the court of the Banī Umayyah, where he served in several religious and administrative positions.

that time, and none of the Banū Hāshim did either. Only when Imam ʿAlī was **compelled** to pledge allegiance, he did so, and then the Banū Hāshim also pledged allegiance."[58]

Imam ʿAlī ؑ believed in his right for the caliphate and accused Abū Bakr and his companions of despotism and went as far on the record to having said: "We have a right in this matter, but you have deprived us of it."[59]

In *Ṣaḥīḥ al-Bukhārī*, it is noted that Imam ʿAlī ؑ did not pledge allegiance to Abū Bakr during the lifetime of Lady Fāṭima al-Zahrā' ؑ, however, after six months, when she passed away, Imam ʿAlī ؑ pursued reconciliation and pledged allegiance to Abū Bakr.[60]

---

[58] *Tārīkh al-Rusul wa al-Mulūk*, Vol. 3, Pg. 208.

[59] Ibid., The Arabic text of this is as follows:

إنّ لنا في هذا الأمر حقًّا فاستبددتم به علينا

[60] *Ṣaḥīḥ al-Bukhārī*, Vol. 5, Pp. 82-83. The Arabic text of this is as follows [Arabic and English taken from www.sunnah.com]:

حَدَّثَنَا يَحْيَى بْنُ بُكَيْرٍ حَدَّثَنَا اللَّيْثُ عَنْ عُقَيْلٍ عَنِ ابْنِ شِهَابٍ عَنْ عُرْوَةَ عَنْ عَائِشَةَ أَنَّ فَاطِمَةَ عَلَيْهَا السَّلاَمُ بِنْتَ النَّبِيِّ صَلَّى اللَّهُ عَلَيْهِ وَسَلَّمَ أَرْسَلَتْ إِلَى أَبِي بَكْرٍ تَسْأَلُهُ مِيرَاثَهَا مِنْ رَسُولِ اللَّهِ صَلَّى اللَّهُ عَلَيْهِ وَسَلَّمَ مِمَّا أَفَاءَ اللَّهُ عَلَيْهِ بِالْمَدِينَةِ وَفَدَكَ وَمَا بَقِيَ مِنْ خُمُسِ خَيْبَرَ فَقَالَ أَبُو بَكْرٍ إِنَّ رَسُولَ اللَّهِ صَلَّى اللَّهُ عَلَيْهِ وَسَلَّمَ قَالَ: لاَ نُورَثُ مَا تَرَكْنَا صَدَقَةٌ إِنَّمَا يَأْكُلُ آلُ مُحَمَّدٍ صَلَّى اللَّهُ عَلَيْهِ وَسَلَّمَ فِي هَذَا الْمَالِ. وَإِنِّي وَاللَّهِ لاَ أُغَيِّرُ شَيْئًا مِنْ صَدَقَةِ رَسُولِ اللَّهِ صَلَّى اللَّهُ عَلَيْهِ وَسَلَّمَ عَنْ حَالِهَا الَّتِي كَانَ عَلَيْهَا فِي عَهْدِ رَسُولِ اللَّهِ صَلَّى اللَّهُ عَلَيْهِ وَسَلَّمَ وَلأَعْمَلَنَّ فِيهَا بِمَا عَمِلَ بِهِ رَسُولُ اللَّهِ صَلَّى اللَّهُ عَلَيْهِ وَسَلَّمَ فَأَبَى أَبُو بَكْرٍ أَنْ يَدْفَعَ إِلَى فَاطِمَةَ مِنْهَا شَيْئًا فَوَجَدَتْ فَاطِمَةُ عَلَى أَبِي بَكْرٍ فِي ذَلِكَ فَهَجَرَتْهُ فَلَمْ تُكَلِّمْهُ حَتَّى تُوُفِّيَتْ وَعَاشَتْ بَعْدَ النَّبِيِّ صَلَّى اللَّهُ عَلَيْهِ وَسَلَّمَ سِتَّةَ أَشْهُرٍ، فَلَمَّا تُوُفِّيَتْ دَفَنَهَا زَوْجُهَا عَلِيٌّ لَيْلاً وَلَمْ يُؤْذِنْ بِهَا أَبَا بَكْرٍ وَصَلَّى عَلَيْهَا وَكَانَ لِعَلِيٍّ مِنَ النَّاسِ وَجْهٌ حَيَاةَ فَاطِمَةَ فَلَمَّا

تُوُفِّيَتِ اسْتَنْكَرَ عَلِيٌّ وُجُوهَ النَّاسِ فَالْتَمَسَ مُصَالَحَةَ أَبِي بَكْرٍ وَمُبَايَعَتَهُ وَلَمْ يَكُنْ يُبَايِعُ تِلْكَ الأَشْهُرَ فَأَرْسَلَ إِلَى أَبِي بَكْرٍ أَنِ ائْتِنَا وَلَا يَأْتِنَا أَحَدٌ مَعَكَ كَرَاهِيَةً لِمَحْضَرِ عُمَرَ. فَقَالَ عُمَرُ لَا وَاللَّهِ لَا تَدْخُلُ عَلَيْهِمْ وَحْدَكَ. فَقَالَ أَبُو بَكْرٍ وَمَا عَسَيْتَهُمْ أَنْ يَفْعَلُوا بِي وَاللَّهِ لآتِيَنَّهُمْ. فَدَخَلَ عَلَيْهِمْ أَبُو بَكْرٍ، فَتَشَهَّدَ عَلِيٌّ فَقَالَ إِنَّا قَدْ عَرَفْنَا فَضْلَكَ وَمَا أَعْطَاكَ اللَّهُ وَلَمْ نَنْفَسْ عَلَيْكَ خَيْرًا سَاقَهُ اللَّهُ إِلَيْكَ، وَلَٰكِنَّكَ اسْتَبْدَدْتَ عَلَيْنَا بِالأَمْرِ، وَكُنَّا نَرَى لِقَرَابَتِنَا مِنْ رَسُولِ اللَّهِ صَلَّى اللَّهُ عَلَيْهِ وَسَلَّمَ نَصِيبًا. حَتَّى فَاضَتْ عَيْنَا أَبِي بَكْرٍ، فَلَمَّا تَكَلَّمَ أَبُو بَكْرٍ قَالَ وَالَّذِي نَفْسِي بِيَدِهِ لَقَرَابَةُ رَسُولِ اللَّهِ صَلَّى اللَّهُ عَلَيْهِ وَسَلَّمَ أَحَبُّ إِلَيَّ أَنْ أَصِلَ مِنْ قَرَابَتِي، وَأَمَّا الَّذِي شَجَرَ بَيْنِي وَبَيْنَكُمْ مِنْ هَٰذِهِ الأَمْوَالِ، فَلَمْ آلُ فِيهَا عَنِ الْخَيْرِ، وَلَمْ أَتْرُكْ أَمْرًا رَأَيْتُ رَسُولَ اللَّهِ صَلَّى اللَّهُ عَلَيْهِ وَسَلَّمَ يَصْنَعُهُ فِيهَا إِلَّا صَنَعْتُهُ. فَقَالَ عَلِيٌّ لأَبِي بَكْرٍ مَوْعِدُكَ الْعَشِيَّةُ لِلْبَيْعَةِ. فَلَمَّا صَلَّى أَبُو بَكْرٍ الظُّهْرَ رَقِيَ عَلَى الْمِنْبَرِ، فَتَشَهَّدَ وَذَكَرَ شَأْنَ عَلِيٍّ، وَتَخَلُّفَهُ عَنِ الْبَيْعَةِ، وَعُذْرَهُ بِالَّذِي اعْتَذَرَ إِلَيْهِ، ثُمَّ اسْتَغْفَرَ، وَتَشَهَّدَ عَلِيٌّ فَعَظَّمَ حَقَّ أَبِي بَكْرٍ، وَحَدَّثَ أَنَّهُ لَمْ يَحْمِلْهُ عَلَى الَّذِي صَنَعَ نَفَاسَةً عَلَى أَبِي بَكْرٍ، وَلَا إِنْكَارًا لِلَّذِي فَضَّلَهُ اللَّهُ بِهِ، وَلَٰكِنَّا نَرَى لَنَا فِي هَٰذَا الأَمْرِ نَصِيبًا، فَاسْتَبَدَّ عَلَيْنَا، فَوَجَدْنَا فِي أَنْفُسِنَا، فَسُرَّ بِذَٰلِكَ الْمُسْلِمُونَ وَقَالُوا أَصَبْتَ. وَكَانَ الْمُسْلِمُونَ إِلَى عَلِيٍّ قَرِيبًا، حِينَ رَاجَعَ الأَمْرَ الْمَعْرُوفَ.

Fāṭima, the daughter of the Prophet ﷺ, sent someone to Abū Bakr (when he was a caliph), asking for her inheritance of what Allah's Messenger ﷺ had left of the property bestowed on him by Allah from the *Fai* (i.e. booty gained without fighting, thus considered as a gift) in Madina; and Fadak, and what remained of the *Khumus* of the Khaybar booty. On that, Abū Bakr said: "Allah's Messenger ﷺ said: 'Our property is not inherited. Whatever we leave, is *Ṣadaqa*, but the family of (the Prophet) Muḥammad can eat of this property.' By Allah, I will not make any change in the state of the *Ṣadaqa* of Allah's Messenger ﷺ and will leave it as it was during the lifetime of Allah's Messenger ﷺ and will dispose of it as Allah's Messenger ﷺ used to do." So Abū Bakr refused to give anything of that to Fāṭima. So, she became angry with Abū Bakr and kept away from him and did not talk to

---

him until she died. She remained alive for six months after the death of the Prophet. When she died, her husband ʿAlī, buried her at night without informing Abū Bakr, and he said the funeral prayer by himself. When Fāṭima was alive, the people used to respect ʿAlī much, but after her death, ʿAlī noticed a change in the people's attitude towards him. So ʿAlī sought reconciliation with Abū Bakr and gave him an oath of allegiance. ʿAlī had not given the oath of allegiance during those months (i.e. the period between the Prophet's death and Fāṭima's death). ʿAlī sent someone to Abū Bakr saying, "Come to us, but let nobody come with you," as he disliked that ʿUmar should come. ʿUmar said (to Abū Bakr), "No, by Allah, you shall not enter upon them alone." Abū Bakr said, "What do you think they will do to me? By Allah, I will go to them' So Abū Bakr entered upon them, and then ʿAlī uttered tashahhud and said (to Abū Bakr), "We know well your superiority and what Allah has given you, and we are not jealous of the good what Allah has bestowed upon you, but you did not consult us in the question of the rule and we thought that we have got a right in it because of our near relationship to Allah's Messenger ﷺ." Thereupon Abū Bakr's eyes flowed with tears. And when Abū Bakr spoke, he said, "By Him in Whose Hand my soul is to keep good relations with the relatives of Allah's Messenger ﷺ is dearer to me than to keep good relations with my own relatives. But as for the trouble which arose between me and you about his property, I will do my best to spend it according to what is good and will not leave any rule or regulation which I saw Allah's Messenger ﷺ following, in disposing of it, but I will follow." On that ʿAlī said to Abū Bakr, "I promise to give you the oath of allegiance in this afternoon." So when Abū Bakr had offered the *Ẓuhr* prayer, he ascended the pulpit and uttered the *Tashahhud* and then mentioned the story of ʿAlī and his failure to give the oath of allegiance, and excused him, accepting what excuses he had offered; Then ʿAlī (got up) and praying (to Allah) for forgiveness, he uttered *Tashahhud*, praised Abū Bakr's right, and said, that he had not done what he had done because of jealousy of Abū Bakr or as a protest of that Allah had favoured him with. ʿAlī added: "But we used to consider that we too had some right in this affair (of rulership) and that he (i.e. Abū Bakr)

Now, more clearly, we will explain the position of the Ahlul Bayt ﷺ in this matter, and the threats and intimidations of the Saqīfah faction.

Attack, Assault, and Threats of Arson

The attack on the house of Imam ʿAlī ﷺ and Lady Fāṭima ﷺ, and the threats and intimidations for their allegiance are well-documented in history, indicating their opposition to the caliphate of Abū Bakr.

In this regard, several examples are mentioned in the history books.

Ibn Abī Shaybah narrates the following with an authentic chain of narrators in his book, *Al-Muṣannaf*: "When Abū Bakr took allegiance after the passing away of the Messenger of Allah, ʿAlī and Zubayr went to Fāṭima and engaged in conversation and consultation with her, and news of this reached ʿUmar ibn al-Khaṭṭāb.

ʿUmar went to the house of Fāṭima and said: 'O daughter of the Messenger of Allah! By Allah, no one is more beloved to us than your father, and after him, you are the most beloved among the people to us! But by Allah, this love will not prevent us from burning down the house if these people gather in your house.'

ʿUmar continued and said: 'By Allah, that will not prevent us if they gather at your place; I will order the house to be set on fire.'[61]

When ʿAlī and Zubayr returned home, the beloved daughter of the Prophet said to ʿAlī and Zubayr: 'ʿUmar came here and took an

did not consult us in this matter and therefore caused us to feel sorry." On that all the Muslims became happy and said, "You have done the right thing." The Muslims then became friendly with ʿAlī as he returned to what the people had done (i.e. giving the oath of allegiance to Abū Bakr)."

[61] The Arabic text of this is as follows:

وايم اللّهِ ما ذاك بمانعي إن اجتمع هؤلاء النّفر عندك أن أمرتُهم أن يحرق عليهم البيت.

oath that if this gathering were to happen again in his presence, he would set the house on fire.'

Then Fāṭima al-Zahrā' added: 'By Allah, he will carry out what he has sworn.'"⁶²

According to Balādhurī, Abū Bakr asked Imam 'Alī ؑ for his allegiance, but Imam 'Alī ؑ refused to give it. After that, 'Umar approached the house of Imam 'Alī ؑ with a flaming torch and met Lady Fāṭima ؑ near the door. She said to him: "O son of Khaṭṭāb, have you come to burn my door?!"⁶³

'Umar bluntly replied: "Yes, and that is stronger than what your father brought."⁶⁴

The meaning of 'Umar ibn al-Khaṭṭāb by this statement was that this act is in accordance with the wishes of the father of Fāṭima al-Zahrā' ؑ – the Prophet of Allah ﷺ [as if this is what his teachings were all about – to force people to submit to commands!].

According to Ṭabarī, 'Umar ibn al-Khaṭṭāb went to the house of Imam 'Alī ؑ, where Ṭalḥa, Zubayr, and a group of the *Muhājirūn* were present, and said to them: "By Allah, I will set fire to your house unless you come out to pay allegiance."⁶⁵ Zubayr came out with his drawn sword, however, he slipped and dropped his sword and

---

⁶² *Al-Muṣannaf*, Vol. 8, Pg. 572. The Arabic text of this is as follows:

وأيمُ اللهِ ليمضينّ لما حلف عليه.

⁶³ The Arabic text of this is as follows:

يَابْنَ الْخَطَّابِ أَتُرَاكَ مُحْرِقًا عَلَيَّ بَابِي؟

⁶⁴ *Ansāb al-Ashrāf*, Vol. 1, Pg. 586. The Arabic text of this is as follows:

نَعَمْ وَذَلِكَ أَقْوَى فِيمَا جَاءَ بِهِ أَبُوكَ.

⁶⁵ The Arabic text of this is as follows:

وَاللهِ لأحرقنّ عليكم أو لتخرجنّ إلى البيعة.

immediately, those present [on the side of ʿUmar ibn al-Khaṭṭāb] jumped on top of him and apprehended him.[66]

The renowned historian, Ibn Qutayba al-Dīnawarī, provides a more detailed account of this incident and writes the following: "Abū Bakr approached those who had refrained from pledging allegiance to him who had gathered at the house of ʿAlī, and he sent ʿUmar after them.

ʿUmar arrived at the house of ʿAlī and called everyone to come out, but they refused to leave the house. At that moment, ʿUmar asked for firewood and said: 'By the life of ʿUmar, if you do not come out, then I will set the house on fire![67] ... I swear by Allah, I will set the house on fire if they gather in it.'

Someone said to ʿUmar: 'O Abū Ḥafṣ, Fāṭima is in there.'[68]

But he replied: 'So be it!'[69]

Fāṭima al-Zahrāʾ stood behind the door and said: 'I have never seen a group worse than you! You who abandoned the Prophet's funeral to pursue your own agenda, who refused to accept our leadership, and are now denying us our rights.'

ʿUmar returned to Abū Bakr and asked him: 'Should we not hold this man (referring to ʿAlī) accountable for his defiance?!'

Abū Bakr said to Qunfudh:[70] 'Go and call ʿAlī!'

---

[66] *Tārīkh al-Rusul wa al-Mulūk*, Vol. 3, Pg. 202.

[67] The Arabic text of this is as follows:

وَ الَّذِي نَفْسُ عُمَرَ بِيَدِهِ لَتَخْرُجَنَّ أَوْ لَأُحْرِقَنَّهَا عَلَى مَنْ فِيهَا.

[68] The Arabic text of this is as follows:

يَا أَبَا حَفْصٍ إِنَّ فِيهَا فَاطِمَةَ.

[69] The Arabic text of this is as follows:

وَإِنْ.

[70] He was a slave who belonged to ʿUmar ibn al-Khaṭṭāb. (Tr.)

Qunfudh went to the house and said to ʿAlī: 'The successor of the Messenger of Allah is calling you.'

ʿAlī replied: 'How fast you resort to lying about [the statements of the] Messenger of Allah![71] How quickly you turned away from the truth and called Abū Bakr his successor!'

Qunfudh returned and conveyed the words of ʿAlī [to ʿUmar and Abū Bakr].

ʿUmar again said: 'Do not give this man who defies the allegiance any respite.'

Qunfudh went to ʿAlī once more, but ʿAlī did not pay any attention to him."

Dīnawarī continues in his narration and states: "This time ʿUmar went with a group and reached the house of Fāṭima. When Fāṭima heard their voices, she shouted: 'O my father, O Messenger of Allah, what difficulties have we faced after you from the son of Khaṭṭāb and the son of Abī Quḥāfah!'[72]

Some of that group turned back upon hearing the voice of Fāṭima and her weeping, however, ʿUmar and a few others stayed there. They dragged ʿAlī outside, brought him to Abū Bakr, and told him: 'Pledge allegiance!'

ʿAlī asked: 'If I do not do it, then what will happen?'[73]

They said: 'Then, by Allah, whom there is no deity except Him,

---

[71] The Arabic text of this is as follows:

لَسَرِيعُ مَا كَذَبْتُهُمْ عَلَى رَسُولِ اللّٰهِ.

[72] A reference to Abū Bakr. (Tr.) The Arabic text of this is as follows:

يَا أَبَتِ يَا رَسُولَ اللّٰهِ. مَاذَا لَقِينَا بَعْدَكَ مِنِ ابْنُ الْخَطَّابِ وَابْنِ أَبِي قُحَافَةَ.

[73] The Arabic text of this is as follows:

إِنْ أَنَا لَمْ أَفْعَلْ فَمَهُ؟

we will strike your neck with our swords.'[74]

'Alī replied: 'Then you will have killed the servant of Allah and the brother of the Messenger of Allah!'[75]

'Umar said: 'We accept that you are a servant of Allah, but we do not accept that you are the brother of the Messenger of Allah.'

During these discussions and conflicts, Abū Bakr remained silent and did not speak, then at that moment, 'Umar said to Abū Bakr: 'Why don't you give us your orders? (i.e., to force 'Alī to pledge allegiance)?' Abū Bakr replied: 'As long as Fāṭima is alive, we have no business with 'Alī.'

Then they released 'Alī who went to the Prophet's grave while crying and said: 'O son of my mother (O my brother), indeed, these people have humiliated and weakened me (considered me weak), and they almost killed me.'"[76]

---

[74] The Arabic text of this is as follows:

إِذًا وَاللهِ الَّذِي لَا إِلَهَ إِلَّا هُوَ نضرِ عُنُقِكَ.

[75] The Arabic text of this is as follows:

إِذًا تَقْتُلُونَ عَبْدُ اللهِ وَأَخَا رَسُولِهِ.

[76] The Arabic text of this is as follows:

يابن أمّ إنّ القوم استضعفوني و كادوا يقتلونني.

This is in reference to Sūrah al-A'rāf (7), Verse 150:

﴿...قَالَ ٱبْنَ أُمَّ إِنَّ ٱلْقَوْمَ ٱسْتَضْعَفُونِى وَكَادُوا۟ يَقْتُلُونَنِى...﴾

"...He (referring to Prophet Hārūn) said: 'O son of my mother, indeed, the people overpowered me and were about to kill me...'"

After Prophet Mūsā ﷺ returned to his people from the appointed time with Allah ﷻ, he observed that the Children of Isrā'īl had turned to idol worshipping. He held his brother, Prophet Hārūn ﷺ, accountable for this,

Dīnawarī continues in his narration and states that: "ʿUmar said to Abū Bakr: 'Let us go to Fāṭima together because we have angered her.'

The two of them went to Fāṭima's house and requested permission to enter, but she did not grant them permission.

They went to Imam ʿAlī and asked for his help, and with his permission, they entered the house. When they entered, Lady Fāṭima turned her face away from them, and did not even respond to their greetings (of *salām*). Abū Bakr spoke some words to console her, but Fāṭima replied: 'If I narrate a saying of the Messenger of Allah that you have heard, will you testify to it?'

They answered: 'Yes.'

Fāṭima then said: 'I swear by Allah and His angels that both of you have angered me and have not pleased me. When I meet the Prophet, I will complain about both of you to him.'"[77]

According to these documented accounts that are all narrated from prominent sources of the Ahlul Sunnah, the position of Imam ʿAlī ؑ and Lady Fāṭima al-Zahrāʾ ؑ regarding the caliphate of Abū Bakr was very clear, and the Saqīfah group were seeking their allegiance in any way possible. As we saw, they even resorted to severe threats; and according to some historians, these threats were carried out due to the refusal of Imam ʿAlī ؑ to pledge allegiance to Abū Bakr.

In this regard, we will mention several historical narrations.

When the Prophet ﷺ informed Imam ʿAlī ؑ about his future offspring, he also recounted to him the incident that would take place

---

to which Hārūn ؑ replied: "O son of my mother (O my brother), indeed, the people oppressed me (considered me weak) and were about to kill me."

[77] *Al-Imāmah wa al-Siyāsah*, Vol. 1, Pp. 30-31 (summarized). The Arabic text of this is as follows:

فإني أُشهد الله وملائكته أنّكما أسخطتماني وما أرضيتماني ولئن لقيت النبيّ لأشكونّكما إليه.

in the future of the attack and assault on Lady Fāṭima al-Zahrā', as well as on their house.

According to a reliable narration mentioned by Juwaynī found in the book, *Farā'id al-Simṭayn*, Ibn ʿAbbās narrated: "One day, the Messenger of Allah was sitting when his grandson, Ḥasan ibn ʿAlī, entered. Upon seeing Ḥasan, tears welled up in the eyes of the Messenger of Allah. Then, Ḥusayn ibn ʿAlī came, and when the Messenger of Allah saw him, he cried. Fāṭima and ʿAlī also came, and upon seeing them, the Prophet wept.

When they asked the reason for his weeping, he replied: 'When I saw her (Fāṭima al-Zahrā'), I remembered what will befall her after me. It was as if I could see disgrace entering her house, her sanctity violated, her rights usurped, her inheritance denied, her side broken, and her fetus miscarried, while she calls out: 'O Muḥammad!' But no one will answer her cries for help.'"78

The remorse of Abū Bakr and the regret he felt towards the end of his life serve as a testimony to his involvement in the attack on the house of Lady Fāṭima and the other atrocities against her.

Historians have written that in the final moments of his life, Abū Bakr could be heard saying: "I wish I had not done three things." One of those three things which he wished he had not done was: "I wish I had not violated the sanctity of the house of Fāṭima, and had nothing to do with it, even if it had led to war."79

---

78 The Arabic text of this is as follows:

وَأَنِّي لَمَّا رَأَيْتُهَا ذَكَرْتُ مَا يُصْنَعُ بِهَا بَعْدِي كَأَنِّي بِهَا وَقَدْ دَخَلَ الذُّلُّ بَيْتَهَا وَانْتُهِكَتْ حُرْمَتُهَا وَغُصِبَتْ حَقَّهَا وَمُنِعَتْ إِرْثَهَا وَكُسِرَ جَنْبُهَا [وَكُسِرَتْ جَنْبَتُهَا] وَأَسْقَطَتْ جَنِينَهَا وَهِيَ تُنَادِي يَا مُحَمَّدَاهْ فَلَا تُجَابُ وَتَسْتَغِيثُ فَلَا تُغَاثُ.

79 The Arabic text of this is as follows:

وَدَدْتُ أَنِّي لَمْ أَكُنْ أَكْشِفْ بَيْتَ فَاطِمَةَ وَتَرَكْتُهُ وَإِنْ أُغْلِقَ عَلَى الْحَرْبِ.

This statement has also been reported with various expressions and wordings attributed to Abū Bakr.

For example, Maṣʿūdī reports that Abū Bakr said: "I wish I had not searched Fāṭima's house, and in that regard, I said many things."[80]

These historical accounts and statements illustrate the remorse and regret expressed by Abū Bakr for his involvement in the attack on the house of Lady Fāṭima.

These regretful statements indicate the occurrence of an attack on her house, and suggest that upon Abū Bakr's orders, an assault was carried out on her, and individuals entered her house without permission. Naturally, these oppressors did not show any respect, manners, or composure, which led Abū Bakr to express remorse.

There are additional statements attributed to Abū Bakr on this matter, as mentioned in the narrations given by Maṣʿūdī. However, the narrator refrained from quoting these words to preserve the dignity of the caliphate. It is possible that if those words were not omitted, we would have seen another dimension of the attack on the house of Fāṭima from Abū Bakr's own words.

ʿAbdul Karīm al-Shahrastānī, a renowned Sunnī scholar and author of the book, *Al-Milal wa al-Niḥal*, quotes Ibrāhīm ibn al-Sayyār, also known as Naẓẓām al-Muʿtazilī, due to his eloquence in

---

[80] *Farāʾid al-Simṭayn*, Vol. 2, Pg. 34, Tradition 371; *Tārīkh al-Islam*, Vol. 3, Pp. 117-118; *Al-Muʿjam al-Kabīr*, Vol. 1, Pg. 63; *Mizān al-ʿItidāl*, Vol. 3, Pg. 109; *Lisān al-Mizān*, Vol. 4, Pg. 189; *Sharḥ Nahj al-Balāgha,* Vol. 2, Pp. 47-46; *Murūj al-Dhahab*, Vol. 2, Pg. 301; *Tārīkh al-Yaʿqūbī*, Vol. 2, Pg. 137. These statements of Abū Bakr with slight variations can also be found in the following books: *Tārīkh al-Rusul wa al-Mulūk*, Vol. 3, Pg. 430; *Ansāb al-Ashrāf*, Vol. 10, Pg. 346; *Kanz al-ʿUmmāl*, Vol. 5, Pg. 631; *Al-Imāmah wa al-Siyāsah*, Vol. 1, Pg. 36; *Tārīkh Madina Dimashqī*, Vol. 30, Pg. 418; *Al-ʿAqd al-Farīd*, Vol. 4, Pg. 268. The Arabic text of this is as follows:

فَوَدَدْتُ أَنِّي لَمْ أَكُنْ فتّشتُ بَيْتَ فَاطِمَةَ وَذَكَرَ فِي ذٰلِكَ كَلَامًا كَثِيرًا.

poetry and prose. He reports that Ibrāhīm ibn al-Sayyār said: "On the day of allegiance, 'Umar struck the stomach of Fāṭima, causing her to miscarry the fetus she was carrying."[81]

Unfortunately, present day Sunnī scholars are not willing to share these pieces of evidence with their followers.

Why is that?

One of the statements that indicates the dissatisfaction of Imam ʿAlī ﷺ with the selection of Abū Bakr is a statement attributed to him after the incident of Saqīfah.

In *Nahj al-Balāgha*, it is mentioned that when the news of the event at Saqīfah reached Imam ʿAlī ﷺ after the demise of the Messenger of Allah ﷺ, the Imam asked: "'What did the *Anṣār* say in response to the proposal of the *Muhājirūn* for caliphate?' They replied: 'The *Anṣār* said: 'We have our leader *(amīr)*, and you have your leader. Leadership belongs to us and to you.'"

The Imam responded with a statement to the *Anṣār* that they could not become leaders.

Then he asked: "What argument did the Quraysh present?"

They said: "Their argument (for their priority in the caliphate) was that both of them (Abū Bakr and 'Umar) are from the Quraysh, and they are both related to the Messenger of Allah."

The Imam replied: "They argued with lineage, but they lost the

---

[81] *Al-Milal wa al-Niḥal*, Vol. 1, Pg. 57; Safādī in *Al-Wafī bil Wafāyāt*, Vol. 6, Pg. 15, quotes the statement of Naẓẓām. For further information on the sources of the attack on the house of Lady Fāṭima al-Zahrā' ﷺ refer to the Chapter, *Fire in the House of Revelation*, found in this anthology. The Arabic text of this is as follows:

إِنَّ عُمَرَ ضَرَبَ بَطْنِ فَاطِمَةَ يَوْمَ الْبَيْعَةِ حَتَّى أُلْقَتِ الْجَنِينِ مِنْ بَطْنِهَا.

fruit (result)."[82]

This points out that if the connection to the lineage of Prophet Muḥammad ﷺ through a tribe is the reason for their priority for the caliphate, then why should the close kinship with the Prophet ﷺ not be given preference?

We know that both Imam ʿAlī ﵇ and the Messenger of Allah ﷺ

---

[82] In *Nahj al-Balāgha*, in Sermon 67, titled *Imāmah and Politics*, the following statement attributed to Imam ʿAlī ﵇ is mentioned:

قَالَ عَلِيٌّ: مَا قَالَتِ الْأَنْصَارُ؟ قَالُوا: قَالَتْ مِنَّا أَمِيرٌ وَمِنْكُمْ أَمِيرٌ. قَالَ عَلِيٌّ: فَهَلَّا احْتَجَجْتُمْ عَلَيْهِمْ بِأَنَّ رَسُولَ اللّٰهِ وَصَّى بِأَنْ يُحْسَنَ إِلَى مُحْسِنِهِمْ وَيُتَجَاوَزَ عَنْ مُسِيئِهِمْ. قَالُوا: وَمَا فِي هٰذَا مِنَ الْحُجَّةِ عَلَيْهِمْ؟ فَقَالَ لَوْ كَانَ الْإِمَامَةُ فِيهِمْ لَمْ تَكُنِ الْوَصِيَّةُ بِهِمْ. ثُمَّ قَالَ: فَمَا ذَا قَالَتْ قُرَيْشٌ؟ قَالُوا: احْتَجَّتْ بِأَنَّهَا شَجَرَةُ الرَّسُولِ. فَقَالَ احْتَجُّوا بِالشَّجَرَةِ وَأَضَاعُوا الثَّمَرَةَ.

[After the death of the Messenger of Allah ﷺ, when reports of the fathering at the Saqīfah of Banū Sāʿida reached the Commander of the Faithful] he asked: "What did the *Anṣār* say?"

Those who had brought him the reports of what had happened replied: "The *Anṣār* proposed: 'There should be a commander chosen from our side and another chosen from yours.'"

ʿAlī responded: "Did you not remind them about the Messenger's order to recompense those who do good among them, and pardon those who transgress?"

Those reporting asked: "How is that evidence against their claim [to leadership]?"

ʿAlī replied: "The instruction would not be about them if they had the right to command." Then he asked: "How did the Quraysh respond?"

The people answered: "They argued that they are the Messenger's tree."

ʿAlī exclaimed: "They argue for the tree but forget about its fruit!"

In *Nahj al-Balāgha*, under the Short Sayings, it is also stated: "You have taken this matter (caliphate) by force from the *Anṣār*, and we, the people of the Prophet's household, are also being deprived of it."

were from the tribe of Banū Hāshim. In addition, they were cousins, and they later became son-in-law and father-in-law. In this regard, we quote a poem from Imam ʿAlī ﷺ:

"If you, Abū Bakr, became the ruler of their affairs through consultation,
Then what kind of consultation is this in which those who should be consulted, like me and others like me, were absent?
If you presented your argument against their opposition based on your proximity to the Prophet,
Then others are even more deserving and closer to the Prophet [than you]."[83]

ʿAbbās, the uncle of the Prophet, also addressed Abū Bakr and ʿUmar, who came to him to force him to pledge allegiance, and said the following in response to their statement: "The Messenger of Allah is from us and from you.[84] Indeed, he (ʿAlī) is from a tree of which we are its branches, and you are its neighbours."[85]

The Role of ʿUmar in Solidifying the Caliphate of Abū Bakr

[83] *Nahj al-Balāgha*, Short Saying 190. The Arabic text of this is as follows:

فكيف بهذا والمشيرون غُيَّب	فإن كنتَ بالشّورىٰ مَلَكْتَ أمورهم
فغيرك أولى بالنّبيّ وأقربُ	وإن كنت بالقربى حجَجْت خصيمَهم

[84] The Arabic text of this is as follows:

إِنَّ رَسُولَ اللهِ مِنَّا وَمِنْكُمْ.

[85] *Al-Imāmah wa al-Siyāsah*, Vol. 1, Pg. 33; *Tārīkh al-Yaʿqūbī*, Vol. 2, Pg. 126. The Arabic text of this is as follows:

فإنّه قد كان من شجرة نحن أغصانها وأنتم جيرانها.

The Event of Saqīfah and its consequences vividly depict the role of the second caliph in the selection and consolidation of the caliphate of Abū Bakr. Even during the time of the Messenger of Allah ﷺ, due to their friendship, closeness, and various similarities, these two individuals (Abū Bakr and 'Umar) established a brotherly bond with one another.

Ḥākim al-Naysābūrī, in his book, *Mustadrak 'alā al-Ṣaḥīḥḥayn*, narrates from 'Abdullāh ibn 'Umar that the Messenger of Allah ﷺ established brotherhood among his companions. From this bond, Abū Bakr and 'Umar became brothers, as well as Ṭalḥa and Zubayr, and likewise 'Uthmān and 'Abdul Raḥmān ibn 'Awf.[86]

The mutual support between Abū Bakr and 'Umar is evident and well-demonstrated in the incident of Saqīfah. Until the arrival of Abū Bakr, 'Umar denied the death of the Messenger of Allah ﷺ. However, upon the arrival of Abū Bakr and him reciting certain verses of the Quran, 'Umar accepted the Prophet's ﷺ demise.

When 'Umar heard the news about the gathering of the *Anṣār* at Saqīfah, he called upon Abū Bakr, and they went there together. At first, Abū Bakr proposed that 'Umar or Abū 'Ubādah al-Jarrah should become the caliph – however, 'Umar, relying on Abū Bakr's companionship with the Prophet ﷺ in the cave [on the migration from Mecca to Madina] and considering him to be older, gave in and pledged allegiance to Abū Bakr. From then on, 'Umar would approach anyone he encountered, extending their hands to Abū Bakr as a sign of allegiance.

'Umar suppressed any opponents of Abū Bakr during the

---

86 *Mustadrak 'alā al-Ṣaḥīḥḥayn*, Vol. 3, Pg. 14. In the book, *Ṭabaqāt al-Kubrā*, Vol. 3, Pg. 174, it is also mentioned that brotherhood was established between different companions in various circumstances and times. It has been narrated that Abū Bakr and Kharijah ibn Zayd also formed a bond of brotherhood. See *Fatḥ al-Bārī fī Sharḥ Ṣaḥīḥ al-Bukhārī*, Vol. 7, Pg. 210.

gathering at Saqīfah by attacking Saʿd ibn ʿUbādah and insulting him. He also threatened the members of the Banū Hāshim, such as Zubayr and others, and even attacked the house of Imam ʿAlī ﷺ and Lady Fāṭima al-Zahrāʾ ﷺ, assaulted them both, and violated their privacy – as we previously noted.

Ibn Abī al-Ḥadīd, a Sunnī Muʿtazilī scholar, openly admits and writes: "It was ʿUmar who solidified the allegiance of Abū Bakr and suppressed their opponents. When Zubayr drew his sword, ʿUmar broke his sword, and struck it against the chest of Miqdād. He trampled Saʿd ibn ʿUbādah at Saqīfah and said: 'Kill Saʿd! May Allah kill Saʿd!' He shattered the nose of Ḥabāb ibn al-Mundhīr, and he threatened anyone seeking refuge in the house of Fāṭima from the Banū Hāshim and forcefully expelled them from the house. If it were not for him, nothing would have been established for Abū Bakr, and nothing would have remained for him."[87]

Therefore, Imam ʿAlī ﷺ, in response to ʿUmar's threats and pressures to pledge allegiance to Abū Bakr, addressed him saying: "Milk it for him, a milking in which you keep half for yourself, and make his matter firm so that he will return it to you tomorrow."[88]

---

[87] *Sharḥ Nahj al-Balāgha*, Vol. 1, Pg. 174. The Arabic text of this is as follows:

وعمر هو الّذي شدّ بيعة أبي بكر ووقم المخالفين فيها فكسر سيف الزّبير لـمّا جرّده ودفع في صدر المقداد ووطئ في السقيفة سعد بن عبادة وقال: اقتلوا سعدًا قتل اللّٰه سعدًا وحطّم أنف الحباب بن المنذر ... وتوعّد من لجأ إلى دار فاطمة من الهاشميّين أخرجهم منها ولو لاه لم يثبت لأبي بكر أمر ولا قامت له قائمة.

[88] *Al-Imāmah wa al-Siyāsah*, Vol. 1, Pg. 29. This is a famous expression from Imam ʿAlī ﷺ warning that there is a deal or arrangement being made in such a way that both parties' benefit, and to ensure the matter is managed

Conclusion

With careful examination of the following points, several important conclusions can be drawn:

1. The gathering at Saqīfah was not an elected council; rather, a group of *Anṣār* who formed a social assembly to secure the caliphate for themselves, and some of the *Muhājirūn* competed with them. Through cunning manipulation of the competition between the tribes of Aws and Khazraj, they achieved their desired outcome.
2. There was a clash in choosing the caliph at Saqīfah; Saʿd ibn ʿUbādah was attacked and insulted, and ʿUmar labelled him a hypocrite. Saʿd, in turn, grabbed ʿUmar by the beard, to which ʿUmar threatened to break his teeth.
3. The arguments presented by both the *Anṣār* and the *Muhājirūn* demonstrated that there was serious competition between them for seizing power, and their reasoning reflected their worldly ambitions, rather than focusing on spiritual criteria. It appears that they were dividing an inheritance, each claiming a share. On the other hand, Abū Bakr and ʿUmar were so occupied in negotiating with influential individuals to secure allegiance and remove opponents from the scene that they missed the opportunity to participate in the burial of the Messenger of Allah ﷺ.
4. Abū Bakr's selection occurred suddenly, amidst turmoil and conflict, and ʿUmar himself admits that the allegiance to Abū Bakr was hasty and lacked careful consideration. However, as ʿUmar claimed, Allah ﷻ protected the Muslims from further

---

in a cunning way so that the favour or benefit is reciprocated in the future. (Tr.) The Arabic text of this is as follows:

احلب حلبًا لك شطره واشدد له امره يردده عليك غدًا.

harm of that situation! ʿUmar therefore issued a threat, stating: "No one has the right to give allegiance to anyone else without consulting the Muslims, or else such a person will be subject to death."

ʿUmar did not necessarily accept the selection process that was used to bring Abū Bakr to power, and he considered anyone who were to use such a process of selecting the caliph as deserving of death. He acknowledged that the caliphate of Abū Bakr was established without consulting the Muslims.

5. If Abū Bakr and ʿUmar had arrived a little later to Saqīfah, or if there had not been any dispute between the Aws and Khazraj, the first caliph would have been Saʿd ibn ʿUbādah. If the *Muhājirūn* had agreed to divide power, then the Islamic world would have witnessed a consultative caliphate after the Messenger of Allah ﷺ.
6. Imam ʿAlī ؑ regarded ʿUmar's efforts to consolidate Abū Bakr's caliphate as self-serving, and in return for these efforts, Abū Bakr appointed him as the caliph after himself, which indeed happened.
7. It is very clear that a group of well-known companions opposed Abū Bakr's selection. As well, the Banū Hāshim, who were the closest individuals to the Messenger of Allah ﷺ were not present at Saqīfah, mainly because they were busy with the burial arrangements of the final Prophet ﷺ. However, they openly expressed their opposition afterwards when they found out about what had transpired. History testifies that ʿUmar suppressed the opponents to consolidate the matter of caliphate; and he treated Lady Fāṭima عليها السلام, the beloved daughter of the Messenger of Allah ﷺ, with extreme disrespect and audacity, even resorting to threats and violence. Intense intimidation was also used against the dissenters. These facts are well-documented in the books of the Sunnī Muslims and

were clearly shown in this work.

8. Abū Bakr and ʿUmar acted to silence ʿAbbās, the uncle of the Prophet ﷺ, and distance him from Imam ʿAlī ؑ through persuasion – however, they were met with disappointment.

With this summary, several questions arise:

1. Which Islamic criteria were compatible with the method of selecting the first caliph? Can the caliphate be obtained without consulting respected companions, or by threatening a group and persuading others collectively?
2. How is the use of insults and provocation of two tribes, and igniting ancient rivalries between Aws and Khazraj, justified in attaining power? What criteria does it align with?
3. With respect to Bashīr ibn Saʿd al-Asī, who pledged allegiance to Abū Bakr and attributed it to the absence of disputes among them, did he not know that there were, among the *Muhājirūn* and the *Anṣār*, people who were more worthy of this position? What about Imam ʿAlī ؑ, with all his background qualities and exceptional virtues? Was he not the most deserving of leadership? Why did he remain silent in the face of the group slogan that said: "We will not pledge allegiance to anyone except ʿAlī"?
4. Is consent of the one pledging allegiance a condition for allegiance?
5. Do the threats, intimidation against Imam ʿAlī ؑ, violation of the house of Imam ʿAlī ؑ and Lady Fāṭima ؑ, and the assaults against them for the purpose of obtaining allegiance have any roots in the principles of the *sharīʿah*?
6. Can a caliph, who has angered the beloved daughter of the Messenger of Allah ﷺ – the same daughter whose satisfaction is considered the satisfaction of the Prophet ﷺ himself, as well as the satisfaction of Allah ﷻ; and whose anger is considered the anger of the Prophet ﷺ himself, as well as the anger of

Allah ﷻ – ever be considered as a rightful caliph of the Muslims?

7. If Saʿd had not been ill, and had caused chaos in Madina, expelled the migrants from there, and become the caliph of the Muslims, would it still be believed that his caliphate was legitimate, and would it have been necessary to follow him?
8. Are the methods used to select the first caliph worthy of emulation in the present Muslim world? Can we proceed with such a method of selecting leaders in Islamic countries, considering the belief of the Sunnī scholars who consider the actions of the companions as having legal authority?
9. Was the Messenger of Allah ﷺ not aware of the mentality of his companions, and that they might create disturbances and cause problems in choosing a caliph after him? If we assume that he was unaware of this mentality, then we cast doubt on the intelligence and foresight of the Messenger of Allah ﷺ.
10. Lastly, if the Noble Prophet ﷺ had foreseen the events that would transpire after him, would he not have provided guidance to his nation and the Muslims?
    a. Would he not have shown them the right path?
    b. Did the wise and intelligent Messenger of Islam ﷺ abandon or neglect them?
    c. Should it not be accepted that the Prophet ﷺ did indeed introduce a caliph with clear conditions and prominent qualities to the people – which transpired at Ghadir Khumm?
    d. Should it not be acknowledged that the final Messenger ﷺ established a reference point to resolve conflicts and prevent people from going astray – namely by following the reference point of the Ahlul Bayt (عليهم السلام) – as was emphasized in the *Ḥadīth of Thaqalayn?*

In conclusion, the theory of appointment and introduction of an exceptional figure who can continue the goals and ideologies of the Noble Prophet Muḥammad ﷺ is the most logical, especially if Allah ﷻ already designated that leader. Its proof goes beyond the many verses of the Quran and the numerous narrations, aligns with logic and reason, and is the same theory advocated by the school of Ahlul Bayt عليهم السلام.

Bibliography

The Noble Quran.

ʿAbdul Barr, Abū ʿUmar Yūsuf ibn ʿAbdullāh ibn Muḥammad ibn, *Al-Istīʿāb fī Maʿrifah al-Aṣḥāb* (Beirut: Dār al-Jīl, Beirut, 1st Edition, 1412 AH - Edited by ʿAlī Muḥammad al-Bajawī).

Andalūsī, Ibn ʿAbd Rabbih, *Al-ʿIqd al-Farīd* (Beirut, Dār al-Kutub al-Arabi, 1403 AH).

ʿAsqalānī, Aḥmad ibn ʿAlī ibn Ḥajr al-, *Muqaddimah Fatḥ al-Bārī* (Beirut: Dār al-Maʿārifah, 2nd Edition, n.d.).

ʿAsqalānī, Aḥmad ibn Nūr al-Dīn ʿAlī ibn Muḥammad ibn Ḥajr al-, *Fatḥ al-Bārī fī Sharḥ Ṣaḥīḥ al-Bukhārī* (Beirut: Dār al-Maʿārifah, 2nd Edition, n.d.).

ʿAsqalānī, ʿAlī ibn Muḥammad ibn Ḥajr al-, *Lisān al-Mizān* (Beirut: Muʾassasah al-Alami, 2nd Edition, 1390 AH).

ʿAynī, Badr al-Dīn al-, *ʿUmdat al-Qārī* (Beirut: Dār Iḥyāʾ al-Turāth al-Arabi, n.d.).

Balādhurī, Aḥmad ibn Yaḥyā ibn Jābir al-, *Ansāb al-Ashrāf* (Beirut: Dār al-Fikr, 1st Printing, 1417 AH, Researched by Suhail Zukkār).

Bayhaqī, Aḥmad ibn Ḥusayn ibn ʿAlī ibn Mūsā al-Khusrawjirdī al-, *Sunan al-Kubrā* (Dār al-Fikr, Beirut, n.d.).

Bukhārī, Muḥammad ibn Ismāʿīl al-, *Ṣaḥīḥ al-Bukhārī* (Beirut: Dār al-Jīl, n.d.).

Dārimī, ʿAbdullāh ibn ʿAbdul Raḥmān al-, *Sunan al-Dārimī*.

Dhahabī, Muḥammad ibn Aḥmad ibn ʿUthmān al-, *Mizān al-ʿItidāl* (Beirut: Dār al-Maʿārif, Edited by ʿAlī Muḥammad al-Bajawī, n.d.).

Dhahabī, Shams al-Dīn al-, *Tārīkh al-Islām* (Beirut: Dār al-Kutub al-ʿArabī, 2nd Edition, 1413 AH - Edited by ʿUmar ʿAbdul Salām).

Dimashqī, Abūl Fiḍāʾ ʿImād al-Dīn Ismāʾīl ibn ʿUmar ibn Kathīr al-

Qurayshī al-, *Al-Bidāyah wa al-Nihāyah* (Beirut: Dār al-Fikr, 1st Edition, 1407 AH).

Dimashqī, Abūl Fiḍā' ʿImād al-Dīn Ismāʿīl ibn ʿUmar ibn Kathīr al-Qurayshī al-, *Al-Sīrah al-Nabawiyyah* (also known as *Sīrah Ibn Kathīr*), (Beirut: Dār al-Maʿārif, n.d.).

Dīnawarī, Abū Muḥammad ʿAbdullāh ibn Muslim ibn Qutayba al-, *Al-Imāmah wa al-Siyāsah* (Beirut: Dār al-Adwā, Beirut, 1st Edition, 1410 AH - Edited by ʿAlī Shirī).

Ḥamawī, Yāqūt Shihāb ibn ʿAbdullāh al-Rūmī al-, *Muʿjam al-Buldān* (Beirut: Dār Sader, 2nd Edition, 1995 AH).

Dhuhlī, Abū ʿAbdillāh Aḥmad ibn Muḥammad ibn Ḥanbal al-, *Musnad Aḥmad* (Beirut: Dār al-Sādir, n.d.).

Haythamī, ʿAlī ibn Ḥajr al-, *Al-Ṣawā'iq al-Muḥriqah* (Egypt: Muḥammadīyyah Edition, n.d.).

Ḥibbān, Muḥammad ibn, *Ṣaḥīḥ Ibn Ḥibbān* (Al-Risālah Foundation, 2nd Edition, 1414 AH - Edited by Shuʿayb al-Arnaout).

Hindī, ʿAla al-Din ʿAlī ibn ʿAbdul Malik Husām al-Dīn al-Muttaqī al-, *Kanz al-ʿUmmāl* (Beirut: Mu'assasah al-Risālah, 1409 AH).

Ibn ʿAsākir, *Tārīkh al-Dimashqī* (Beirut, 1415 AH).

Jawzī, ʿAbdul Raḥmān ibn ʿAlī ibn Muḥammad Abūl Farash ibn al-, *Al-Muntazam fi Tārīkh al-Rusul wa al-Mulūk* (Beirut: Dār al-Kutub al-ʿIlmīyyah, 1st Edition, 1412 AH - Edited by Muḥammad ʿAbdul Qādir ʿAtā).

Jazarī, ʿIzz al-Dīn ibn al-Athīr al-, *Usd al-Ghābah fi Maʿrifah al-Ṣaḥābah* (Beirut: Dār al-Fikr, 1409 AH).

Juwaynī, Ibrāhīm ibn Muḥammad al-Muyyad al-, *Farā'id al-Simtayn* (Beirut: Mu'assasah al-Maḥmūdī, 1400 AH).

Khaldūn, ʿAbdul Raḥmān ibn Muḥammad ibn al-, *Tārīkh Ibn Khaldūn* (Dār al-Fikr, 2nd Edition, 1408 AH - Researched by Khalīl Shahādah).

Khuzaymah, Abū Bakr Muḥammad ibn Isḥāq ibn, *Ṣaḥīḥ Ibn Khuzaymah* (The Islamic Bureau, 1412 AH - Edited and Commentary by Dr. Muḥammad Muṣṭafā al-Adhamī).

Kūfī, Ibn Abī Shaybah al-, *Al-Muṣannaf* (Beirut: Dār al-Fikr, 1st Edition, 1409 AH - Edited by Saʿīd al-Lahham).

Maṣʿūdī, Abūl Ḥasan ʿAlī ibn al-Ḥusayn ibn ʿAlī al-, *Murūj al-Ḍhahab* (Qum: Dār al-Hijrah, 1409 AH - Edited by Asad Dagher).

Muʿtazilī, Ibn Abī al-Ḥadīd al-, *Sharḥ Nahj al-Balāgha* (Beirut: Dār Iḥyāʾ al-Kutub al-Arabiyyah, n.d. - Edited by Muḥammad Abul Fadl Ibrāhīm).

Nahj al- Balāgha (with research and annotation of Ṣubḥī Ṣāliḥ).

Nasāʾī, Aḥmad ibn Shuʿayb ibn ʿAlī ibn Sinān al-, *Sunan al-Kubrā* (Beirut: Dār al-Kutub al-ʿIlmīyyah, 1st Edition, 1411 AH - Researched by Dr. ʿAbdul Ghaffār Sulaymān).

Naysābūrī, Ḥākim al-, *Al-Mustadrak ʿalā al-Ṣaḥīḥḥayn* (Edited by Yūsuf ʿAbdul Raḥmān al-Murshilī, n.d.).

Naysābūrī, Muslim ibn Ḥajjāj al-, *Ṣaḥīḥ Muslim* (Beirut: Dār al-Fikr, n.d.).

Ṣafādī, Ṣalāḥ al-Dīn Khalīl ibn Aybak al-, *Al-Wafī bil Wafāyāt* (Dār Iḥyāʾ al-Turāth, 1420 AH - Edited by Aḥmad al-Arnaut and Turki Muṣṭafā).

Ṣanaʿāī, ʿAbdul Razzāq al-, *Al-Muṣannaf* (Manshūrāt al-Majlis al-ʿIlmī, n.d. - Researched by Ḥabīb al-Raḥmān al-Aʿaẓamī).

Shahrastānī, ʿAbdul Karīm al-, *Al-Milal wa al-Niḥal* (Egypt: Maktabat Muṣṭafā al-Bābī wa Awlāduh, 1387 AH - Edited by Muḥammad Sayed Kilānī).

Shaybānī, ʿAlī ibn Muḥammad ibn Muḥammad al-, also known as Ibn Athīr, *Al-Kāmil fī al-Tārīkh* (Beirut: Dār Sader, 1385 AH).

Sulaymān, Nūr al-Dīn ʿAlī ibn Abī Bakr ibn, *Majmūʿ al-Zawāʾid* (Dār al-Kutub al-ʿIlmīyyah, n.d.).

Suyūṭī, Jalāl al-Dīn al-, *Al-Durr al-Manthūr* (Beirut: Dār al-Fikr, 1423 AH).

Ṭabarānī, Sulaymān ibn Aḥmad al-, *Al-Muʿjam al-Kabīr* (Beirut: Dār Iḥyāʾ al-Turāth, 2nd Edition, 1404 AH - Edited by Ḥamdī ʿAbdul Majīd al-Salafī).

Ṭabarī, Muḥammad ibn Jarīr ibn al-, *Tārīkh al-Ṭabarī* (Beirut: Daār al-Turāth, 2nd Edition, 1387 AH - Edited by Muḥammad Abūl Faḍl Ibrāhīm).

Tirmidhī, Abū ʿIsā al-, *Sunan Tirmidhī* (Beirut: Dār al-Fikr, 1st Printing, 1424 AH - Researched by ʿAbdul Raḥmān Muḥammad ʿUthmān).

Yaʿqūb, Aḥmad ibn Abī, *Tārīkh al-Yaʿqūbī* (Beirut: Dār Sader, n.d.).

Chapter Three

Fire in the House of Revelation

Myth Or Reality: An Introduction

Recently, a person ignorant about Islamic history authored an article about the beloved daughter of Prophet Muḥammad ﷺ, titled: *The Legend of Fāṭima al-Zahrā's Martyrdom.* In this article, after mentioning the merits and virtues of Lady Fāṭima ؏, he tried to deny her martyrdom and disregard the atrocities done to her. In summary, this article proved to be a clear distortion of the established Islamic history and prompted us to respond and prove that the martyrdom of the Lady of Light, Fāṭima al-Zahrā' ؏ is an undeniable, historical fact.

In this research, we will shed some light on the following areas:

1. Fāṭima al-Zahrā' ؏ in the words of the Messenger of Allah ﷺ.

2. Respecting the physical house of Lady Fāṭima al-Zahrā' ؏ in the teachings of the Quran and established *Sunnah* of Prophet Muḥammad ﷺ.

3. Desecration of the house of Lady Fāṭima al-Zahrā' ؏.

We hope that by clarifying these three points, the author of the article will realize the errors in his claims and make amends for his work.

Once again, it is important to note that all the sources referred to in this book have been taken from authentic Sunnī works of *Ḥadīth* and history.

Fāṭima al-Zahrā' ؏ in the Words of the Prophet ﷺ

The beloved daughter of the Noble Messenger ﷺ has a prominent position in Islam, and the statements of the Prophet ﷺ about his daughter indicate her spiritual proximity to him ﷺ.

For example, the Prophet ﷺ is quoted as saying: "Fāṭima is a part of me, and whoever makes her angry, makes me angry."[1]

---

[1] *Fatḥ al-Bārī fī Sharḥ Ṣaḥīḥ al-Bukhārī,* Vol. 7, Pg. 84; Al-Bukhārī also cites this *ḥadīth* in the section on the Signs of Prophethood, Vol. 6, Pg. 491; and

The anger of Lady Fāṭima al-Zahrā' ﷺ is a source of grief for the Messenger of Allah ﷺ, and the punishment for a person who hurts Prophet Muḥammad ﷺ in any way, shape or form is described in the Noble Quran as follows: "And those who hurt the Messenger of Allah will have a painful torment."[2]

What is a more decisive proof of her virtue and standing in Islam is a *ḥadīth* in which her pleasure is equated to the pleasure of Allah ﷻ, and her anger is equated to the anger of Allah ﷻ. This is seen in a famous *ḥadīth* where Prophet Muḥammad ﷺ is quoted as having said: "O Fāṭima, indeed Allah is angry when you are angry, and He is pleased when you are pleased."[3]

Additionally, her status in Islam is clearly defined in the following *ḥadīth*: "O Fāṭima! Are you not pleased that you are the Chief of the women of the worlds, and that you are the Chief of the women of this nation, and that you are the Chief of [all] the believing women?"[4]

---

at the end of *Al-Maghāzī*, Vol. 8, Pg. 110. The Arabic text of this is as follows:

فَاطِمَةُ بَضْعَةٌ مِنِّي فَمَنْ أَغْضَبَهَا أَغْضَبَنِي.

[2] Quran, Sūrah al-Tawbah (9), Verse 61:

﴿...وَٱلَّذِينَ يُؤْذُونَ رَسُولَ ٱللَّهِ لَهُمْ عَذَابٌ أَلِيمٌ ٦١﴾

[3] *Al-Mustadrak ʿalā al-Ṣaḥīḥḥayn*, Vol. 3, Pg. 154; *Majmaʿ al-Zawāʾid*, Vol. 9, Pg. 203. The *ḥadīth* in Al-Ḥākim's *Mustadrak* is authentic according to the conditions of Al-Bukhārī and Muslim. The Arabic text of this is as follows:

يَا فَاطِمَةُ إِنَّ اللَّهَ لَيَغْضَبُ لِغَضَبِكِ وَيَرْضَى لِرِضَاكِ.

[4] *Al-Mustadrak ʿalā al-Ṣaḥīḥḥayn*, Vol. 3, Pg. 156. The Arabic text of this is as follows:

Respecting the House of Fāṭima al-Zahrā᾿ ﷺ

Ḥadīth experts narrate that when the blessed verse: "(This light can best be obtained and those guided to it are found) In some houses for which Allah has ordered to be raised, and for His Name to be mentioned (praised and invoked) therein; glorifying Him in the mornings and the evenings,"[5] was revealed to the Prophet ﷺ, he began to recite it inside the masjid.

A man stood up and asked: "O beloved Messenger! What are these houses...?"

The Prophet ﷺ replied: "The houses of the Prophets."

Abū Bakr then stood up, while pointing to the house of ʿAlī ﷺ and Fāṭima ﷺ, and asked: "Is this house one of those houses?"

The Prophet ﷺ replied: "Yes, and it is the best (or most superior) of them."[6]

The Noble Prophet ﷺ would come to the door of his daughter's house for nine months straight, and would greet her and her beloved husband, then proceed to read this verse: "Allah only desires to keep

---

يَا فَاطِمَةُ أَلَا تَرْضَيْنَ أَنْ تَكُونِي سَيِّدَةَ نِسَاءِ الْعَالَمِينَ وَسَيِّدَةَ نِسَاءِ هٰذِهِ الْأُمَّةِ وَسَيِّدَةَ نِسَاءِ الْمُؤْمِنِينَ.

[5] Quran, Sūrah an-Nūr (24), Verse 36:

﴿فِي بُيُوتٍ أَذِنَ ٱللَّهُ أَن تُرْفَعَ وَيُذْكَرَ فِيهَا ٱسْمُهُۥ يُسَبِّحُ لَهُۥ فِيهَا بِٱلْغُدُوِّ وَٱلْآصَالِ ۝٣٦﴾

[6] *Al-Durr al-Manthūr*, Vol. 6, Pg. 203; *Tafsīr Rūḥ al-Maʿānī*, Vol. 18, Pg. 174. The Arabic text of this is as follows:

قَرَأَ رَسُولُ اللهِ صَلَّى الله عَلَيْهِ وَآلِهِ هٰذِهِ الآيَةَ: ﴿فِي بُيُوتٍ أَذِنَ اللهُ أَنْ تُرفَعَ...﴾ فَقَامَ إِلَيهِ رَجُلٌ فَقَالَ: أَيُّ بُيُوتٍ هٰذِهِ يَا رَسُولَ اللهِ؟ قَالَ: بُيُوتُ الأَنْبِيَاءِ. فَقَامَ إِلَيهِ أَبُو بَكْرٍ فَقَالَ: يَا رَسُولَ اللهِ، هٰذَا البَيتُ مِنْهَا؟ لِبَيْتِ عَلِيٍّ وَفَاطِمَةَ؟ قَالَ: نَعَمْ مِنْ أَفَاضِلِهَا.

away the uncleanness from you, O People of the House *(Ahlul Bayt)*, and to purify you with a (thorough) purification."[7]

Indeed, her house was one that Allah ﷻ had ordered to dignify, and thus, it had to be highly venerated. A house which enclosed the People of the Cloak *(Aṣḥāb al-Kisā')*, and one in which its inhabitants were revered by Allah ﷻ with majesty and greatness, had to be respected by all Muslims.

However, we must ask the following questions:

1. After the death of Prophet Muḥammad ﷺ, how much was this house honoured?
2. How did some of the Muslims violate the sanctity of that house, and what was their confession later?
3. Who were these desecrators, and what was their reason for destroying the inviolability of such a sacred space?

Desecration of the House of Fāṭima عليها السلام

Unfortunately, despite the strict orders of Allah ﷻ in the Quran, and the clear *ḥadīth* of Prophet Muḥammad ﷺ, some of the 'companions' of the final Messenger, Prophet Muḥammad ﷺ, ignored the sanctity of the noble house of Fāṭima al-Zahrā' عليها السلام after his death, and went on to desecrate it – and this is not an issue that can be covered up or taken lightly.

We quote some texts from the books of the Ahlul Sunnah to make it clear that the desecration of the house of Fāṭima al-Zahrā' عليها السلام and subsequent events are historical, and incontrovertible and undeniable facts – they are not a legend.

In the era of the first three caliphs, there was an extraordinary strictness about writing about the virtues and nobility of the Ahlul

---

[7] Quran, Sūrah al-Aḥzāb (33), Verse 33:

﴿إِنَّمَا يُرِيدُ اللَّهُ لِيُذْهِبَ عَنكُمُ الرِّجْسَ أَهْلَ الْبَيْتِ وَيُطَهِّرَكُمْ تَطْهِيرًا﴾

Bayt ﷺ – however, this truth was still preserved largely in historical and *Ḥadīth* literature.

Opinion of Ibn Abī Shaybah

The Sunnī scholar, Ibn Abī Shaybah (d. 235 AH), author of *Al-Muṣannaf*, documents the following narration with an authentic chain: "After the Messenger of Allah (passed away), when the allegiance was paid to Abū Bakr, ʿAlī and Zubayr used to enter the house of Fāṭima and discuss their plans. When this news reached ʿUmar ibn al-Khaṭṭāb, he went out [into the streets of Madina] and entered the house of Fāṭima, saying: 'O daughter of the Messenger of Allah! By Allah, your father is the most beloved to me; and after him, it is you. But by Allah! This love will not stop me from burning the house down upon them.'

When he left, and when these people, meaning ʿAlī and Zubayr, returned to the house, Fāṭima told them: 'Do you know that ʿUmar came to me and swore by Allah that if you returned, then he would burn down the house? And I swear by Allah that he would do what he has vowed to do!'"[8]

---

[8] The Arabic text of this is as follows:

أَنَّهُ حِينَ بُويِعَ لِأَبِي بَكْرٍ بَعْدَ رَسُولِ اللهِ صَلَّى اللهُ عَلَيْهِ وَسَلَّمَ كَانَ عَلِيٌّ وَالزُّبَيْرُ يَدْخُلَانِ عَلَى فَاطِمَةَ بِنْتِ رَسُولِ اللهِ صَلَّى اللهُ عَلَيْهِ وَسَلَّمَ فَيُشَاوِرُونَهَا وَيَرْتَجِعُونَ فِي أَمْرِهِمْ. فَلَمَّا بَلَغَ ذٰلِكَ عُمَرَ بْنَ الْخَطَّابِ خَرَجَ حَتَّى دَخَلَ عَلَى فَاطِمَةَ فَقَالَ: يَا بِنْتَ رَسُولِ اللهِ وَاللهِ مَا مِنْ أَحَدٍ أَحَبَّ إِلَيْنَا مِنْ أَبِيكِ وَمَا مِنْ أَحَدٍ أَحَبَّ إِلَيْنَا بَعْدَ أَبِيكِ مِنْكِ وَايْمُ اللهِ مَا ذَاكَ بِمَانِعِي إِنِ اجْتَمَعَ هَؤُلَاءِ النَّفَرُ عِنْدَكِ أَنْ أَمَرْتُهُمْ أَنْ يُحَرَّقَ عَلَيْهِمِ الْبَيْتُ. قَالَ: فَلَمَّا خَرَجَ عُمَرُ جَاءُوهَا فَقَالَتْ: تَعْلَمُونَ أَنَّ عُمَرَ قَدْ جَاءَنِي وَقَدْ حَلَفَ بِاللهِ لَئِنْ عُدْتُمْ لَيُحَرِّقَنَّ عَلَيْكُمُ الْبَيْتَ وَايْمُ اللهِ لَيَمْضِيَنَّ لِمَا حَلَفَ عَلَيْهِ.

Opinion of Al-Balādhurī

Aḥmad ibn Yaḥyā ibn Jābir al-Balādhurī (d. 270 AH), a famous Sunnī writer and author of history, narrates this historical event in his book, *Ansāb al-Ashrāf*: "Abū Bakr wanted ʿAlī to give allegiance to him, but when ʿAlī refused the pledge, ʿUmar went to the house with fire. Fāṭima confronted him at the door, saying: 'O Ibn al-Khaṭṭāb! Do you want to burn my door?' He replied: 'Yes, and this is in line with what your father came with.'"[9]

Opinion of Ibn Qutaybah

The famous Sunnī historian, Abū Muḥammad ʿAbdullāh ibn Muslim ibn Qutaybah al-Dīnawarī (d. 276 AH) was one of the pioneers of literature, a prolific writer in the field of Islamic history, and the author of books such as: *Ta'wīl Mukhtalif al-Ḥadīth*, *Kitāb Adab al-Kātib*, and many more. In his book, *Al-Imāmah wa al-Siyāsah*, he writes the following: "Abū Bakr was closely inspecting a group of people who were with ʿAlī who had not yet pledged allegiance to him. ʿUmar [ibn al-Khaṭṭāb] was sent to them. He called them to come outside as they were in the house of ʿAlī, but they refused to come out. So, he (ʿUmar) called for firewood and said: 'By the one who has ʿUmar's soul in his hand, you either come out, or I will burn this house and those inside of it!' It was said to him (ʿUmar): 'O Abū Ḥafṣ, Fāṭima is in there!' He said: 'So be it!'"[10]

---

[9] *Ansāb al-Ashrāf*, Vol. 1, Pg. 586. The Arabic of this text is as follows:

إِنَّ أَبَا بَكْرٍ أَرْسَلَ إِلَى عَلِيٍّ يُرِيدُ الْبَيْعَةَ، فَلَمْ يُبَايِعْ، فَجَاءَ عُمَرُ وَمَعَهُ فَتِيلَةٌ؛ فَلَقِيَتْهُ فَاطِمَةُ عَلَى الْبَابِ، فَقَالَتْ فَاطِمَةُ: يَا ابْنَ الْخَطَّابِ، أَ تُرَاكَ مُحْرِقًا عَلَيَّ بَابِي؟ قَالَ: نَعَمْ، وَذٰلِكَ أَقْوَى فِيمَا جَاءَ بِهِ أَبُوكِ...

[10] *Al-Imāmah wa al-Siyāsah*, Pg. 12. The Arabic of this text is as follows:

Ibn Qutaybah continues to write this event which only becomes more painful to read, in which he narrates: "ʿUmar [ibn al-Khaṭṭāb] got up, and a group of people followed him until they reached the door of [the house of] Fāṭima. They knocked on the door, and when she heard their voices, she called out at the top of her voice: 'O Father, O Messenger of Allah, what do we have to go through after your demise due to ʿUmar ibn al-Khaṭṭāb and Ibn Abī Quḥāfah (Abū Bakr)!'

When the people heard her voice and her crying, (some of them) left, crying, with heavy hearts, and aching pain; however, ʿUmar stayed behind with a few of them. They forcibly brought ʿAlī out of the house and took him to Abū Bakr. Then they said to ʿAlī: 'Pledge allegiance!'

He said: 'And if I do not?'

They said: 'Then, by Allah, besides whom there is no God, we shall strike your neck [with our swords and kill you].'"[11]

This part of history is very unpalatable and unappealing for those who are fond of the two *Shaykhs* – namely Abū Bakr and ʿUmar.

إِنَّ أَبَا بَكْرٍ (رض) تَفَقَّدَ قَوْمًا تَخَلَّفُوا عَنْ بَيْعَتِهِ عِنْدَ عَلِيٍّ كَرَّمَ اللهُ وَجْهَهُ، فَبَعَثَ إِلَيْهِمْ عُمَرُ، فَجَاءَ فَنَادَاهُمْ وَهُمْ فِي دَارِ عَلِيٍّ، فَأَبَوْا أَنْ يَخْرُجُوا، فَدَعَا بِالْحَطَبِ، وَقَالَ: وَالَّذِي نَفْسِ عُمَرَ بِيَدِهِ، لَتَخْرُجَنَّ أَوْ لَأَحْرَقَنَّهَا عَلَى مَنْ فِيهَا. فَقِيلَ لَهُ: يَا أَبَا حَفْصٍ، إِنَّ فِيهَا فَاطِمَةَ؟ فَقَالَ: وَإِنْ.

[11] *Al-Imāmah wa al-Siyāsah*, Pg. 13. The Arabic of this text is as follows:

ثُمَّ قَامَ عُمَرَ فَمَشَى مَعَهُ جَمَاعَةٌ حَتَّى أَتَوْا بَابَ فَاطِمَةَ، فَدَقُّوا الْبَابَ فَلَمَّا سَمِعَتْ أَصْوَاتَهُمْ نَادَتْ بِأَعْلَى صَوْتِهَا: يَا أَبَةَ يَا رَسُولَ اللّٰهَ، مَا ذَا لَقِينَا بَعْدَكَ مِنْ ابْنِ الْخَطَّابِ وَابْنِ أَبِي قُحَافَةَ. فَلَمَّا سَمِعَ الْقَوْمُ صَوْتَهَا وَبُكَاءَهَا انْصَرَفُوا وَبَقِيَ عُمَرُ وَمَعَهُ قَوْمٌ، فَأَخْرَجُوا عَلِيًّا، فَمَضَوْا بِهِ إِلَى أَبِي بَكْرٍ؛ فَقَالُوا لَهُ: بَايِعْ. فَقَالَ: إِنْ أَنَا لَمْ أَفْعَلْ فَمَهْ؟ قَالُوا: إِذَا وَاللّٰهِ الَّذِي لَا إِلٰهَ إِلَّا هُوَ نَضْرِبُ عُنُقَكَ...

Therefore, some people try to doubt the attribution of this book to Ibn Qutaybah, even though Ibn Abī al-Ḥadīd, the Master of History, considers this book to be one of his works and constantly quotes from it.

Unfortunately, this book has suffered distortion, and some parts of its contents were removed during recent printings – however, Ibn Abī al-Ḥadīd preserved the actual wording in his commentary of *Nahj al-Balāgha.*

The Sunnī scholar, Khayr al-Dīn al-Ziriklī, considers this book to be one of Ibn Qutaybah's works, as he expressed in the book, *Al-A'lām*, and added that: "Scholars have opinions (doubts) in this regard."[12]

He is attributing doubts to others, not to himself – although he is the one who doubts this historical event and wants to exonerate certain historical personalities.

Additionally, Elyās Sarkīs also considers this book as one of Ibn Qutaybah's works.[13]

Opinion of Ṭabarī

The famous historian, Muḥammad ibn Jarīr al-Ṭabarī (d. 310 AH) in his book, *Tārīkh al-Rusul wa al-Mulūk,* describes the desecration of the House of Revelation as follows: "'Umar ibn al-Khaṭṭāb came to the house of 'Alī, while Ṭalḥa and Zubayr, and some of the *Muhājirūn* were also in the house. 'Umar shouted: 'By Allah! Either you come out to render the oath of allegiance, or I will set the house on fire!'

Zubayr came out with his sword drawn, but he stumbled (upon something), and the sword fell out from his hand, at which point

---

[12] *Al-A'lām*, Vol. 4, Pg. 137.

[13] *Mu'jam al-Matbu'āt al-'Arabiyyah*, Vol. 1, Pg. 212.

those present jumped on him and arrested him."[14]

This part of history indicates that giving the oath of allegiance to the caliph Abū Bakr was done with threats and intimidation. If that was the case, then we must ask ourselves the question: What is the value or legitimacy of such an allegiance?

It is up to the readers to judge.

Opinion of Ibn ʿAbd Rabbih

Shahhāb al-Dīn Aḥmad, known as Ibn ʿAbd Rabbih al-Andalūsī, the author of *Al-ʿIqd al-Farīd* (d. 463 AH), has given a detailed report about the history of the Event at Ṣaqīfah in his book. He writes the following under the title of: 'Those who Refused to Pay the Pledge of Allegiance to Abū Bakr:' "Those who fell behind in giving the allegiance to Abū Bakr were ʿAlī, ʿAbbās, Zubayr, and Saʿd ibn ʿUbādah, amongst whom ʿAlī, ʿAbbās, and Zubayr were sitting in the house of Fāṭima. At that time, Abū Bakr sent ʿUmar ibn al-Khaṭṭāb with the order that he remove those gathered in the house of Fāṭima, and if they refuse to come out, then to fight them. Thus, ʿUmar brought fire to the house of Fāṭima, and when she met him, she said: 'O Ibn al-Khaṭṭāb! Have you come to set my home on fire?'

He (ʿUmar) replied: 'Yes, unless you people give allegiance to Abū Bakr as the entire Muslim nation has done.'"[15]

---

[14] *Tārīkh al-Rusul wa al-Mulūk*, Vol. 2, Pg. 443. The Arabic of this text is as follows:

أَتَى عُمَرُ بْنُ الْخَطَّابِ مَنْزِلَ عَلِيٍّ وَفِيهِ طَلْحَةُ وَالزُّبَيْرُ وَرِجَالٌ مِنَ الْمُهَاجِرِينَ فَقَالَ: وَاللهِ لَأُحْرِقَنَّ عَلَيْكُمْ أَوْ لَتَخْرُجَنَّ إِلَى الْبَيْعَةِ فَخَرَجَ عَلَيْهِ الزُّبَيْرُ مُصْلِتًا بِالسَّيْفِ فَعَثَرَ فَسَقَطَ السَّيْفُ مِنْ يَدِهِ فَوَثَبُوا عَلَيْهِ فَأَخَذُوهُ.

[15] *Al-ʿIqd al-Farīd*, Vol. 4, Pg. 93. The Arabic of this text is as follows:

So far, we have covered the intention to desecrate the House of Revelation. Now, we move onto the second part of our discussion which shows how this intention was implemented.

Do not think that their intention was merely to threaten Imam ʿAlī ؑ and his companions into pledging allegiance, and that they did not really intend to go through with their threat of burning down the house of Lady Fāṭima al-Zahrāʾ ؑ – even though she was in it.

The quotations only point to the bad intentions of the caliph Abū Bakr, ʿUmar ibn al-Khaṭṭāb, and his companions. However, here are some narrations that show the actual attack and desecration of the house of Lady Fāṭima ؑ.

Opinion of Abū ʿUbayd

Abū ʿUbayd al-Qāsim ibn Salām (d. 224 AH) writes in *Kitāb al-Amwāl*, a reliable book which Sunnī jurists regard as being trustworthy, that: "ʿAbdul Raḥmān ibn ʿAwf says: 'I went to the house of Abū Bakr to visit him when he was sick. After a long conversation, he said: 'Indeed, I do not regret anything except for three things I did which I wish I would not have done; and three things I did not do which I wish I had done; and three things I wish I had asked the Messenger of Allah about. As for the three things I wish I had not done, I wish that I had not violated the sanctity of the house of Fāṭima and left it – even if they would have used it (to

---

فَأَمَّا عَلِيٌّ وَالْعَبَّاسُ وَالزُّبَيْرُ فَقَعَدُوا فِي بَيْتِ فَاطِمَةَ حَتَّى بَعَثَ إِلَيْهِمْ أَبُو بَكْرٍ، عُمَرَ بْنَ الْخَطَّابِ لِيُخْرِجَهُمْ مِنْ بَيْتِ فَاطِمَةَ وَقَالَ لَهُ: إِنْ أَبَوْا فَقَاتِلْهُمْ. فَأَقْبَلَ بِقَبَسٍ مِنْ نَارٍ أَنْ يُضْرِمَ عَلَيْهِمُ الدَّارَ، فَلَقِيَتْهُ فَاطِمَةُ فَقَالَتْ: يَا ابْنَ الْخَطَّابِ أَجِئْتَ لِتَحْرِقَ دَارَنَا؟ قَالَ: نَعَمْ، أَوْ تَدْخُلُوا فِيمَا دَخَلَتْ فِيهِ الْأُمَّةُ.

prepare) for war...'"[16]

When Abū ʿUbayd arrives at this point of the narration, instead of the sentence: "I wish that I had not violated the sanctity of the house of Fāṭima and left it," he writes "such-and-such," and adds that "I do not want to mention it!"

Even though Abū ʿUbayd refused to narrate the truth due to religious prejudice, or possibly other reasons, he writes in the footnote of the same book, *Kitāb al-Amwāl*: "The deleted sentences have been included in the book, *Mizān al-Iʿtidāl,* in the way it was stated."

In addition, al-Ṭabarānī in his work, *Al-Muʿjam al-Kabīr,* and Ibn ʿAbd Rabbih in *Al-ʿIqd al-Farīd,* and others, have included the omitted sentences.

Opinion of Ṭabarānī

Abūl Qāsim Sulaymān ibn Aḥmad al-Ṭabarānī (d. 360 AH) whom al-Dhahabī considers as being reliable in his *Mizān al-Iʿtidāl,*[17] documents in his work, *Al-Muʿjam al-Kabīr,* about the speech of Abū Bakr on his deathbed. In this regard, he writes the following: "At the time of his death, Abū Bakr wished for some things and said: 'I wish I had not done three things, and I wish I had done three things, and I wish I had asked the Messenger of Allah about three things. As for those three things I wish I had not done: I wish I had not violated the

[16] *Kitāb al-Amwāl,* footnote 4; See also Pg. 144 of the same book. *Al-ʿIqd al-Farīd,* Vol. 4, Pg. 93. The Arabic text of this is as follows:

وَدَدْتُ أَنِّي لَمْ أَكُنْ أَكْشِفْ بَيْتَ فَاطِمَةَ وَتَرَكْتُهُ وَإِنْ أُغْلِقَ عَلَى الْحَرْبِ.

[17] Dhahabī, Muḥammad ibn Aḥmad ibn ʿUthmān al-, *Mizān al-Iʿtidāl,* Vol. 2, Pg. 195.

sanctity of the house of Fāṭima and had left it alone!'"[18]

These interpretations clearly show that the threats which ʿUmar ibn al-Khaṭṭāb made were implemented, and the door of the house of the beloved daughter of the Prophet ﷺ was opened by force, and it was set on fire.

Opinion of Ibn ʿAbd Rabbih

Ibn ʿAbd Rabbih al-Andalūsī (d. 463 AH), the author of *Al-ʿIqd al-Farīd,* quotes ʿAbdul Raḥmān ibn ʿAwf in his book as having said: "I visited Abū Bakr during his illness and he said: 'I wish I had not done three things, and one of those three things is that I wish I had not violated the sanctity of the house of Fāṭima for any reason, even if they had closed it for battle.'"[19]

Opinion of Naẓẓām

Abū Isḥāq Ibrāhīm ibn Sayyār Muʿtazilī, popularly known as al-Naẓẓām, due to the beauty of his words in poetry and prose, narrates the incident about the attack on the house of Fāṭima ﷺ in several books. In one of his works, he says: "On the day of swearing the oath of allegiance to Abū Bakr, ʿUmar hit Fāṭima's stomach, which resulted in a miscarriage of her child named Moḥsin."[20]

---

[18] Ṭabarānī, Sulaymān ibn Aḥmad al-, *Al-Muʿjam al-Kabīr,* Vol. 1, Pg. 62, Tradition 36. The Arabic text of this is as follows:

أَمَا الثَّلَاثُ اللَّائِي وَدِدْتُ أَنِّي لَمْ أَفْعَلْهُنَّ: فَوَدِدْتُ أَنِّي لَمْ أَكُنْ أَكْشِفُ بَيْتَ فَاطِمَةَ وَتَرَكْتُهُ.

[19] *Al-ʿIqd al-Farīd,* Vol. 4, Pg. 93. The Arabic text of this is as follows:

وَدِدْتُ أَنِّي لَمْ أَكْشِفْ بَيْتَ فَاطِمَةَ عَنْ شَيْءٍ وَإِنْ كَانُوا أَغْلَقُوهُ عَلَى الْحَرْبِ.

[20] Al-Naẓẓām, *Al-Wāfī bil Wafāyāt,* Vol. 6, Pg. 17, No. 2444; Shahrastānī, ʿAbdul Karīm al-, *Al-Milal wa al-Nihal,* Vol. 1, Pg. 57. Refer to the

Opinion of Mubarrad

Ibn Abī al-Ḥadīd writes: "Muḥammad ibn Yazīd ibn ʿAbdul Akbar al-Baghdādī (d. 285 AH), a writer and famous author of notable works, writes the story of the caliph's wishes in the book, *Al-Kāmil*, narrated from ʿAbdul Raḥmān ibn ʿAwf, and mentions this: 'I wish I had not violated the sanctity of the house of Fāṭima, and should have left it alone even if it was closed for war.'"[21]

Opinion of Maṣʿūdī

Al-Maṣʿūdī (d. 325 AH) in his book, *Murūj al-Dhahab*, writes: "When Abū Bakr was dying, he said: 'I did three things that I wish I had not done; one of those three things was that I wish I had not violated the sanctity of the house of al-Zahrā'.' [In fact,] He said a lot about this."[22]

Even though al-Maṣʿūdī had a positive tendency towards the Ahlul Bayt ﷺ, here he refrained from narrating the full speech of the caliph, Abū Bakr, and rejected it with sarcasm. Of course, only Allah ﷻ knows why he did this, and why he left the speech incomplete.

Biography of al-Naẓẓām in the book, *Buḥūth fī al-Milal wa al-Niḥal*, Vol. 3, Pp. 248–255. The Arabic text of this is as follows:

إِنَّ عُمَرَ ضَرَبَ بَطْنَ فَاطِمَةَ يَوْمَ الْبَيْعَةِ حَتَّى أَلْقَتِ الْمُحْسِنَ مِنْ بَطْنِهَا.

[21] *Sharḥ Nahj al-Balāgha*, Vol. 2, Pp. 46-47. The Arabic text of this is as follows:

وَدَدْتُ أَنِّي لَمْ أَكُنْ كَشَفْتُ عَنْ بَيْتِ فَاطِمَةَ وَتَرَكْتُهُ وَلَوْ أُغْلِقَ عَلَى الْحَرْبِ.

[22] Maṣʿūdī, ʿAlī ibn al-Ḥusayn ibn ʿAlī al-, *Murūj al-Ḍhahab*, Vol. 2, Pg. 301. The Arabic text of this is as follows:

فَوَدَدْتُ أَنِّي لَمْ أَكُنْ فَتَّشْتُ بَيْتَ فَاطِمَةَ وَذَكَرَ فِي ذٰلِكَ كَلَامًا كَثِيرًا.

Opinion of Dhahabī

Al-Dhahabī in *Mizān al-ʿItidāl* documented a narration from Muḥammad ibn Aḥmad al-Kūfī al-Ḥāfiẓ who reported that this narration was read in the presence of Aḥmad ibn Muḥammad, popularly known as Ibn Abī Dārim (d. 357 AH), a *muḥaddith* (narrator of *Ḥadīth*) from the city of Kūfa, that: "ʿUmar kicked Fāṭima, and the child in her womb named Moḥsin was miscarried!"[23]

Opinion of ʿAbdul Fattāḥ ʿAbdul Maqṣūd

ʿAbdul Fattāḥ ʿAbdul Maqṣūd mentioned the attack on the house of revelation two times in his book entitled *Al-Imām ʿAlī ibn Abī Ṭālib* - we will limit ourselves to quoting one of them.

In his narration, he states: "ʿUmar said: 'By Him in whose hand is ʿUmar's life, they must either come out, or I will burn the house together with those in it!' A group who feared Allah and cared for the Messenger of Allah turned back on their heels and said to him: 'O Abū Ḥafṣ, there is Fāṭima in the house!' He shouted: 'I do not care. So be it!' He approached and knocked on the door, then slammed it, and barged into it. ʿAlī was found... And at that time the voice of al-Zahrāʾ rang at the entrance of the house as she was calling for help...'"[24]

---

[23] *Mizān al-Iʿtidāl*, Vol. 1, Pg. 139, No. 552. The Arabic text of this is as follows:

إِنَّ عُمَرَ رَفَسَ فَاطِمَةَ حَتَّى أَسْقَطَتْ بِـمُحْسِنٍ.

[24] Maqṣūd, ʿAbdul Fattāḥ ʿAbdul, *Al-Imām ʿAlī ibn Abī Ṭālib*, Vol. 4, Pp. 276-277. The Arabic text of this is as follows:

وَالَّذِي نَفْسُ عُمَرَ بِيَدِهِ، لَيَخْرُجَنَّ أَوْ لَأَحْرِقَنَّهَا عَلَى مَنْ فِيهَا ... قَالَتْ لَهُ طَائِفَةٌ خَافَتِ اللَّهَ ورَعَتِ الرَّسُولَ فِي عَقِبِهِ: يَا أَبَا حَفْصٍ، إِنَّ فِيهَا فَاطِمَةَ ... فَصَاحَ: لَا يُبَالِي وَإِنْ ... وَاقْتَرَبَ وَقَرَعَ الْبَابَ،

We end this discussion – although there are still many things left unsaid – with a final narration from Muqātil ibn ʿAṭiyyah in the book, *Al-Imāmah wa al-Khilāfah*. He writes in this book: "Abū Bakr, after taking the pledge of allegiance to himself from the people with terror, sword, and force, sent ʿUmar and Qunfudh, and a group to the house of ʿAlī and Fāṭima. ʿUmar gathered firewood for the house of Fāṭima and burned the door of the house."[25]

In addition to these narrations, there are several other narrations that the pen cannot even express, and so we leave this discussion at this point.

Conclusion

Despite unmistakable evidence quoted from Sunnī sources, some of them use the term "the fable of the martyrdom," and consider this tragic incident to be a hoax! If it was not for their insistence on denying these facts, we would not have expanded the discussion to this extent.

We hope that the revelation of these facts will wake up the sleeping minds so that they do not hide historical facts amidst prejudice or deny them altogether.

Allah ﷻ says in the Quran: "And not upon us (our duty) is except

---

ثُمَّ ضَرَبَهُ وَاقْتَحَمَهُ ... وَبَدَالَهُ عَلِيٌّ ... وَرَنَّ حِينَذَاكَ صَوْتُ الزَّهْرَاءِ عِنْدَ مَدْخَلِ الدَّارِ ... فَإِنْ هِيَ إِلَّا طَنِينَ اسْتِغَاثَةٍ...

[25] ʿAṭiyyah, Maqātil ibn, *Al-Imāmah wa al-Khilāfah*, Pp. 160-161. Introduction by Dr. Hamed Dawud, Professor of ʿAyn al-Shams, University of Cairo. The Arabic text of this is as follows:

إِنَّ أَبَا بَكْرٍ بَعْدَ مَا أَخَذَ الْبَيْعَةَ لِنَفْسِهِ مِنَ النَّاسِ بِالْإِرْهَابِ وَالسَّيْفِ وَالْقُوَّةِ أَرْسَلَ عُمَرَ وَقُنْفُذًا وَجَمَاعَةً إِلَى دَارِ عَلِيٍّ وَفَاطِمَةَ وَجَمَعَ عُمَرُ الْحَطَبَ عَلَى دَارِ فَاطِمَةَ وَأَحْرَقَ بَابَ الدَّارِ.

to convey (the clear message)."[26]

[26] Quran, Sūrah Yāsīn (36), Verse 17:

﴿وَمَا عَلَيْنَآ إِلَّا ٱلْبَلَٰغُ ٱلْمُبِينُ ١٧﴾

Chapter Four

An Analysis of the Life of ʿUmar ibn al-Khaṭṭāb

An Analysis of the Life of ʿUmar ibn al-Khaṭṭāb

One of the issues that has kept the minds of the youth who are busy searching for the true visage of Islam and has also preoccupied the unbiased researchers of Islamic thought is the inconsiderate behavioural pattern of the second caliph, ʿUmar ibn al-Khaṭṭāb. This discussion is significant, and as we will mention, the necessity for this study is based on two reasons:

1. The Quran refers to the noble ethical traits of the final Messenger of Allah, Muḥammad ﷺ, and describes him as merciful and lenient, and negates any semblance of harshness in his character [and thus, it stands to reason that anyone who claims to be his successor and the leader of the Muslim nation must also display the same qualities and characteristics in their life – from the beginning to the end].[1]

2. The demonstration of compassion and love on the part of the Muslims in relation to one another is established in the Quran as being one of the traits of the followers of Prophet Muḥammad ﷺ. The Quran notes that it is only in the face of the belligerent disbelievers that the Muslims must stand their ground – however, in the presence of one another, they should be extremely compassionate in their interactions.[2]

With that said, in the life of the second caliph – as has been clearly

---

[1] Quran, Sūrah Āle ʿImrān (3), Verse 159:

﴿فَبِمَا رَحْمَةٍ مِّنَ اللَّهِ لِنتَ لَهُمْ ۖ وَلَوْ كُنتَ فَظًّا غَلِيظَ الْقَلْبِ لَانفَضُّوا مِنْ حَوْلِكَ...﴾

"Only through the Divine Mercy have you (Muḥammad) been able to deal with your followers so gently. If you had been stern and hard-hearted, then they would all have deserted you a long time ago..."

[2] Quran, Sūrah al-Fatḥ (48), Verse 29:

﴿مُّحَمَّدٌ رَّسُولُ اللَّهِ ۚ وَالَّذِينَ مَعَهُ أَشِدَّاءُ عَلَى الْكُفَّارِ رُحَمَاءُ بَيْنَهُمْ...﴾

"Muḥammad is the Messenger of Allah, and those with him are stern with the disbelievers, yet merciful among themselves..."

mentioned in the well-known books of the Ahlul Sunnah, and as we will see in this section – he was an extremely abrasive individual towards other people, especially Muslims; and would sometimes even act this way with Prophet Muḥammad ﷺ himself.

It is natural that an honest researcher may ask oneself that with the sheer number of examples that have been mentioned in the books of history and *Ḥadīth*, can someone with such negative characteristics and destructive traits really be a successor of the final Messenger of Allah ﷺ and a caliph to guide humanity?

Can an individual with such a personality claim to be a role model and exemplar for other Muslims to follow?

Unfortunately, the attitude that was characterized by the second caliph had, and still has, an impact on some Muslims – particularly a group from amongst the unsympathetic "Wahhābis" who use callous and punitive methods against the general Muslim population, and even against those outside of Islam who do not follow their dogma. In addition, through engaging in blatant acts of terrorism and killing innocent men, women, and children, such individuals have given the religion of Islam a highly negative reputation around the world today.

Therefore, we feel that the scholars and thinkers from within the Ahlul Sunnah community must conduct a thorough and unbiased scrutiny of the unhospitable attitude of the second caliph and clearly label such behaviour as being antithetic to the pure Islam brought by Prophet Muḥammad ﷺ.

By doing so, they will be able to save the youth who are seeking the truth behind this ideological conflict that sets as rivals the attitude of the second caliph face-to-face with the magnificent demeanour of Prophet Muḥammad ﷺ.

Once the youth and others can sift through this quagmire of conflicting approaches, they will then be able to acquaint everyone with the beautiful Prophetic teachings and true Islamic conduct.

In addition, through this, a large part of the anger and rage that has been meted out to Muslims of various denominations *(madhāhib)* by those who themselves claim to be Muslims will be reduced, and all Muslims will be able to live in harmony with one another.

Even though ideological and jurisprudential differences may still exist, the Muslims will be able to develop into a powerful force in the world and stand together in the face of the oppressors and egotistical global powers.

Rather than expending their energies fighting against one another, the Muslims will be able to work alongside each other in areas of common interest. Through reciprocal love, and by exploiting their collective strengths, they will be able to – with one united voice – defend the faith of Islam and free their occupied countries.

The Character of the Second Caliph

The investigation into the character of the second caliph will be carried out in the following four stages, and will cover ʿUmar ibn al-Khaṭṭāb's:

1. Temperament and actions during the lifetime of Prophet Muḥammad ﷺ.
2. Role in the Event at Ṣaqīfah.
3. Interaction with other Muslims during his caliphate.
4. Relationship with his own family.

In this investigation, we have endeavoured to ensure that all references and resources quoted are taken directly from the most well-known books of the Ahlul Sunnah so that we are not looked upon as being prejudicial in our research.

During the Lifetime of Prophet Muḥammad ﷺ

The harsh character that the second caliph exemplified during the lifetime of the Messenger of Allah ﷺ has been clearly noted in the books of history. This can be seen in his crass method of interaction with others, and even his attitude in the presence of the Messenger of Allah ﷺ. In this regard, we present a few examples.

Assaulting his Female Muslim Servant

In his book on history, the well-known historian, Ibn Athīr, has written about individuals who were physically assaulted due to their acceptance of Islam, and he presents one of them as being a woman named Labībah, a slave from the tribe of Banī Muʾammil, who also happened to be a servant of ʿUmar ibn al-Khaṭṭāb.

Regarding Labībah, he writes: "She (Labībah) accepted Islam before ʿUmar ibn al-Khaṭṭāb came into Islam; and during that time [before he accepted Islam] he used to harass her and try to get her to leave the faith [of Islam], and finally [when he got tired of attempting to get her to revert back to her previous faith], he left her alone and said: 'I am now leaving you to be as you are [as a Muslim] because I am exhausted from constantly striking you.'"[3]

Ibn Hishām, the famous historian, also related the same event and further stated that: "ʿUmar used to hit her [Labībah] so much that he himself became drained of energy and would say [to her]: 'I seek your pardon [that I am not able to continue hitting you], and I am not dissuaded from this except that I am completely exhausted [due

[3] *Al-Kāmil fī al-Tārīkh*, Vol. 2, Pg. 69. The Arabic text of this is as follows:
أَسْلَمَتْ قَبْلَ إِسْلَامَ عُمْرَ بْنَ الْخَطَّابَ وَكَانَ يُعَذِّبُهَا حَتَّى تُفْتَنَ ثُمَّ يَدْعُهَا وَيَقُولُ: إِنِّي لَمْ أَدْعُكِ إِلَّا سَآمَةَ.

to hitting you so much].'"[4]

At this point, Ibn Hishām continued the discussion and mentioned: "One day, Abū Bakr saw what was happening [between ʿUmar and his slave-girl], so he [Abū Bakr] purchased her and freed her."[5]

Another well-known historian, Ibn Kathīr, also related a similar event in the section of his book on history in which he recounts other individuals whom Abū Bakr purchased and then freed.[6]

Physically Attacking his Own Sister

When the discussion concerning how ʿUmar ibn al-Khaṭṭāb accepted Islam is brought up in many of the biographical and historical accounts, a story is related that clearly shows his harsh nature: "When ʿUmar was informed about his sister, Fāṭima, and (her husband) his brother-in-law, Saʿīd ibn Zayd, accepting the religion of Islam, it is reported that he went to their house. They had some writings of the Quran which they were reciting from, and when they saw him [enter the house], they hid them at which point, he (ʿUmar) said to them: 'I heard that you have become a follower of the religion of Muḥammad?!' He then proceeded to physically attack his brother-in-law, Saʿīd, and in this scuffle, his sister Fāṭima tried to intervene

[4] The Arabic text of this is as follows:

إِنِّي أَعْتَذِرُ إِلَيْكِ. إِنِّي لَمْ أَتْرُكْكِ إِلَّا مَلَالَةً.

[5] *Al-Sīrah al-Nabawiyyah*, Vol. 1, Pg. 319.

[6] *Al-Bidāyah wa al-Nihāyah*, Vol. 3, Pg. 58. Before accepting Islam, ʿUmar was very harsh with those who had accepted Islam, and therefore when speaking about him in *Ansāb al-Ashrāf*, Vol. 10, Pg. 301, the famous scholar, Balādhurī states:

فَكَانَتْ فِيهِ غِلْظَةٌ عَلَى الْمُسْلِمِينَ.

"He [ʿUmar] was very harsh against the Muslims."

and protect her husband, however ʿUmar hit her so badly that she began to bleed due to her injuries.[7] It is stated that after this, he [ʿUmar ibn al-Khaṭṭāb] felt remorse over his actions and that upon seeing the verses of the Quran, he immediately accepted Islam."[8]

Attacking Abū Hurayrah and Directly Objecting to Prophet Muḥammad ﷺ

In a *ḥadīth* that Muslim has narrated in his *Ṣaḥīḥ*, it is mentioned from Abū Hurayrah that: "We were sitting around the Messenger of Allah. Abū Bakr and ʿUmar were also there among the audience. In the meanwhile, the Messenger of Allah got up and left us, and he delayed in coming back to us, which caused us anxiety that he might be attacked by some enemy when we were not with him; so being alarmed we got up.

I was the first to be alarmed. I therefore, went out to look for the Messenger of Allah and came to a garden belonging to the Banū al-Najjār, a section of the *Anṣār*, and went around it, looking for a gate, but failed to find one [to enter the area].

Seeing a *rabīʿ* (i.e. streamlet) flowing into the garden from a well outside, I drew myself together, like a fox, and slinked into (the place) where Allah's Messenger was.

He (the Noble Prophet) said: 'Is it Abū Hurayrah?'

I (Abū Hurayrah) replied: 'Yes, O Messenger of Allah.'

He (the Noble Prophet) said: 'What is the matter with you?'

I replied: 'You were amongst us but got up and went away and

---

[7] The Arabic text of this is as follows:

فَقَامَتْ فَاطِمَةُ لِتَكُفَّهُ عَنْهُ فَضَرَبَهَا فَشَجَّهَا.

[8] *Ansāb al-Ashrāf*, Vol. 1, Pp. 287-288; *Al-Bidāyah wa al-Nihāyah*, Vol. 3, Pg. 80; *Al-Kāmil fī al-Tārīkh*, Vol. 2, Pg. 85 & 414; *Al-Sīrah al-Nabawiyyah*, Vol. 1, Pg. 344; *Kanz al-ʿUmmāl*, Vol. 12, Pg. 607.

delayed for a time, so fearing that you might be attacked by some enemy when we were not with you, we became alarmed. I was the first to be alarmed. So, when I came to this garden, I drew myself together as a fox does, and these people are following me.'

He addressed me as Abū Hurayrah and gave me his sandals and said: 'Take away these sandals of mine, and when you meet anyone outside this garden who testifies that there is no god but Allah, being assured of it in his heart, gladden him by announcing that he shall go to Paradise.'

Now the first one I met was 'Umar. He asked: 'What are these sandals, Abū Hurayrah?'

I replied: 'These are the sandals of the Messenger of Allah with which he has sent me to gladden anyone I meet who testifies that there is no god but Allah, being assured of it in his heart, with the announcement that he would go to Paradise.'

Thereupon 'Umar struck me on the chest and I fell on my back. He then said: 'Go back, Abū Hurayrah,' so I returned to the Messenger of Allah, and was about to break into tears.

'Umar followed me closely and there he was behind me. The Messenger of Allah said: 'What is the matter with you, Abū Hurayrah?'

I said: 'I happened to meet 'Umar and conveyed to him the message with which you sent me. He struck me on my chest [with such force that it] made me fall upon my back and ordered me to go back [to you].'

Upon this the Messenger of Allah said: 'What prompted you to do this, 'Umar?'

He said: 'O Messenger of Allah, may my mother and father be sacrificed for you, did you send Abū Hurayrah with your sandals to gladden anyone he met, and whoever testified that there is no god except Allah, and being assured of it in his heart, with the tidings that he would go to Paradise?'

He said: 'Yes.'

ʿUmar said: 'Please do it not, for I am afraid that people will trust in it alone; let them go on doing (good) deeds.'

The Messenger of Allah said: 'Well, let them.'"[9]

---

[9] *Ṣaḥīḥ Muslim*, Vol. 1, Pp. 44-45, Section on "The One who meets Allah with Faith and has no Doubts." The Arabic text of this is as follows:

قَالَ حَدَّثَنِي أَبُو هُرَيْرَةَ قَالَ: كُنَّا قُعُودًا حَوْلَ رَسُولِ اللهِ صَلَّى اللهُ عَلَيْهِ وَسَلَّمَ مَعَنَا أَبُو بَكْرٍ وَعُمَرُ فِي نَفَرٍ فَقَامَ رَسُولُ اللهِ صَلَّى اللهُ عَلَيْهِ وَسَلَّمَ مِنْ بَيْنِ أَظْهُرِنَا فَأَبْطَأَ عَلَيْنَا وَخَشِينَا أَنْ يُقْتَطَعَ دُونَنَا وَفَزِعْنَا فَقُمْنَا فَكُنْتُ أَوَّلَ مَنْ فَزِعَ فَخَرَجْتُ أَبْتَغِي رَسُولَ اللهِ صَلَّى اللهُ عَلَيْهِ وَسَلَّمَ حَتَّى أَتَيْتُ حَائِطًا لِلْأَنْصَارِ لِبَنِي النَّجَّارِ فَدُرْتُ بِهِ هَلْ أَجِدُ لَهُ بَابًا فَلَمْ أَجِدْ فَإِذَا رَبِيعٌ يَدْخُلُ فِي جَوْفِ حَائِطٍ مِنْ بِئْرٍ خَارِجَةٍ وَالرَّبِيعُ الْجَدْوَلُ فَاحْتَفَزْتُ كَمَا يَحْتَفِزُ الثَّعْلَبُ فَدَخَلْتُ عَلَى رَسُولِ اللهِ صَلَّى اللهُ عَلَيْهِ وَسَلَّمَ فَقَالَ أَبُو هُرَيْرَةَ: فَقُلْتُ: نَعَمْ يَا رَسُولَ اللهِ. قَالَ: مَا شَأْنُكَ. قُلْتُ: كُنْتَ بَيْنَ أَظْهُرِنَا فَقُمْتَ فَأَبْطَأْتَ عَلَيْنَا فَخَشِينَا أَنْ تُقْتَطَعَ دُونَنَا فَفَزِعْنَا فَكُنْتُ أَوَّلَ مَنْ فَزِعَ فَأَتَيْتُ هٰذَا الْحَائِطَ فَاحْتَفَزْتُ كَمَا يَحْتَفِزُ الثَّعْلَبُ وَهٰؤُلَاءِ النَّاسُ وَرَائِي. فَقَالَ يَا أَبَا هُرَيْرَةَ وَأَعْطَانِي نَعْلَيْهِ قَالَ: اذْهَبْ بِنَعْلَيَّ هَاتَيْنِ فَمَنْ لَقِيتَ مِنْ وَرَاءِ هَذَا الْحَائِطِ يَشْهَدُ أَنْ لَا إِلٰهَ إِلَّا اللهُ مُسْتَيْقِنًا بِهَا قَلْبُهُ فَبَشِّرْهُ بِالْجَنَّةِ. فَكَانَ أَوَّلَ مَنْ لَقِيتُ عُمَرُ فَقَالَ: مَا هَاتَانِ النَّعْلَانِ يَا أَبَا هُرَيْرَةَ؟ فَقُلْتُ: هَاتَانِ نَعْلَا رَسُولِ اللهِ صَلَّى اللهُ عَلَيْهِ وَسَلَّمَ بَعَثَنِي بِهِمَا مَنْ لَقِيتُ يَشْهَدُ أَنْ لَا إِلٰهَ إِلَّا اللهُ مُسْتَيْقِنًا بِهَا قَلْبُهُ بَشَّرْتُهُ بِالْجَنَّةِ . فَضَرَبَ عُمَرُ بِيَدِهِ بَيْنَ ثَدْيَيَّ فَخَرَرْتُ لِاسْتِي فَقَالَ: ارْجِعْ يَا أَبَا هُرَيْرَةَ فَرَجَعْتُ إِلَى رَسُولِ اللهِ صَلَّى اللهُ عَلَيْهِ وَسَلَّمَ فَأَجْهَشْتُ بُكَاءً وَرَكِبَنِي عُمَرُ فَإِذَا هُوَ عَلَى أَثَرِي فَقَالَ لِي رَسُولُ اللهِ صَلَّى اللهُ عَلَيْهِ وَسَلَّمَ: مَا لَكَ يَا أَبَا هُرَيْرَةَ؟ قُلْتُ: لَقِيتُ عُمَرَ فَأَخْبَرْتُهُ بِالَّذِي بَعَثْتَنِي بِهِ فَضَرَبَ بَيْنَ ثَدْيَيَّ ضَرْبَةً خَرَرْتُ لِاسْتِي قَالَ ارْجِعْ. فَقَالَ لَهُ رَسُولُ اللّٰهِ صَلَّى اللهُ عَلَيْهِ وَسَلَّمَ: يَا عُمَرُ مَا حَمَلَكَ عَلَى مَا فَعَلْتَ؟ قَالَ: يَا رَسُولَ اللهِ بِأَبِي أَنْتَ وَأُمِّي أَبَعَثْتَ أَبَا هُرَيْرَةَ بِنَعْلَيْكَ مَنْ لَقِيَ يَشْهَدُ أَنْ لَا إِلٰهَ إِلَّا اللهُ مُسْتَيْقِنًا بِهَا قَلْبُهُ بَشَّرَهُ بِالْجَنَّةِ؟ قَالَ: نَعَمْ. قَالَ: فَلَا تَفْعَلْ فَإِنِّي أَخْشَى أَنْ يَتَّكِلَ النَّاسُ عَلَيْهَا فَخَلِّهِمْ يَعْمَلُونَ. قَالَ رَسُولُ اللهِ: صَلَّى اللهُ عَلَيْهِ وَسَلَّمَ فَخَلِّهِمْ.

In this *ḥadīth*, we see that to encourage people towards the belief in Monotheism *(Tawḥīd)*, the Messenger of Allah ﷺ gave them the glad tidings of Paradise.

Obviously, this announcement was meant to stimulate their interest in accepting the faith of Islam, which would then be coupled with certainty in the heart – and alongside this, acting according to the religious precepts would also be required [however, this would come gradually, in stages].

However, ʿUmar ibn al-Khaṭṭāb stood up and opposed the words of the Messenger of Allah ﷺ to such an extent that he even physically attacked Abū Hurayrah, then he directly criticized the Messenger of Allah ﷺ to his face for issuing such a declaration.

Direct Onslaught Against the Messenger of Allah ﷺ

When the well-known hypocrite *(munāfiq)* ʿAbdullāh ibn Ubayy died, his son came to Prophet Muḥammad ﷺ and asked if he, the Prophet ﷺ, would perform the funeral prayers over his father.

Keeping in mind that ʿAbdullāh ibn Ubayy was at least openly a Muslim who had pronounced the two testimonies to accept Islam *(Shahādatayn)*, and that the Messenger of Allah ﷺ had not yet been given any formal commandment (from Allah ﷻ) on how to deal with him and the likes of him (the hypocrites), Prophet Muḥammad ﷺ attended the funeral prayers of ʿAbdullāh ibn Ubayy.

In this regard, it is mentioned in a *ḥadīth* found in the authentic books of the Ahlul Sunnah; in some versions, it is related from ʿAbdullāh ibn ʿUmar [the son of ʿUmar ibn al-Khaṭṭāb]; while in another version, it is related directly from ʿUmar ibn al-Khaṭṭāb himself – that ʿUmar went to the Messenger of Allah ﷺ and launched a vicious attack against him (the Prophet ﷺ), and prevented the Prophet ﷺ from performing the funeral prayers over ʿAbdullāh ibn Ubayy.

According to a narration from Bukhārī, ʿAbdullāh ibn ʿUmar

states that: "Just when he [the Messenger of Allah ﷺ] wanted to perform the [funeral] prayers over him [ʿAbdullāh ibn Ubay], ʿUmar took a hold of him [the Messenger of Allah ﷺ and pulled him aside]."

The tradition goes on to mention that ʿUmar then told Prophet Muḥammad ﷺ: "Allah has prohibited you from performing the funeral prayers over the hypocrites!"

To this, the Messenger of Allah ﷺ replied: "Allah has left this decision up to me and He has said: 'Whether you ask forgiveness for them or do not ask forgiveness for them – even if you were to ask forgiveness for them seventy times, Allah will never forgive them.'"[10]

This verse means that the Prophet ﷺ praying over such an individual will have no impact or benefit for that person (and as such, it conveys the meaning in this historical event that the Prophet ﷺ attended the funeral of ʿAbdullāh ibn Ubayy for a specific reason, and we need to trust his actions).[11]

According to another *ḥadīth*, it has been mentioned that: "ʿUmar ibn al-Khaṭṭāb grabbed him [Prophet Muḥammad ﷺ] by his clothes and said to him: 'Are you going to pray over him while he is a known hypocrite?'"[12]

In yet another *ḥadīth* which has been related directly from ʿUmar, he has been quoted as saying: "I ran towards him [Prophet Muḥammad ﷺ] and said to him: 'Why are you performing the

---

[10] Quran, Sūrah al-Tawbah (9), Verse 80:

﴿إِسْتَغْفِرْ لَهُمْ أَوْ لاَ تَسْتَغْفِرْ لَهُمْ إِنْ تَسْتَغْفِرْلَهُمْ سَبْعِينَ مَرَّةٍ فَلَنْ يَغْفِرُ اللهُ لَهُمْ﴾

[11] *Ṣaḥīḥ al-Bukhārī*, Vol. 2, Pg. 76. This verse was later abrogated after the revelation of Verse 84, in which the Messenger of Allah ﷺ was ordered to never pray over the hypocrites.

[12] Ibid., Vol. 5, Pg. 207. The Arabic of this is as follows:

فَأَخَذَ عُمْرُ بْنُ أَلْخَطَّابِ بِثَوْبِهِ فَقَالَ: تُصَلِّي عَلَيْهِ وَهُوَ مُنَافِقُ.

funeral prayers over him?!' The Prophet smiled and said: 'Move aside.' However, I ['Umar] continued to persist [in asking him this question]."[13]

As 'Umar relates this incident, he then adds that he stated [to the Prophet ﷺ]: "I was amazed [with myself] that I had such courage to stand up to the Messenger of Allah in this way!"[14]

This event has also been mentioned in other well-known and reliable books by the Ahlul Sunnah.[15]

We know for a fact that the Messenger of Allah ﷺ would never perform any action without the explicit direction of Allah ﷻ, and thus, every action, word, or life characteristic he exemplified stemmed from revelation. As such, the Muslims had no right to question or criticize anything he did, and the Noble Quran was clear on this: "It is not for a believing man or a believing woman, whenever Allah and His Apostle have decided a matter, that they should (thereafter) have any choice about their affair. And [thus], whoever rebels against Allah and His Apostle has most obviously, gone astray."[16]

In addition, we read the following: "O you who believe! Do not raise your voices above the voice of the Prophet, and neither speak loudly to him, as you would speak loudly to one another, lest (all)

---

[13] *Ṣaḥīḥ al-Bukhārī*, Vol. 5, Pg. 206.

[14] Ibid., Pg. 207. The Arabic of this is as follows:

فَعَجِبْتُ مِنْ جُرْأَتِي عَلَىٰ رَسُولِ اللّٰهِ.

[15] *Ṣaḥīḥ Muslim*, Vol. 7, Pg. 116; Vol. 8, Pg. 120; *Sunan al-Tirmidhī*, Vol. 4, Pg. 343; *Musnad Aḥmad*, Vol. 2, Pg. 18; and other books.

[16] Quran, Sūrah al-Aḥzāb (33), Verse 36:

﴿وَمَا كَانَ لِمُؤْمِنٍ وَلَا مُؤْمِنَةٍ إِذَا قَضَى اللّٰهُ وَرَسُولُهُ أَمْرًا أَنْ يَكُونَ لَهُمُ الْخِيَرَةُ مِنْ أَمْرِهِمْ ۗ وَمَنْ يَعْصِ اللّٰهَ وَرَسُولَهُ فَقَدْ ضَلَّ ضَلَالًا مُبِينًا﴾

your [good] deeds become worthless without you perceiving it."[17]

In the above quoted incident, carefully note that the second caliph's defiance of the Messenger of Allah ﷺ continued to such a point that he ended up pulling at the clothes of the Prophet ﷺ and persisted in his demands to the final Messenger ﷺ to desist. Later, when he reminisced about the event, ʿUmar ibn al-Khaṭṭāb recalled what show of "bravery" and "courage" he displayed in opposing the greatest creation of Allah ﷻ – namely Prophet Muḥammad ﷺ.

Unduly Accusations Against the Prophet ﷺ

One of the bitter events that took place in early Islamic history is known as *The Tragedy of Thursday*[18] which transpired near the end of the life of Prophet Muḥammad ﷺ.

It was on a Thursday when the Prophet ﷺ was lying sick in his bed, a few days before he passed away. During this illness, with the companions gathered around him, he asked the people: "Bring me a pen and something to write upon so that I may write something for you after which you will never go astray after me."

In direct opposition to this wish of the Messenger of Allah ﷺ, ʿUmar ibn al-Khaṭṭāb replied: "The Prophet's sickness has taken over him [and he has no clue about what he is speaking about], and anyway, the Book of Allah is with us, and it is sufficient for us."[19]

---

[17] Quran, Sūrah al-Ḥujurāt (49), Verse 2:

﴿يَا أَيُّهَا الَّذِينَ آمَنُوا لَا تَرْفَعُوا أَصْوَاتَكُمْ فَوْقَ صَوْتِ النَّبِيِّ وَلَا تَجْهَرُوا لَهُ بِالْقَوْلِ كَجَهْرِ بَعْضِكُمْ لِبَعْضٍ أَنْ تَحْبَطَ أَعْمَالُكُمْ وَأَنْتُمْ لَا تَشْعُرُونَ﴾

[18] This event has been covered in detail in this book in Chapter One entitled: *The Event of the Pen and Paper.* (Tr.)

[19] The Arabic text of this is as follows:

إِنَّ النَّبِيَّ غَلَبَهُ الْوَجْعَ وَ عِنْدَنَا كِتَابُ اللهِ حَسْبُنَا.

The individuals there began to argue in the presence of the Messenger of Allah ﷺ – one group of individuals demanded that the Prophet ﷺ be permitted to write what he wished, while another group that was present repeated the statement that was made by ʿUmar ibn al-Khaṭṭāb. It was in such an environment that Prophet Muḥammad ﷺ eventually ordered everyone present to exit his house and leave him alone.

Do not assume that this is a fictitious event or something that has been narrated in the books of *Ḥadīth* only a limited number of times *(khabar al-wāḥid)*.[20] Rather, according to the various wordings that have been related regarding this event in the *Ṣiḥāḥ* and *Masānīd*[21] of the Ahlul Sunnah, this event has been narrated consecutively.

One author, al-Bukhārī, himself narrates this event in six unusual places within his collection of *aḥādīth* (sometimes he narrates it lucidity with the name of ʿUmar ibn al-Khaṭṭāb mentioned; while at other times, he uses the plural pronoun while describing this event without taking names).

Muslim, in his book of *Ḥadīth*, *Ṣaḥīḥ*, has also narrated this incident three times.[22]

---

[20] *Khabar al-Wāḥid:* According to the Science of *Ḥadīth*, this is a *ḥadīth*, a saying of Prophet Muḥammad ﷺ, or according to the school of the Ahlul Bayt ؑ, a verbal statement from Prophet Muḥammad ﷺ, Lady Fāṭima al-Zahrā' ؑ, or one of the 12 immaculate Imams ؑ – which is **not** regarded as *mutawātir* (a *ḥadīth* reported numerously by different narrators and through various chains of transmission in a way that substantiates its authenticity).

[21] Plural of *Musnad:* refers to a collection of *Ḥadīth* – such as *Musnad Aḥmad*, etc.

[22] *Ṣaḥīḥ al-Bukhārī*, Book of Knowledge, Section 39 (Section on the Writing of Knowledge), Tradition 4; Book of Al-Jihād and Al-Sayr, Section 175, Tradition 1; Book of al-Jizya, Section 6, Tradition 3; Book of al-Maghāzī,

How can anyone bear to read such "reliable" and "acknowledged" statements? Even more than that, what reasonable explanation can be given for such an utterance of ʿUmar ibn al-Khaṭṭāb? We leave it up to the judgement of the reader with an awakened consciousness to determine.

For further elaboration on this event and the various references that speak about this historical account, one can refer to the section in this book on *The Event of the Pen and Paper.*

The Event at Ṣaqīfah[23]

In the history of Islam, the Event at Ṣaqīfah is a lengthy narrative and one that raises many questions such that, if we to discuss it in complete depth, it would require an entirely separate book. However, what is clear in this historical incident is that the anger of the second caliph was evident during that event and what transpired after it.

The books of history mention that at the death of Prophet Muḥammad ﷺ, a group of the *Anṣār* gathered in the *ṣaqīfah* (tent) of the clan of Banī Sāʿida, and began to discuss amongst one another regarding the caliphate, and the news of this gathering reached ʿUmar ibn al-Khaṭṭāb.

ʿUmar ibn al-Khaṭṭāb took Abū Bakr and Abū ʿUbaydah al-Jarrāḥ along with him and arrived at the Ṣaqīfah of Banī Sāʿida. Once there, Abū Bakr proceeded to deliver a sermon, and thereafter a heated discussion ensured between Ḥubāb ibn Mundhīr and ʿUmar ibn al-

---

Section 84 (Section on the Sickness of the Prophet and his Death), Traditions 4 and 5; *Book of al-Marḍā,* Section 18 (Section of his [Prophet Muḥammad] Statement to 'Get up and leave.'), Tradition 1; *Ṣaḥīḥ Muslim, Book of al-Waṣīyyah,* Section 6, Traditions 6, 7, and 8.

[23] This event has been discussed in detail in Chapter Two entitled: *The Legitimacy of the Event at Ṣaqīfah.*

Khaṭṭāb in which they ended up threatening one another with violence.

In the end, due to a long-standing enmity between the tribes of Aws and Khazraj – both of whom were present at Ṣaqīfah – to ensure that the caliphate did not reach to Saʿd ibn ʿUbādah and his tribe of the Khazraj, those from the tribe of Aws rushed to hurriedly pledge allegiance to Abū Bakr as their caliph.

In narrating this event, when the well-known Sunnī historian Ṭabarī gets to the part where the people who were present at Ṣaqīfah rushed to pledge their allegiance to Abū Bakr, amongst them being Saʿd ibn ʿUbādah who ended up being trampled, he writes the following: "Someone yelled out: 'Be careful of Saʿd that you do not trample him!' At this point, ʿUmar stated: 'Kill him! May Allah kill him!'"[24]

At this point, ʿUmar ibn al-Khaṭṭāb stood above Saʿd, who was lying on the ground, and said to him: "I had planned to trample upon you to such an extent that the bones in your arm would have turned to dust!"[25]

According to the narration of Bukhārī, ʿUmar ibn al-Khaṭṭāb offered the following report about what happened on that day: "When Saʿd ibn ʿUbādah was being trampled upon, a group of people proclaimed: 'You have killed Saʿd ibn ʿUbādah!' I (ʿUmar) said: 'May

---

[24] The Arabic text of this is as follows:

أُقْتُلُوهُ قَتَلَهُ اللّٰهُ.

[25] *Tārīkh al-Rusul wa al-Mulūk*, Vol. 3, Pg. 223; A similar quotation has been mentioned in *Tārīkh ibn Khaldūn*, Vol. 2, Pg. 488. The Arabic text of this is as follows:

قَتَلَ اللّٰهُ سَعْدَ بْنَ عُبَادَةَ.

Allah kill Saʿd ibn ʿUbādah.'"[26]

With such a behaviour, we can see that ʿUmar ibn al-Khaṭṭāb instigated some people to act in this way towards Saʿd – a man who was a companion of Prophet Muḥammad ﷺ.

According to another narration of this event, ʿUmar ibn al-Khaṭṭāb has been quoted as saying: "May Allah kill him! Indeed, he is a hypocrite!"[27]

In continuation of this event, the pledging of allegiance, and cementing the caliphate of Abū Bakr, the sternness of ʿUmar ibn al-Khaṭṭāb was unmistakable and evident for all to witness.

According to the narration from the well-known historian of the Ahlul Sunnah, Ṭabarī, some of the *Anṣār* who were present stated: "'We will not pledge our allegiance to anyone except for ʿAlī [ibn Abī Ṭālib].' ʿUmar ibn al-Khaṭṭāb, who was informed that some of the companions had gathered at the house of ʿAlī, went towards his house. Some people, such as Ṭalḥa, Zubayr, and others from among the *Muhājirīn* were already present there (as they had refused to pledge the oath of allegiance to Abū Bakr); thus, when he reached there, ʿUmar said to them: 'I swear by Allah! I will burn all of you [alive], or I will force you all to come and pledge allegiance [to Abū Bakr].'"[28]

According to the narrative which has been mentioned by

---

[26] *Ṣaḥīḥ al-Bukhārī*, Vol. 8, Pp. 27-28; also see *Musnad Aḥmad*, Vol. 1, Pg. 56; *Tārīkh al-Ṭabarī*, Vol. 3, Pg. 206; *Al-Bidāyah wa al-Nihāyah*, Vol. 5, Pg. 246.

[27] *Tārīkh al-Rusul wa al-Mulūk*, Vol. 3, Pg. 223. The Arabic text of this is as follows:

قَتَلَهُ اللّٰهُ! إِنَّهُ مُنَافِقٌ.

[28] Ibid., Pg. 202. The Arabic text of this is as follows:

وَاللّٰهِ لَأُحْرِقَنَّ عَلَيْكُمْ أَوْ لَتَخْرُجَنَّ إِلىٰ الْبَيْعَةِ.

Balādhurī, ʿUmar ibn al-Khaṭṭāb went with a torch towards the house of ʿAlī ﷺ. He arrived and saw Fāṭima al-Zahrāʾ ﷺ standing near the door, at which point Fāṭima ﷺ said to him: "O son of al-Khaṭṭāb! Do you want to burn my door [of the house] down?"[29]

To this, ʿUmar immediately replied: "Yes! And this [what I want to do] is the same goal for which your father came [meaning that this was the same role that Prophet Muḥammad ﷺ came to do, according to ʿUmar – that is, to spread fear and fright in the people], and it is something extremely important [for me]."[30]

According to the narration of Ibn Abī Shaybah, ʿUmar said to Fāṭima al-Zahrāʾ ﷺ: "I swear by Allah that this issue (the love which we have for your father and for you) will never stop us from this [burning your house], and if those few people (ʿAlī, Zubayr, etc.) come close to you [to protect you], I will give the command to burn your house!"[31]

It is due to this insensitive and wrathful nature that according to a *ḥadīth* mentioned by Bukhārī, after the death of Lady Fāṭima ﷺ, when Imām ʿAlī ﷺ sent for Abū Bakr to talk to him, he said to Abū Bakr that he should come alone and not bring anyone with him because Imām ʿAlī ﷺ did not like to be in the presence of ʿUmar ibn al-Khaṭṭāb: "So then he (Imam ʿAlī) sent someone to Abū Bakr and asked him to come to see them (Imām ʿAlī and the others), and (Abū

---

29 The Arabic text of this is as follows:

يَابْنَ الْخَطَّابِ! أَتَرَاكَ مُحَرِّقًا عَلَيَّ بَابِي.

30 *Ansāb al-Ashrāf*, Vol. 1, Pg. 586. The Arabic text of this is as follows:

نَعَمْ وَذٰلِكَ أَقْوىٰ فِيمَا جَاءَ بِهِ أَبُوكِ.

31 *Al-Muṣannaf Ibn Abī Shaybah*, Vol. 8, Pg. 572. The Arabic text of this is as follows:

وايم الله ما من ذاك بمانعي إن اجتمع هولاء النفر عندك أن أمرتهم أن يحرق عليهم البيت.

Bakr) was told to ensure that no one else comes with him (Abū Bakr) as he (Imam ʿAlī) did not like to be in the presence of ʿUmar."[32]

In the narration mentioned by Ṭabarī and Ibn Kathīr, an even clearer statement has been mentioned in which Imam ʿAlī ﷺ said to Abū Bakr: "'Come on your own,' as he did not want ʿUmar to be with him as ʿAlī was well-aware of the harsh nature of ʿUmar."[33]

The crass and severe attitude displayed by ʿUmar ibn al-Khaṭṭāb during the Event at Ṣaqīfah has been covered in Chapter Two of this book.

We once again emphasize the fact that what we have stated above, and what is mentioned in other discussions in this book, have all been taken from the most well-known sources of the Ahlul Sunnah.

Harsh Attitude During His Caliphate

In introducing the second caliph, the well-known Sunnī scholar, Ibn Abī al-Ḥadīd al-Muʿtazilī, writes the following: "ʿUmar was extremely ill-tempered and unmerciful; he was continuously frowning and believed that [being like] this was a praiseworthy trait and [behaving in any way] other than this was a defect [in a person's character]."[34]

---

[32] *Ṣaḥīḥ al-Bukhārī*, Vol. 5, Pg. 83. The Arabic text of this is as follows:

فَأَرْسَلَ إِلىٰ أَبِي بَكْرٍ أَنْ أَئْتِنَا وَلاَ يَأْتِنَا أَحَدٌ مَعَكَ كَرَاهِيَّةً لِمَحْضَرِ عُمْرَ.

[33] *Tārīkh al-Rusul wa al-Mulūk*, Vol. 3, Pg. 208; *Al-Bidāyah wa al-Nihāyah*, Vol. 5, Pg. 286. The Arabic text of this is as follows:

وره أن يأتيه عمر لما علم من شدّة عمر.

[34] *Sharḥ Nahj al-Balāgha*, Vol. 6, Pg. 372. The Arabic text of this is as follows:

The harsh nature of ʿUmar was so well-known that even when he was appointed as the caliph by Abū Bakr on his death bed, the people began to complain about this appointment.

Ibn Abī Shaybah, a well-known Sunnī author who wrote the book, *Al-Muṣannaf*, writes: "When Abū Bakr was approaching his death, he ordered that ʿUmar be brought to him so he [Abū Bakr] may appoint him [ʿUmar] as his caliph. The people said to Abū Bakr: 'Are you going to appoint someone [to come after you, as your caliph] over us who is very stern and harsh? If he is put in charge over us, then he will be even sterner and harsher [than he currently is].'"[35]

In addition, according to the narration from Ibn Abī al-Ḥadīd, the well-known companion, Ṭalḥa, went to Abū Bakr and complained to him and said: "Tomorrow [on the Day of Reckoning], what answer will you give to your Lord having appointed someone who is stern and harsh over us [as the next caliph]!?"[36]

كان عمر شديد الغلظة وعر الجانب خشن الملمس دائم العبوس كان يعتقد أن ذلك هو الفضيلة وأن خلافه نقص.

[35] *Al-Muṣannaf Ibn Abī Shaybah*, Vol. 7, Pg. 485, Tradition 46. The Arabic text of this is as follows:

أَتَسْتَخْلِفُ عَلَيْنَا فَظًّا غَلِيظًا فَلَوْ مَلَكْنَا كَانَ أَفَظَّ وَأَغْلَظَ.

[36] *Sharḥ Nahj al-Balāgha*, Vol. 1, Pg. 164. The Arabic text of this is as follows:

مَا أَنْتَ قَائِلٌ لِرَبِّكَ غَدًا وَقَدْ وُلِّيتَ عَلَيْنَا فَظًّا غَلِيظًا.

It is interesting to note that the terms 'فظا' and 'غليظا' are the same two words which ʿUmar used to describe his own father! Historians narrate that when ʿUmar was returning to Madina from his final *Ḥajj* pilgrimage, when he reached the vicinity of Ḍhajnān (a mountain area which was about 40 km from Madina), he spoke about his father in the following manner: "There

In addition, in the Sermon of *Shiqshiqīyyah* (Sermon Three in *Nahj al-Balāgha*), the Commander of the Faithful, ʿAlī ﷺ also alluded to this point and stated: "This one [Abū Bakr] put it [the caliphate] in a tough enclosure [ʿUmar] where the utterance was haughty, and the touch was rough."[37]

It is for this reason that ʿUmar himself – according to the narration of Ibn Saʿd, a well-known scholar of the Ahlul Sunnah in his book, *Al-Ṭabaqāt* – states that after ʿUmar attained the post of caliphate, the first statement he made after ascending the pulpit *(mimbar)* was: "O Allah! Indeed, I am harsh, so make me soft; and I am weak, so give me strength; and I am miserly, so make me generous."[38]

However, when studying the life of ʿUmar ibn al-Khaṭṭāb during the period of his caliphate, we can conclude that he was never able to get rid of this negative quality – his harsh and stern character.

At this point, let us review some other instances from his life that have been mentioned in the well-known books of the Ahlul Sunnah

---

was a time when I brought a camel here for my father, al-Khaṭṭāb." At this point, ʿUmar began to describe his father for those present and said:

وَكَانَ فَظًّا غَلِيظًا يَتْعَبَنِي إِذَا عَمِلْتُ وَيَضْرِبُنِي إِذَا قَصَرْتُ.

"He [my father] was stern and harsh. Whenever I would do anything, he would apply so much pressure upon me, that I would be run down, and anytime I made a mistake, he would strike me." See *Al-Istīʿāb*, Vol. 3, Pg. 1157; *Tārīkh al-Rusul wa al-Mulūk*, Vol. 4, Pg. 219; *Ansāb al-Ashrāf*, Vol. 10, Pg. 299.

[37] The Arabic text of this is as follows:

فصيرها في حوزة خشناء يغلظ كلمها ويخشن مسّها.

[38] *Al-Ṭabaqāt al-Kubrā*, Vol. 8, Pg. 339. The Arabic text of this is as follows:

أَللّٰهُمَّ إِنِّي شَدِيدٌ (غَلِيظٌ) فَلَيِّنِي وَإِنِّي ضَعِيفٌ فَقَوِّنِي وَإِنِّي بَخِيلٌ فَسَخِّنِي.

about his abrasive nature.

Brutal Whippings

ʿUmar's physical attacks on people with the whip and his ferocious attitude with the masses are so well-known that according to a narration from Shurbaynī and Shirwānī, two major jurists *(fuqahāʾ)* of the Ahlul Sunnah, the physical lashes of ʿUmar were more frightful than the sword of Ḥajjāj ibn Yūsuf al-Thaqafī.[39] They report: "The lashes from the whip of ʿUmar were more frightful than the sword of Ḥajjāj."[40]

In addition, ʿUmar has been described as the first person who used to carry a whip around with him, which he would use on the people

---

[39] Ḥajjāj ibn Yūsuf al-Thaqafī (d. 95/714) was the ruler of Iraq and Ḥijāz in the Umayyad period and was hostile to the Shīʿa and played a significant role in the establishment of the Umayyad government. His loyalty to the Umayyad dynasty and his services to protect their government made him highly respected by the Umayyads. Upon his death, ʿAbdul Malik ibn Marwān recommended his son, Walīd ibn ʿAbdul Malik, to respect Ḥajjāj. Moreover, he named one of his sons Ḥajjāj.

He is known as a ruthless, brutal person who slaughtered his opponents so excessively that he was even reprimanded by ʿAbdul Malik ibn Marwān. Historians have estimated the number of people slaughtered by Ḥajjāj to be up to 130,000 people.

Historians note that he was fond of killing, as he is quoted as saying that he took pleasure in shedding blood and doing things that no one else has ever done.

Ḥajjāj continued the method of his Umayyad predecessors to curse Imam ʿAlī ibn Abī Ṭālib ﷺ and his progeny and killed people who did not curse them. (Tr.)

[40] *Mughnī al-Muḥtāj*, Vol. 4, Pg. 390; *Ḥawāshī* of al-Shirwānī, Vol. 10, Pg. 134. The Arabic of this is as follows:

كانت درّة عمر أهيب من سيف الحجاج.

at will.[41]

He was known to use his whip to strike both women and men; in fact, children, youth, elders, and even infants were not spared from his whip. Due to the incessant punitive nature of ʿUmar, and his assaulting other people, and the fear that he instilled in the masses, according to some of the narrations that have been stated in the books of history, sometimes even young children would run away when they saw him coming.[42]

Humiliating Children by Striking Them

One day, one of ʿUmar ibn al-Khaṭṭāb's own children came to him with neatly combed hair, wearing a beautiful outfit. ʿUmar began to strike him with his whip to such an extent that the child began to cry.[43] Ḥafṣa, the daughter of ʿUmar, who was witnessing this screamed out: "Why are you hitting him?!" In reply, ʿUmar said: "[For

---

[41] *Tārīkh al-Rusul wa al-Mulūk,* Vol. 4, Pg. 209; *Al-Bidāyah wa al-Nihāyah,* Vol. 7, Pg. 133.

[42] *Al-Ṭabaqāt al-Kubrā,* Vol. 7, Pg. 89. Keep in mind that Prophet Muḥammad ﷺ was known to be so merciful and compassionate to children; and as narrated in the books, sometimes he would be seen playing with young children (*Musnad Aḥmad,* Vol. 3, Pg. 121); he would greet children (*Sunan al-Dāramī,* Vol. 2, Pg. 276; *Sunan Ibn Mājah,* Vol. 2, Pg. 1220); and it is due to his mercy and compassion that when he would return from a journey, the children would all run towards the Prophet ﷺ to greet and welcome him back home (*Ṣaḥīḥ al-Bukhārī,* Vol. 5, Pg. 136). Sometimes, the Prophet ﷺ would allow the children to climb on top of him to play with him, and it has even been related that children would boast with one another if they were chosen to climb on the back of the Prophet ﷺ to play (*Musnad Aḥmad,* Vol. 4, Pg. 5).

[43] The Arabic text of this is as follows:

فَضَرَبَهُ عُمَرُ بِالدِّرَّةِ حَتّٰى أَبْكَاهُ.

no other reason except that] I saw that he was extremely jubilant and happy [due to having his hair combed nicely and the beautiful clothes he was wearing], so I wanted to humiliate him!”[44]

Striking Mourning Women

After the death of Abū Bakr, his family gathered to lament and cry over his demise. ʿUmar ibn al-Khaṭṭāb requested them to remain quiet in their program as they remembered him, but they did not pay any heed to his request. ʿUmar ordered that they be forcefully removed from the home, and when Umm Farwah, the sister of Abū Bakr, was dragged out of the house and brought into the court of the second caliph, ʿUmar began to physically assault her.[45]

According to a *ḥadīth* narrated in *Kanz al-ʿUmmāl*, as each woman began to leave the house, ʿUmar proceeded to strike them with his whip.[46]

---

[44] *Al-Muṣannaf* of ʿAbdul Razzāq, Vol. 10, Pg. 416, Tradition 19548. The Arabic text of this is as follows:

رَأَيْتُهُ قَدِ أَعْجَبَتْهُ نَفْسُهُ فَأَحْبَبْتُ أَنْ أَصْغَرُهَا إِلَيْهِ.

[45] *Tārīkh al-Rusul wa al-Mulūk, Vol.* 3, Pg. 423; *Ansāb al-Ashrāf,* Vol. 10, Pg. 95; *Al-Kāmil fī al-Tārīkh,* Vol. 2, Pg. 419. The Arabic text of this is as follows:

فعلاها بالدّرّة فضربها ضربات.

[46] *Kanz al-ʿUmmāl,* Vol. 15, Pg. 732, Tradition 42911. After relating this tradition from Ibn Rāhwiyyah, Muttaqī al-Hindī notes that he considers this tradition as being authentic *(ṣaḥīḥ).* In *Ṣaḥīḥ al-Bukhārī,* there is also an allusion to this event (see *Ṣaḥīḥ al-Bukhārī,* Vol. 3, Pg. 91). In addition, Ibn Ḥajr al-ʿAsqalānī in his commentary of *Ṣaḥīḥ al-Bukhārī* relates a tradition with a correct *(ṣaḥīḥ)* chain of narrators from *Ṭabaqāt al-Kubrā of Ibn Saʿd* in detail regarding this (See *Fatḥ al-Bārī fī Sharḥ Ṣaḥīḥ al-Bukhārī,* Vol. 5, Pg. 54).

After the death of Khālid ibn al-Walīd, a group of women gathered in the house of Maymūnah, one of the wives of the Messenger of Allah ﷺ, and began to weep and lament over his death. With his whip in hand, ʿUmar, along with Ibn ʿAbbās, went to the house, and ʿUmar said to Ibn ʿAbbās: "Enter the house and tell the Mother of the Believers (Maymūnah) to put on her covering *(ḥijāb)*, and then pull every single woman out of the house!"

It is reported that Ibn ʿAbbās entered the house and removed every woman, and as they came out, ʿUmar began to strike them with his whip.[47]

While he was hitting these women as they were leaving the house, the head covering of one of the women fell off, exposing her hair. Some of those who were present said to ʿUmar: "O Commander of the Faithful! Her head covering has come off!" He replied: "Leave it alone, she does not deserve to be respected!"[48]

After relating this incident, ʿAbdul Razzāq al-Ṣanaʿānī narrates a statement from his teacher, Muʿammar which states: "Muʿammar was surprised at his [ʿUmar's] statement that she (the lady whose head covering fell off) does not deserve to be respected!"[49]

According to a narration mentioned in *Musnad Aḥmad*, after the

---

[47] The Arabic text of this is as follows:

فجعل يخرجهن عليه وهو يضربهنّ بالدّرّة.

[48] The Arabic text of this is as follows:

فَقَالُوا: يَا أَمِيرَ الْمُؤْمِنِينَ! خِمَارَهَا! فَقَالَ: دَعُوهَا وَلَا حُرْمَتَ لَهَا.

[49] *Al-Muṣannaf* of ʿAbdul Razzāq, Vol. 3, Pg. 557, Tradition 6681. The same can be seen in Tradition 6682. The Arabic text of this is as follows:

كان معمر يعجب من قوله: لا حرمة لها.

death of Ruqayyah, a daughter[50] of the Messenger of Allah ﷺ, the women of Madina lamented over her death. ʿUmar was present at that gathering and struck them with his whip.[51] The Messenger of Allah ﷺ said to ʿUmar: "Leave them alone to cry!"[52]

Of course, when it came to showing grief over the departed ones, the Prophet ﷺ did prevent the women from doing anything which went against the religious standards of mourning and was not appropriate.[53]

---

50 There are varying reports in the books of history as to the number of daughters that Prophet Muḥammad ﷺ had. Some *ḥadīth* state that he had only one, Fāṭima al-Zahrāʾ ؑ, while others state that he had three more, Ruqayyah, Umm Kulthūm, and Zaynab. Other reports note that these there were the daughters of the sister of Khadījah binte Khuwaylid ؑ, and that Prophet Muḥammad ﷺ and his wife, Lady Khadījah ؑ used to take care of them after her sister passed away, so they are "thought of" as being his daughters. (Tr.)

51 The Arabic text of this is as follows:

فَجَعَلَ عُمَرُ يَضْرِبُهُنَّ بِسَوْطِهِ.

52 The Arabic text of this is as follows:

دَعْهُنَّ يَبْكِينَ.

53 *Musnad Aḥmad*, Vol. 1, Pg. 335; *Majmaʿ al-Zawāʾid*, Vol. 3, Pg. 17; *Al-Iṣābah*, Vol. 8, Pg. 138; *Al-Ṭabaqāt al-Kubrā*, Vol. 8, Pg. 30. Note that in other instances, the Messenger of Allah ﷺ also prevented ʿUmar from prohibiting women to cry [when someone passes away], however, ʿUmar continued to act in the same way. In *Musnad Aḥmad*, Vol. 2, Pg. 110, it is narrated that Abū Hurayrah came and said: "Someone from the family of the Prophet has died. The women gathered to cry and lament over the death, when suddenly ʿUmar ibn al-Khaṭṭāb decided that he wanted to stop them from this action. The Prophet ﷺ said to him: 'O son of Khaṭṭāb! Indeed, the eyes flow (with tears) and the spiritual heart laments, and the grief of the close ones is fresh [in their memory].'"

This event clearly shows that even during the lifetime of the Messenger of Allah ﷺ, ʿUmar acted in the same fashion, and if anything, every event that occurred which was not correct in his opinion would be met with violence, even without seeking permission from the Messenger of Allah ﷺ, as he would simply do whatever he pleased.

Out of Fear, a Woman...

In one of his books, ʿAbdul Razzāq al-Ṣanaʿānī mentions that once, ʿUmar ibn al-Khaṭṭāb passed by a group of women and smelled a pleasant fragrance emanating from one of the ladies, so he said: "If only I knew which of you women was using perfume, I would have done this and that to you [physically assaulted you]."[54]

ʿUmar continued and then said to this group of women: "Every woman must perfume herself for her husband [alone], however, when they leave their house, they must change their clothing and wear the old rags which their female servants would normally wear [so as to not attract the attention of men whom they are not related to]."

The individual who has narrated this event then states that ʿUmar said the following: "Information has reached me that the woman who had perfumed herself, due to fear [of me] has urinated in her clothing [due to the fear which I brought to that group of women]!"[55]

---

[54] The Arabic text of this is as follows:

لو أعلم أيتكن هي لفعلت ولفعلت.

[55] *Al-Muṣannaf* of ʿAbdul Razzāq, Vol. 4, Pg. 373, Tradition 8117. The Arabic text of this is as follows:

بَلَغَنِي أَنَّ الْمَرْأَةَ الَّتِي كَانَتْ تَطَيَّبَتْ بَالَتْ فِي ثِيَابِهَا مِنَ الْفَرَقِ.

A Woman Miscarries her Child

In the books of Islamic Jurisprudence related to the monetary compensation that must be offered in certain legal cases *(Kitāb al-Diyyāt)*, jurists of the Ahlul Sunnah have narrated that one day, ʿUmar ibn al-Khaṭṭāb went in search of a particular woman who was pregnant as he sought to investigate claims made against her of supposed infidelity. When the woman heard that ʿUmar was looking for her, she stated: "O woe is me! What does she (pointing to herself) have to do with ʿUmar [that he is looking for me]?"[56]

She proceeded to go to where ʿUmar was, however, while on the way to see him, due to the extreme fear and anxiety that she was feeling, she ended up having a miscarriage.[57]

When ʿUmar found out about this, he asked the companions of the Messenger of Allah ﷺ as to what the legal ruling for such an issue is, to which some of them replied saying: "There is nothing which you must do."

Imam ʿAlī ﵇ was present in the gathering, however, he remained silent and did not say a word. ʿUmar turned towards the Imam ﵇ and asked him: "What is your opinion?"

Imam ʿAlī ﵇ replied to him: "If their [the companion's] opinion is as they have stated [that you are not to blame and nothing is pending on you], then indeed they have all erred in their judgement; and if they stated this merely due to their attachment and family relations to you, then indeed they are not people who want the best for you. The ruling for this is that the financial compensation *(diyah)*

---

[56] The Arabic text of this is as follows:

يا وَلِيِّهَا مَالِهَا وَلِعَمْرَ.

[57] The Arabic text of this is as follows:

فَأَلْقَتْ وَلَدًا فَصَاحَ الصَّبِيِّ صَيْحَتَيْنِ ثُمَّ مَاتَ.

which is payable for an abortion is incumbent upon you to pay, because the woman was afraid of you, and she had a miscarriage and lost her child due to the fear she had of you."[58]

Afraid to Speak One's Mind

There are numerous instances in history which bear witness to that fact that there were some companions who, out of fear of the second caliph, ʿUmar ibn al-Khaṭṭāb, refused to impart their opinions or even speak their minds.

Sometimes when they would express their opinions, they encountered a harsh response from ʿUmar – and thus ended up taking a back seat in society. We relate the following incidents to better illustrate this reality of Islamic history.

1. Ibn Abī al-Ḥadīd al-Muʿtazilī has narrated that during the period of the caliphate of ʿUmar ibn al-Khaṭṭāb, ʿAbdullāh ibn ʿAbbās never had the courage to question the statements of ʿUmar – in this specific example, it was regarding the religious ruling on inheritance. However, after the death of ʿUmar, he finally spoke his mind, and it has been narrated that one day, it was said to ʿAbdullāh ibn ʿAbbās: "Why did you never mention this during the time of [the caliphate] of ʿUmar?"[59]

He replied: "I was afraid of him [to say anything which went

---

[58] *Al-Majmūʿ* of al-Nawawī, Vol. 19, Pg. 11; *Al-Mughnī* of Ibn Qudāmah, Vol. 9, Pg. 579; *Kashshāf al-Qanāʿah*, Vol. 6, Pg. 18; This event has also been related in the books of *Ḥadīth* of the Ahlul Sunnah such as the *Al-Muṣannaf* of ʿAbdul Razzāq, Vol. 9, Pg. 458 and *Kanz al-ʿUmmāl*, Vol. 15, Pg. 84, Tradition 40201. The Arabic text of this is as follows:

لِأَنَّكَ أَنْتَ أَفْزَعْتَهَا فَأَلْقَتْ.

[59] The Arabic text of this is as follows:

هلّا قلت هذا في أيّام عمر.

against his opinion]."[60]

2. After the death of ʿUmar ibn al-Khaṭṭāb, Abū Hurayrah stated: "I [now] relate traditions *(aḥādīth)*, which had I spoken these during the time [of the caliphate] of ʿUmar, or mentioned them while in the presence of ʿUmar, he would have split my head open."[61]

Abū Salama stated that he heard Abū Hurayrah say: "We did not have the ability to say: 'The Messenger of Allah said,' until after ʿUmar left this world."[62]

3. Muslim, in his *Ṣaḥīḥ* has narrated that one day, a man came to ʿUmar and said: "I have become ritually impure *(junub)*, and I was not able to find water [to purify myself, so what is my responsibility]?"

To this, ʿUmar replied: "Do not perform your obligatory prayers *(ṣalāt)!*"

---

[60] *Sharḥ Nahj al-Balāgha*, Vol. 6, Pg. 343. The Arabic text of this is as follows:

قال هبته.

[61] *Al-Bidāyah wa al-Nihāyah*, Vol. 8, Pg. 107. The Arabic text of this is as follows:

إِنِّي لَأُحَدِّثُ أَحَادِيثِ لَوْ تَكَلَّمْتُ بِهَا فِي زَمَنِ عُمَرَ أَوْ عِنْدَ عُمَرَ لَشَجَّ رَأْسِي.

[62] Ibid., Vol. 8, Pg. 107. The Arabic text of this is as follows:

مَا كُنْتُ نَسْتَطِيعُ أَنْ نَقُولَ: قَالَ رَسُولُ اللهِ حَتَّى قُبِضَ عُمَرُ.

In other traditions, it is mentioned that Abū Hurayrah used to say:

لَوْ كُنْتُ أُحَدِّثُ فِي زَمَانِ عُمَرُ مِثْلَ مَا أُحِدِّثُكُمْ لَضَرَبَنِي بِـمَخْفَقَتِهِ.

"If I were to relate *ḥadīth* to you during the time [of the caliphate] of ʿUmar as I relate such *ḥadīth* to you today, certainly he would have hit me with his whip." See *Tadhkira al-Ḥuffāẓ*, Vol. 1, Pg. 7. A similar narration can be found from Ibn ʿAbdul Birr in *Jāmiʿ al-Bayān al-ʿIlm wa Fadhluhu*, Vol. 2, Pg. 121.

The well-known companion, ʿAmmār ibn Yāsir who was present said: "O Commander of the Faithful [ʿUmar]! Do you not remember that day when you and I were participating in a battle (alongside the Messenger of Allah ﷺ) and we entered a state of ritually impurity *(janābah)*, and were not able to find any water to perform the ritual washing *(ghusl)* with? You did not perform your obligatory prayers *(ṣalāt)*, however, I performed the spiritual purification with dirt *[tayammum]* and performed my obligatory prayers *(ṣalāt)*, (and after that we both went to meet the Messenger of Allah ﷺ and spoke to him about what had happened) and the Messenger ﷺ replied to us: 'It is sufficient that (if you do not find any water) to strike your hands on the ground and then blow on them [to remove any excess dirt] and wipe your face and the back of your two hands with the dirt [to complete the act of the *tayammum*].'

At this point, ʿUmar, after hearing what ʿAmmār had said and what the Prophet ﷺ had clearly stated, it is as if ʿUmar wanted to continue with his own opinion about the rulings of Islam, so he said: "O ʿAmmār! Be afraid of Allah (and do not repeat such things)!"[63]

ʿAmmār replied: "If you wish, I can refrain from repeating such statements."[64]

---

[63] The Arabic text of this is as follows:

فَقَالَ عُمَرُ: إِتَّقِ اللّٰهَ يَا عَمَّارَ.

[64] *Ṣaḥīḥ Muslim*, Vol. 1, Pg. 193, Section on *Tayammum*. The Arabic text of this is as follows:

حَدَّثَنِي عَبْدُ اللّٰهِ بْنُ هَاشِمٍ الْعَبْدِيُّ، حَدَّثَنَا يَحْيىٰ، يَعْنِي ابْنَ سَعِيدٍ الْقَطَّانَ عَنْ شُعْبَةَ، قَالَ حَدَّثَنِي الْحَكَمُ، عَنْ ذَرٍّ، عَنْ سَعِيدِ بْنِ عَبْدِ الرَّحْمٰنِ بْنِ أَبْزىٰ، عَنْ أَبِيهِ، أَنَّ رَجُلًا، أَتىٰ عُمَرَ فَقَالَ إِنِّي أَجْنَبْتُ فَلَمْ أَجِدْ مَاءً. فَقَالَ لَا تُصَلِّ. فَقَالَ عَمَّارٌ أَمَا تَذْكُرُ يَا أَمِيرَ الْمُؤْمِنِينَ إِذْ أَنَا وَأَنْتَ فِي سَرِيَّةٍ فَأَجْنَبْنَا فَلَمْ نَجِدْ مَاءً فَأَمَّا أَنْتَ فَلَمْ تُصَلِّ وَأَمَّا أَنَا فَتَمَعَّكْتُ فِي التُّرَابِ وَصَلَّيْتُ. فَقَالَ النَّبِيُّ صَلَّى اللّٰه عَلَيْهِ وَسَلَّمَ

We know that in this event, the right is with ʿAmmār and the command of the Messenger of Allah ﷺ completes the argument of what is the correct ruling in such an issue; and in addition, the Quran also clearly mentions this ruling that when a person is in such a situation, then one must perform *tayammum*.[65]

إِنَّمَا كَانَ يَكْفِيكَ أَنْ تَضْرِبَ بِيَدَيْكَ الْأَرْضَ ثُمَّ تَنْفُخَ ثُمَّ تَمْسَحَ بِهِمَا وَجْهَكَ وَكَفَّيْكَ. فَقَالَ عُمَرُ اتَّقِ اللَّهَ يَا عَمَّارُ . قَالَ إِنْ شِئْتَ لَمْ أُحَدِّثْ بِهِ. قَالَ الْحَكَمُ وَحَدَّثَنِيهِ ابْنُ عَبْدِ الرَّحْمَنِ بْنِ أَبْزَى عَنْ أَبِيهِ مِثْلَ حَدِيثِ ذَرٍّ قَالَ وَحَدَّثَنِي سَلَمَةُ عَنْ ذَرٍّ فِي هَذَا الإِسْنَادِ الَّذِي ذَكَرَ الْحَكَمُ فَقَالَ عُمَرُ نُوَلِّيكَ مَا تَوَلَّيْتَ.

"It has been narrated to me from ʿAbdullāh ibn Hāshim al-ʿAbdī that it was related to us from Yaḥyā – meaning Ibn Saʿīd al-Qaṭṭān from Shuʿbah that he said it was related to me from al-Ḥakam from Dhurr from Saʿīd ibn ʿAbdul Raḥmān ibn Abzā narrated on the authority of his father that a man once came to ʿUmar and said: 'I am (at times) affected by seminal emission, but find no water [to purify myself]. He (ʿUmar) told him not to say his prayer.' ʿAmmār then said: 'Do you remember, O Commander of the Faithful, when I and you were in a military detachment and we had had a seminal emission and did not find water (for taking bath) and you did not say your prayers, but as for myself, I rolled in the dust and said my prayer, and (when it was mentioned before) the Apostle ﷺ, he said: 'It was enough for you to strike the ground with your hands, then blow (the dust) and then wipe your face and palms.'' Umar said: 'O ʿAmmār, fear Allah.' He (ʿAmmār) said: 'If you so like, I will not narrate it.'

A tradition like this has been transmitted with the same chain of transmitters except for the words: ʿUmar said: 'We hold you responsible for what you claim.'" From http://sunnah.com/muslim/3.

65 Sūrah al-Nisāʾ (4), Verse 43, the Quran clearly states (in the second portion of this verse):

These few examples from history clearly show that some of the companions were truly frightened of ʿUmar and restored to pious dissimulation *(taqiyyah),*[66] or they would outright just not mention

---

﴿وَإِنْ كُنْتُمْ مَرْضَىٰ أَوْ عَلَىٰ سَفَرٍ أَوْ جَاءَ أَحَدٌ مِنْكُمْ مِنَ الْغَائِطِ أَوْ لَامَسْتُمُ النِّسَاءَ فَلَمْ تَجِدُوا
مَاءً فَتَيَمَّمُوا صَعِيدًا طَيِّبًا فَامْسَحُوا بِوُجُوهِكُمْ وَأَيْدِيكُمْ ۗ إِنَّ اللَّهَ كَانَ عَفُوًّا غَفُورًا﴾

"But if you are ill, or are travelling, or have just satisfied a want of nature, or have cohabited with a woman, and can find no water - then take resort to pure dust, passing [it therewith lightly] over your face and your hands. Indeed, Allah is the Absolver of Sins (Ever-Pardoning), All-Forgiving."

After reading the event that transpired, a question should come into the minds of the readers. If the second caliph was so resolute on his own beliefs and considered them to be above the rulings of Allah ﷻ and His Prophet ﷺ, and believed that if a person was in a state of ritual impurity *(janābah)* and was not able to find water to purify himself, they must not perform the obligatory prayers *(ṣalāt)*, then during the many years of his life in which he would travel, whether it be to the house of Allah ﷻ in Mecca for the pilgrimage, or along with his soldiers on military campaigns, or to visit the cities that were under his governance during his caliphate, and if he was ever in need of water to perform a *ghusl,* but was not able to find it, then in these instances, did the caliph of the entire Muslim community simply refuse to perform his obligatory prayers *(ṣalāt)* to Allah ﷻ? Truly only Allah ﷻ knows what this man did in such circumstances!

[66] *Taqiyyah* is a term that refers to concealing or disguising one's beliefs, convictions, ideas, feelings, opinions, or strategies when there is a threat of persecution or compulsion. It allows Muslims to profess outwardly a different religious belief than their own in situations where revealing their faith could put them in danger.

The concept of *taqiyyah* is derived from verses in the Quran that instruct believers to conceal their faith when faced with potential harm or compulsion. It is seen to protect oneself or avoid greater evil in difficult circumstances. (Tr.)

any Islamic rulings, or since they knew his harsh and crass nature, they simply took a back seat in discussing Islamic Jurisprudence and its rulings when in the presence of ʿUmar ibn al-Khaṭṭāb.

Imprisoning Companions

History has shown that ʿUmar ibn al-Khaṭṭāb prevented people from narrating *aḥādīth* of the Messenger of Allah ﷺ, and was very harsh in dealing with companions who tried to do so – to the point of even imprisoning some of them!

Al-Dhahabī narrates that ʿUmar imprisoned three prominent companions – Ibn Maṣʿūd, Abul Dardā', and Abū Maṣʿūd al-Anṣārī due to their frequently relating *aḥādīth* of the Messenger of Allah ﷺ.[67]

Ḥākim al-Naysābūrī has also narrated that the second caliph had forbidden three individuals, Ibn Maṣʿūd, Abul Dardā', and Abū Dharr al-Ghifārī from leaving Madina due to their frequently relating *aḥādīth,* and that this prohibition of them leaving the city remained until the death of ʿUmar.[68]

The Authority of Allah ﷻ on Earth

According to the narration of Balādhurī and Ṭabarī, someone had brought some wealth to ʿUmar ibn al-Khaṭṭāb so that he could distribute it amongst the people. Thus, ʿUmar gathered the people together – however, the well-known companion, Saʿd ibn Abīl Waqqāṣ pushed all the people present in the gathering aside and made his way to sit beside ʿUmar. When he reached near ʿUmar, he (ʿUmar) began to hit him with his whip and said to him: "Do you dare approach me in such a way!? It is as if you have no fear of Allah's

---

[67] *Tadhkira al-Ḥuffāẓ*, Vol. 1, Pg. 7.

[68] *Mustadrak ʿalā al-Ṣaḥiḥḥayn*, Vol. 1, Pg. 101.

authority on the Earth!?"[69]

Taking Pleasure in Always Looking Stern

According to a narration from Ibn ʿAbd Rabbah al-Andalūsī, a man by the name of Rabīʿ ibn Ziyād al-Ḥārithī said: "During the time of ʿUmar, I was the representative of Abū Mūsā al-Ashʿarī (the Governor of Baṣrah) in the region of Bahrain. ʿUmar wrote a letter to Abū Mūsā and wanted him to come to Madina along with all his representatives and workers. When we all arrived in Madina, before I went to meet ʿUmar, I proceeded to go and meet Yarfaʾ who was a servant of ʿUmar, and asked him what traits does ʿUmar like to see in his workers?"

Yarfaʾ replied to me: "He loves to see sternness."

"Therefore, when I proceeded to meet ʿUmar, I did so with a stern, harsh look on my face, and indeed, he was pleased to see me like this, and asked Abū Mūsā to ensure that he reappoint me as the representative for that region."[70]

Waited for One Year...

Both Bukhārī and Muslim narrate the following incident in their respective books of *Ḥadīth* from Ibn ʿAbbās that he said: "I waited for one year to be able to ask ʿUmar a question regarding the history of revelation of one verse of the Quran. However, I could not ask him due to the awe and fear which I had of him[71] until the

---

[69] *Ansāb al-Ashrāf*, Vol. 10, Pg. 339; *Tārīkh al-Rusul wa al-Mulūk*, Vol. 4, Pg. 212. The Arabic text of this is as follows:

إنك أقبلت لاتهاب سلطان الله في الأرض.

[70] *Al-ʿUqd al-Farīd*, Vol. 1, Pp. 14-15 (summary presented here).

[71] The Arabic text of this is as follows:

فَمَا أَسْتَطِيعُ أَنْ أَسْأَلَهُ هَيْبَةً لَهُ.

opportunity came that I was able to travel on the *Ḥajj* with him. While returning from the trip, in the middle of the journey, a point came when he had to go and relieve himself, so he went behind some trees. I waited for him to finish and when he returned, we continued our journey. (At this time) I found the ideal opportunity to pose my question and said to him: 'O Commander of the Faithful! Who are those two wives of the Messenger of Allah who conspired with one another against him [which the Quran speaks about in Sūrah al-Taḥrīm]?'[72]

To my question, ʿUmar replied: 'Those two women are Ḥafṣa [his own daughter] and ʿĀyesha [the daughter of Abū Bakr].'"

To this, Ibn ʿAbbās replied: "I swear by Allah! It has been one year that I wanted to ask you this question about this verse of the Quran, however, since I feared you, I could not ask you about it!"[73]

An Attack against Abū Maṭar

An individual named Khaythama ibn Musajjaʿ, whose epithet is Abū Maṭar, went to the second caliph, and almost immediately, ʿUmar

---

[72] This verse, from Sūrah al-Taḥrīm (66), Verse 4 reads:

﴿إِنْ تَتُوبَا إِلَى اللهِ فَقَدْ صَغَتْ قُلُوبُكُمَا ۖ وَإِنْ تَظَاهَرَا عَلَيْهِ فَإِنَّ اللهَ هُوَ مَوْلَاهُ وَجِبْرِيلُ وَصَالِحُ الْمُؤْمِنِينَ ۖ وَالْمَلَائِكَةُ بَعْدَ ذَٰلِكَ ظَهِيرٌ﴾

"If both of you (women – ʿĀyesha and Ḥafṣa) turn to Allah repentant, (then He will accept your repentance) for your hearts are already inclined. But if you support (each other) against him (the Prophet ﷺ), (then bear in mind that) Allah is his Protector (and Helper), as is Jibrāʾīl, and the righteous among the believers, and furthermore all the angels are also his helpers."

[73] *Ṣaḥīḥ al-Bukhārī*, Vol. 6, Pg. 69; *Ṣaḥīḥ Muslim*, Vol. 4, Pg. 190. The Arabic text of this is as follows:

وَاللهِ! إِنْ كُنْتُ لَأُرِيدُ أَنْ أَسْأَلَكَ عَنْ هٰذَا مُنْذُ مِنَّةٍ فَمَا أَسْتَطِيعُ هَيْبَةً لَكَ.

began to hit him with his whip – however, Abū Maṭar was able to escape.[74] When Abū Maṭar was later asked as to why he ran away, he replied: "How can I not flee from someone who is hitting me while I have not hit him!?"[75]

Although he himself narrated this event, Balādhurī does not go into the details about why ʿUmar began to attack Abū Maṭar.

It leaves one to wonder why this event occurred, and why it had to be narrated in the books of history.

Attack with the Whip - Even at Prayer Time

Balādhurī in *Ansāb al-Ashrāf,* as well as Ibn Saʿd in his book, *Al-Ṭabaqāt,* as well as other historians have narrated that ʿUmarū ibn Maymūn once asked the second caliph to explain the method of establishing the Congregational Prayers *(Ṣalāt al-Jamāʿat),* and the narration states: "The way of ʿUmar [in leading the Congregational Prayers] was that he would not pronounce the opening *takbīr (takbīratul iḥrām)* [to initiate the *ṣalāt*], until he looked at the people praying in the first row. If he saw any of the people in the first row had either moved forward too much or had lagged a bit, he would strike them with his whip [so that they would make their proper way into the rows of the worshippers]."[76]

---

[74] The Arabic text of this is as follows:

فَحَمَلَ عَلَيْهِ بِالدُّرَّةِ فَهَرَبَ مِنْ بَيْنِ يَدَيهِ.

[75] *Ansāb al-Ashrāf, Vol.* 13, Pg. 51. The Arabic text of this is as follows:

وَكَيْفَ لَا أَهْرُبَ مِنْ بَيْنَ يَدَيْ مَنْ يَضْرِبُنِي وَلَا أَضْرِبُهُ.

[76] *Ansāb al-Ashrāf,* Vol. 10, Pg. 418; *Al-Ṭabaqāt al-Kubrā,* Vol. 3, Pg. 259; *Fatḥ al-Bārī fī Sharḥ Ṣaḥīḥ al-Bukhārī,* Vol. 7, Pg. 49; *Kanz al-ʿUmmāl,* Vol. 12, Pg. 679. The Arabic text of this is as follows:

Forced Marriages

ʿĀtikah binte Zayd was the wife of ʿAbdullāh ibn Abū Bakr. Her husband, ʿAbdullāh, left a large sum of wealth with her so that after his death, she would not have to remarry – a condition that she accepted.

After the death of ʿAbdullāh, history narrates that many men came and asked for her hand in marriage, but she remained committed to the promise that she had made to her late husband, and she turned down all marriage requests.

The second caliph, ʿUmar ibn al-Khaṭṭāb, said to the guardian of ʿĀtikah: "Take my marriage proposal to her."

However, ʿĀtikah also rejected the caliph's marriage proposal. When this answer came, ʿUmar said to the guardian of ʿĀtikah: "Marry me (ʿUmar) to her (ʿĀtikah),"[77] and the man did as he was ordered to by ʿUmar [imposing marriage on her without her consent].

The narration continues and states: "ʿUmar then went to her house (and as ʿĀtikah had no desire to be with him, she naturally rejected all of his sexual advancements), ʿUmar got into a fight with her and overpowered her and ended up forcefully having sexual intercourse with her."[78]

After concluding his sexual relations with ʿĀtikah, the second

---

وَ كَانَ عُمَرُ لَا يُكَبِّرَ حَتَّى يَسْتَقْبِلُ الصَّفُّ الْمُتَقَدِّمِ بِوَجْهِهِ فَإِنْ رَأَى رَجُلًا مُتَقَدِّمًا مِنَ الصَّفِّ أَوْ مُتَأَخِّرًا ضَرَبَهُ بِالدِّرَّةِ.

[77] The Arabic text of this is as follows:

زَوِّجْنِيهَا.

[78] The Arabic text of this is as follows:

فأتاها عمر فدخل عليها فعاركها حتّى غلبها على نفسها فتكحها.

caliph began to say: "Woe be upon me! Woe be upon me! Woe be upon me!"[79]

After saying this, he (ʿUmar) displayed his indignation with ʿĀtikah and left her, and did not come back to her, until the day when her servant sent a message to ʿUmar from ʿĀtikah asking him (ʿUmar) for him to come back to her as the servant had gotten her ready (for ʿUmar to have intimate relations with her).[80]

Splitting Open the Head of ʿUthmān ibn Ḥunayf

Dhahabī, in his well-known book, narrates that one day, ʿUmar ibn al-Khaṭṭāb and ʿUthmān ibn Ḥunayf were speaking to one another in the *masjid,* and their conversation eventually grew into an argument. People began to gather around the two of them when suddenly ʿUmar became enraged and grabbed a handful of rocks from the floor of the *masjid* and hit ʿUthmān in the face with them, splitting ʿUthmān's forehead open![81]

When ʿUmar saw that blood was beginning to pour from the forehead of ʿUthmān and cover his beard, he ordered ʿUthmān saying: "Clean up the blood which has spilt!"[82]

ʿUthmān replied to him: "Do not worry! I swear by Allah that I have never seen such a show of disrespect by anyone towards me as

---

[79] The Arabic text of this is as follows:

أُفٍّ، أُفٍّ، أُفٍّ.

[80] *Al-Ṭabaqāt al-Kubrā*, Vol. 8, Pg. 308; *Kanz al-ʿUmmāl*, Vol. 13, Pg. 633, Tradition 37,604.

[81] The Arabic text of this is as follows:

فقبض من حصباء المسجد قبضة ضرب بها وجه عثمان فشجّ الحصى بجبهته آثارًا من شجاج.

[82] The Arabic text of this is as follows:

فَلَمَّا رَأَى عُمَرُ كَثْرَةَ تسرّب الدُّمُ عَلَىٰ لِحْيَتِهِ قَالَ: أَمْسَحَ عَنِ الدَّمِ.

you have done to me, not even by those in that region which you sent me to [administer over]."[83]

Get Away from Me, Ibn ʿAbbās!

Ṭabarī and Ibn Athīr both relate in their respective books of history that Ibn ʿAbbās has narrated that one day, ʿUmar asked him: "Do you know why, after [Prophet] Muḥammad, the caliphate was taken away from your community (meaning the Banū Hāshim)?"

Ibn ʿAbbās said: "I did not want to respond to him, so therefore I said to him: 'If I do not know the reason for this, O Commander of the Faithful (meaning ʿUmar), then please inform why.'"

To this ʿUmar stated: "It is because the people did not want Prophethood and caliphate to be combined in one family because if that were to happen, then you [your family and lineage] would be able to boast over the people. Therefore, the Quraysh determined who the caliph would be, and that too, they were successful in achieving this.'"

Ibn ʿAbbās said: "If you permit me to speak and agree that you will not get upset at me, then I would like to share with you what I feel is the reason for this."[84]

Ibn ʿAbbās said that ʿUmar gave him the permission, so he began to speak and said: "That what you have said that the Quraysh chose the caliph and that too they were successful in achieving this – if the

---

[83] *History of Islam*, Vol. 4, Pp. 80-81. ʿUthmān ibn Ḥunayf had been sent by ʿUmar ibn al-Khaṭṭāb to review the situation in the regions of ʿIrāq which were under Muslim control, and to measure the size of the lands which were there to determine the amount of *Jizya* and *Kharāj* (land taxes) which had to be levied. (Refer to *Al-Istīʿāb fī Maʿrifah al-Aṣḥāb*, Vol. 3, Pg. 1033, discussion on the circumstances of ʿUthmān ibn Ḥunayf).

[84] The Arabic text of this is as follows:

إن تأذّن لي في الكلام وتمط عنّي الْغضب تكلّمت.

Quraysh had chosen that person whom Allah had already chosen [meaning Imam ʿAlī],[85] then you are right in saying that you were successful in achieving [what you set out to achieve]; however, if you mean that the Quraysh did not want to see caliphate and Prophethood combined in the same family, then you must know that in the Quran, Allah Himself, speaks about people who do not like to follow the commandments of Allah, and has reprimanded them, when He says: 'That is because they hated what Allah revealed, so He rendered their deeds null.'"[86]

Upon hearing this, the second caliph got extremely upset and said to him: "I swear by Allah that your hearts, that is, the Banū Hāshim, and filled with nothing other than jealousy, plots, and intrigues which will never go away!"[87]

Upon hearing this, Ibn ʿAbbās replied: "Take it easy, Commander of the Faithful [ʿUmar]! Do not describe the hearts of those individuals whom Allah has protected from all forms of spiritual contaminants and whom He has purified with a thorough

---

[85] This statement from Ibn ʿAbbās is yet another proof of the truthfulness of the Event at Ghadīr Khumm and the Divine appointment of Imam ʿAlī to the post of leadership after the Prophet , especially given the fact that ʿUmar himself did **not** deny this.

[86] Quran, Sūrah Muḥammad (47), Verse 9:

﴿ذَٰلِكَ بِأَنَّهُمْ كَرِهُوا مَا أَنزَلَ اللَّهُ فَأَحْبَطَ أَعْمَالَهُمْ﴾

[87] The Arabic text of this is as follows:

أبت والله قلوبكم يا بني هاشم إلّا حسدا ما يحول وضعنا وغشّا ما يزول.

purification,[88] with jealousy and intrigues."[89]

At this point, ʿUmar became extremely angry, and in response to such a logical reply from Ibn ʿAbbās, said: "Get away from me, O Ibn ʿAbbās!"[90]

Ibn ʿAbbās states that: "I got up to leave that gathering when ʿUmar stopped me and said: 'Stay,' then he continued to speak to me with jovial words."[91]

It is important to note that it was the caliph himself who started this discussion, and only after seeking permission and ensuring that ʿUmar would not get upset, did Ibn ʿAbbās speak and reply to him.

However, the caliph was still not pleased with the logical response that Ibn ʿAbbās gave him, and so he proceeded to level baseless accusations against him.

You Speak to the Caliph!

Eventually, the Muslims were frustrated and fed up with the harsh character of the second caliph which, according to the narrations of

---

[88] This is a reference to Verse 33 from Sūrah al-Aḥzāb (33) in which Allah says:

﴿إِنَّمَا يُرِيدُ اللَّهُ لِيُذْهِبَ عَنكُمُ الرِّجْسَ أَهْلَ الْبَيْتِ وَيُطَهِّرَكُمْ تَطْهِيرًا﴾

"Allah only desires to keep away the uncleanness from you, O people of the House, and to purify you with a (thorough) purification."

[89] The Arabic text of this is as follows:

مَهْلًا يَا أَمِيرَ الْمُؤْمِنِينَ! لَا تَصِفْ قُلُوبَ قَوْمٍ أَذْهَبَ اللهُ عَنْهُمُ الرِّجْسَ وَطَهَّرَهُمْ تَطْهِيرًا بِالْحَسَدِ وَالْغِشِّ.

[90] The Arabic text of this is as follows:

إِلَيْكَ عَنِّي يَا ابْنَ عَبَّاسٍ.

[91] *Tārīkh al-Rusul wa al-Mulūk,* Vol. 4, Pp. 223-224; *Al-Kāmil fī al-Tārīkh,* Vol. 3, Pp. 63-64 (summarized).

Ṭabarī and Balādhurī, reached such a level that one day, a group of Muslims went to ʿAbdul Raḥmān ibn ʿAwf and said to him: "Please have a word with ʿUmar (and convey our message to him) that he scares us to such an extent that we do not even dare raise our eyes to look at him."[92]

It is interesting to note that when Abū Bakr was dying, he asked ʿAbdul Raḥmān ibn ʿAwf about ʿUmar, and on that day, he (ʿAbdul Raḥmān) said: "In him (ʿUmar) is sternness."[93]

To this, Abū Bakr replied: "The reason [he deals with others which such harshness] is because he found me to be soft and lenient, however, if it [the caliphate] reaches him, then you will find that he will leave much of that [harshness] which he has."[94]

However, the above quoted incidents and the numerous examples that have already been mentioned clearly show that the anticipation of Abū Bakr [regarding the attitude of the second caliph] was not correct, and that the second caliph continued to act the same way after he took over the caliphate just as he acted prior to this.

As well, many of the above examples show that the harsh nature of ʿUmar ibn al-Khaṭṭāb existed from way before and was there even during the time of the final Messenger of Allah ﷺ, and his

---

[92] *Tārīkh al-Rusul wa al-Mulūk,* Vol. 4, Pg. 207; *Ansāb al-Ashrāf,* Vol. 1, Pg. 374. The Arabic text of this is as follows:

كلّم عمر فإنه قد أخشانا حَتَّى مَا نَسْتَطِيعُ أَنْ نَدِيمَ إِلَيْهِ أَبْصَارَنَا.

[93] The Arabic text of this is as follows:

فِيهِ غِلْظَةٌ.

[94] *Tārīkh al-Rusul wa al-Mulūk,* Vol. 3, Pg. 428; *Al-Kāmil fī al-Tārīkh,* Vol. 2, Pg. 425; *Al-Muntaḍhim,* Vol. 4, Pg. 125. The Arabic text of this is as follows:

لِأَنَّهُ يَرَانِي رَقِيقًا وَلَوْ أَفْضَى إِلَيْهِ لترك كَثِيرًا مِمَّا هُوَ عَلَيْهِ.

demeanour had nothing to do with Abū Bakr being too soft or lenient.

Do Not be the Reason for the Persecution

We bring this section to a close by quoting a portion of the words of Ibn Ubay ibn Kaʿb, as narrated in *Ṣaḥīḥ Muslim.*

It has been noted in a *ḥadīth* that Abū Mūsā said he came to ʿUmar and asked permission three times (with various titles of himself) saying: "Abū Mūsā asks permission, al-Ashʿarī asks permission, and ʿAbdullāh ibn Qays asked permission, but it was not granted to him."

Thus, he went away and shortly thereafter, ʿUmar sent for him saying: "Why did you leave?"

He replied: "The Messenger of Allah said: 'When one of you asks permission [to enter to see someone] three times and it is not granted to them; then they should go away.'"

He (ʿUmar) said: "Establish the proof of this [that this saying is from Prophet Muḥammad ﷺ]."

Abū Mūsā went away and came back and said: "This is Ubayy [and he will corroborate my statement of the Prophet ﷺ]."

Ubayy said: "ʿUmar, do not be an agony for the companions of the Messenger of Allah."

ʿUmar said: "I shall not be an agony for the companions of the Messenger of Allah."[95]

---

[95] *Ṣaḥīḥ Muslim*, Vol. 6, Pg. 180; Original Arabic and Translation from http://sunnah.com/abudawud/43/409. The Arabic text of this is as follows: عَنْ أَبِي مُوسَى أَنَّهُ أَتَى عُمَرَ فَاسْتَأْذَنَ ثَلَاثًا فَقَالَ يَسْتَأْذِنُ أَبُو مُوسَى يَسْتَأْذِنُ الأَشْعَرِيُّ يَسْتَأْذِنُ عَبْدُ اللَّهِ بْنُ قَيْسٍ فَلَمْ يُؤْذَنْ لَهُ فَرَجَعَ فَبَعَثَ إِلَيْهِ عُمَرُ مَا رَدَّكَ. قَالَ: قَالَ رَسُولُ اللّٰهِ صَلَّى اللّٰهُ عَلَيْهِ وَسَلَّمَ: يَسْتَأْذِنُ أَحَدُكُمْ ثَلَاثًا فَإِنْ أُذِنَ لَهُ وَإِلَّا فَلْيَرْجِعْ. قَالَ: ائْتِنِي بِبَيِّنَةٍ عَلَىٰ هٰذَا. فَذَهَبَ ثُمَّ رَجَعَ

Anger with his Family

From the point of view of the Islamic teachings, and through an analysis of the lifestyle of Prophet Muḥammad ﷺ, dealing with ones' family with compassion is one of the most noble and spiritual traits of a Muslim.

In this regard, the Messenger of Allah ﷺ has been quoted as saying: "Indeed, the best of all of you is the one who is the most excellent [in dealing] with one's family, and I am the best [among all of you] with regards to my family."[96]

In addition, the Noble Prophet ﷺ has also been quoted as saying: "Indeed, the best of you all are the ones who are the most excellent to their women."[97]

When speaking about the final Messenger ﷺ, it has been narrated from his wife, ʿĀyesha binte Abū Bakr, that she said: "The Messenger of Allah never struck any servant [of his], nor any of his women."[98]

With this being the case, why is it that we see instances in the life and interactions of the second caliph, ʿUmar ibn al-Khaṭṭāb, that involve such harshness with his wives, and events that are

---

فَقَالَ هٰذَا أُبَيٌّ. فَقَالَ أُبَيٌّ: يَا عُمَرُ لَا تَكُنْ عَذَابًا عَلَى أَصْحَابِ رَسُولِ اللّٰهِ صَلَّى اللّٰهُ عَلَيْهِ وَسَلَّمَ. فَقَالَ عُمَرُ: لَا أَكُونُ عَذَابًا عَلَى أَصْحَابِ رَسُولِ اللّٰهِ صَلَّى اللّٰهُ عَلَيْهِ وَسَلَّمَ.

[96] *Sunan Ibn Mājah*, Vol. 1, Pg. 636, Tradition 1977. The Arabic text of this is as follows:

خَيْرُكُمْ خَيْرُكُمْ لِأَهْلِهِ وَأَنَا خَيْرُكُمْ لِأَهْلِي.

[97] Ibid., Tradition 1978. The Arabic text of this is as follows:

خَيْرُكُمْ خَيْرُكُمْ لِنِسَآئِهِمْ.

[98] Ibid., Tradition 1984. The Arabic text of this is as follows:

مَا ضَرَبَ رَسُولُ اللّٰهِ خَادِمًا وَلَا إِمْرَأَةً.

extraordinary regarding his conduct with people from his own family?

Constant Harsh Nature

According to the narration of Balādhurī, Ṭabarī, Ibn Athīr, and Ibn Kathīr, when Yazīd ibn Abū Sufyān died, ʿUmar proposed to his widow, Umm Abān – the daughter of ʿUtbah. It is reported that she turned down the marriage proposal, and when asked why, she retorted: "He [ʿUmar] enters (the house) angry and leaves (the house) angry [meaning that he is always angry, and people fear him]; he closes the doors of the house [he does not allow his women to leave the house, and keeps them locked up all of the time], and there is very little goodness to be seen from him."[99]

An Outcry

Ṭabarī and Ibn Athīr have both narrated that during the time of his reign, ʿUmar proposed in marriage to Umm Kulthūm, the daughter of Abū Bakr, who was an extremely young girl at that time. ʿĀyesha delivered this marriage proposal from the caliph to her sister, Umm Kulthūm, to which she replied: "I have no need of him!"

Upon hearing this, ʿĀyesha replied: "You are not at all attracted to the caliph?"

To this, Umm Kulthūm replied: "Yes [I am in no way attracted to him] – as he is harsh in his day-to-day life, and he is very stern with his women."[100]

---

[99] *Ansāb al-Ashrāf,* Vol. 9, Pg. 368; *Tārīkh al-Rusul wa al-Mulūk,* Vol. 4, Pg. 400; *Al-Kāmil fī al-Tārīkh,* Vol. 3, Pg. 55; *Al-Bidāyah wa al-Nihāyah,* Vol. 7, Pg. 140. The Arabic text of this is as follows:

لِأَنَّهُ يَدْخُلُ عَابِسًا وَيَخْرُجُ عَابِسًا يغلق أبوابه ويقلّ خيره.

[100] The Arabic text of this is as follows:

ʿĀyesha binte Abū Bakr then asked ʿUmarū ʿĀṣ to somehow convey this message to the caliph, ʿUmar, so he (ʿUmarū) approached ʿUmar and after speaking to him for a short while, said to him: "Umm Kulthūm has been brought up under the sisterly affection, care, and love of her sister, the Mother of the Believers, ʿĀyesha; however, you are one who is very stern and harsh, and even we (the men) are afraid of you, and we are not able to get you to change your behaviour and attitude. Thus, if that lady were to go against you in something and you were to launch an attack against her, what would happen!?"[101]

Through this statement of his, he was able to get him (ʿUmar) to rethink his request to marry Umm Kulthūm.[102]

According to the narration from Ibn ʿAbdul Birr, Umm Kulthūm, the daughter of Abū Bakr said to her sister, ʿĀyesha: "Do you really want me to marry a person whom you know is very harsh and stern in his life!?" She then said: "I swear to Allah that if you force me to do this [marry ʿUmar], then I will go to the grave of the Messenger of Allah [to protest this marriage] and will let out a loud scream."[103]

The harshness and anger of the caliph, ʿUmar ibn al-Khaṭṭāb, within his family life was so well-known amongst everyone such

---

نَعَمْ إِنَّهُ خِشْنُ الْعَيْشِ شَدِيدٌ عَلَى النِّسَاءِ.

[101] The statement he mentioned is as follows:

وَفِيكَ غِلْظَةٌ وَنَحْنُ نهابك وَمَا نَقْدِرُ أَنْ نَرُدَّكَ عَنْ خُلُقٍ مِنْ أَخْلَاقِكَ فَكَيْفَ بِهَا إِنْ خَالَفَتْكَ فِي شَيْءٍ فسطوت بِهَا.

[102] *Tārīkh al-Rusul wa al-Mulūk*, Vol. 4, Pg. 199; *Al-Kāmil fī al-Tārīkh*, Vol. 3, Pg. 54.

[103] *Al-Istīʿāb fī Maʿrifah al-Aṣḥāb*, Vol. 2, Pg. 1807. The Arabic text of this is as follows:

وَاللهِ لَئِنْ فَعَلْتَ لَأَخْرُجَنَّ إِلَى قَبْرِ رَسُولِ اللهِ وَلَأُصِيحَنَّ بِهِ.

that even a young girl such as Umm Kulthūm, the daughter of Abū Bakr, knew about his attitude. Since ʿUmar was also the caliph of the Muslims [at the time of this event], and he enjoyed a close relationship with her father, Abū Bakr, he felt that he could have his way with women and marry whomever he wants, however, Umm Kulthūm still refused to marry him.

Physically Assaulting his Wife

In many reliable books of the Ahlul Sunnah, and keep in mind that all of our references in this book have been from the works of the scholars of the Ahlul Sunnah, there is a narration from Ashʿath ibn Qays in which he states: "One evening, I was a guest of ʿUmar [ibn al-Khaṭṭāb], and when half of the night had passed, ʿUmar got up and walked towards his wife and began to physically assault her."[104]

The narration continues, and Ashʿath states: "I got up and went to try and stop what was happening, however, when ʿUmar finally stopped [hitting her] and returned to where we had been sitting, he said to me: 'O Ashʿath! Remember this one thing from me which I heard the Messenger of Allah say: 'A man is never (to be) asked why he physically assaulted his wife.''"[105]

Thus, as one can see, he was indicating that he should never be asked about why he is doing such a thing!

---

[104] The Arabic text of this is as follows:

ضفت عُمَرُ لَيْلَةً فَلَمَّا كَانَ فِي جَوْفِ اللَّيْلِ قَامَ إِلَى إِمْرَأَتِهِ يَضْرِبُهَا فحجزت بَيْنَهُمَا.

[105] *Sunan Ibn Mājah*, Vol. 1, Pg. 639, Tradition 1986; *Sunan al-Kubrā*, Vol. 7, Pg. 357. A similar Tradition can be seen in the *Musnad Aḥmad*, Vol. 1, Pg. 20; *Sunan Abī Dāwūd*, Vol. 1, Pg. 476. The Arabic text of this is as follows:

يَا أَشْعَثُ! إِحْفِظْ عَنِي شَيْئًا سَمِعْتُهُ عَنْ رَسُولِ اللهِ: لَا يُسْأَلُ الرَّجُلُ فِيمَ يَضْرِبُ إِمْرَأَتَهُ.

Marriage on the Condition of No Abuse

ʿĀtikah binte Zayd was the daughter of the uncle of ʿUmar ibn al-Khaṭṭāb [his first cousin]. The historical narratives mention that she was an extremely beautiful woman, and initially she was married to ʿAbdullāh ibn Abū Bakr. After the death of ʿAbdullāh, in the twelfth year after the migration, ʿUmar married her, and after the marriage ceremony concluded, he arranged for a dinner celebration to mark this event.

In this regard, the historians have written: "When ʿUmar initially sent the wedding proposal to her [due to what she had known about the character of ʿUmar] she made a condition with him that he would never prevent her from going to the *Masjid*, and that he would never physically assault her. ʿUmar, very reluctantly, accepted these two conditions."[106]

In the narration which has been provided by Ibn Ḥajr al-ʿAsqalānī, this event has been worded in the following fashion: "She had made a condition with him [ʿUmar] that he would not physically strike her, nor would he prevent her from her rights, nor from performing the *ṣalāt* in the *Masjid* of the Prophet."[107]

It is very well possible that, according to the narration by Ibn Athīr, because of the harsh attitude of ʿUmar ibn al-Khaṭṭāb, whenever he proposed to various women from the families of the Quraysh in Madina, none of them accepted. However, whenever Mughīrah ibn Shuʿbah would send a proposal to any woman, his was

---

[106] The text of this event is mentioned in *Usd al-Ghābah fī Maʿrifah al-Ṣaḥābah*, Vol. 6, Pp. 183-185. The Arabic text of this is as follows:

فلمّا خطبها عمر شرطت عليه أنه لا يمنعها عن المسجد ولا يضربها فأجابها على كره منه.

[107] *Al-Iṣābah*, Vol. 8, Pg. 228. The Arabic text of this is as follows:

شرطت عليه ألاّ يضربها ولا يمنعها من الحق ولا من الصّلاة في المسجد النبويّ.

accepted.[108]

Anger and Snapping at Others

Ibn Abī al-Ḥadīd al-Muʿtazilī has narrated an event in which a person came to ʿUmar ibn al-Khaṭṭāb and complained about ʿUbaydullāh – the son of ʿUmar, and in his complaint, ʿUbaydullāh was referred to with the title of Abū ʿIsā.[109]

Upon hearing this grievance, ʿUmar summoned his son to come to him and began to reprimand him; eventually snapping his hand, then striking him, saying: "ʿIsā [Prophet ʿIsā, the son of Maryam] did not have a father (so why are you choosing the appellation of Abū ʿIsā for yourself!)?"[110]

After narrating this incident, Ibn Abī al-Ḥadīd states: "Zubayr said: 'Anytime ʿUmar became upset with any of his family members, his anger and range could never be controlled until he forcefully took

---

[108] The text of this event, as mentioned in *Usd al-Ghābah fī Maʿrifah al-Ṣaḥābah*, Vol. 3, Pg. 659, is as follows:

إنّ عمر بن الخطّاب خطب إلى قوم من قريش بالمدينة فردّوه وخطب إليهم المغيرة بن شعبة فزوجوه.

[109] The text of this tradition, related by Ibn Athīr as related in *Usd al-Ghābah fī Maʿrifah al-Ṣaḥābah*, Vol. 3, Pg. 423, reads the following: "Regarding the biography of ʿUbaydullāh ibn ʿUmar, he was referred to by the title of Abū ʿIsā which shows that he was well-known by this title during his lifetime."

...وأخذ يده فعضّها ثم ضربه وقال: ويلك. وهل لعيسى أب؟

[110] *Sharḥ Nahj al-Balāgha*, Vol. 6, Pg. 343. By having the title of Abū ʿIsā, this did not mean that the person believed that Prophet ʿIsā ﷺ had a father, and this is clear as the title for the author of the well-known book, *Sunan al-Tirmidhī* was also Abū ʿIsā al-Tirmidhī.

the hand of that individual and snapped it!'"[111]

Etiquette of the Noble Prophet ﷺ

As we close this chapter, we present a selection of traditions that deal with the Prophetic character and etiquette – as Prophet Muḥammad ﷺ is the most perfect example of humanity, and the role model for all Muslims to follow in their daily lives.

Through reviewing this description, the readers – especially the youth – will be able to learn and implement the noble ethical traits within their social and familial relationships, based on the conduct and character of the Prophet of Islam ﷺ. Once again, keep in mind that the traditions that we mention have all been taken from the books of Ahlul Sunnah.

1. ʿĀyesha has narrated the following regarding the character and etiquette of the Prophet ﷺ that: "He was the best of people in terms of his etiquette; he never cursed, never scrutinized, never raised his voice while in the markets, nor did he ever retaliate for evil done against him with evil – rather, he would forgive and exonerate others."[112]
2. Another *ḥadīth* describes the Messenger of Allah ﷺ in the following manner: "Indeed, the Messenger of Allah was merciful, gentle, and forbearing."[113]

---

[111] *Sharḥ Nahj al-Balāgha*, Vol. 6, Pg. 343.

[112] *Musnad Aḥmad*, Vol. 6, Pg. 236; *Sunan al-Tirmidhī*, Vol. 3, Pg. 249, Tradition 2085; *Ṣaḥīḥ Ibn Ḥibbān*, Vol. 14, Pg. 355. The Arabic text of this is as follows:

كَانَ أَحْسَنَ النَّاسِ خُلُقًا لَمْ يَكُنْ فَاحِشًا وَلَا مُتَفَحِّشًا لَا صَخَّابًا بِالْأَسْوَاقِ وَلَا يَجْزِي بِالسَّيِّئَةِ السَّيِّئَةَ وَلٰكِنْ يَعْفُو وَيَصْفَحُ.

[113] *Al-Muʿjam al-Kabīr*, Vol. 19, Pg. 288. The Arabic text of this is as follows:

3. When it comes to observing the rights of women, the Messenger of Allah ﷺ had advised that the men of the Muslim community must deal with them with compassion.[114]
4. Regarding the Prophet ﷺ, Anas ibn Mālik stated: "I have not seen anyone more compassionate to his family than the Messenger of Allah."[115]
5. In addition, when speaking about the morals of the final Prophet ﷺ, we see that the following beautiful expression has been narrated in his regards: "He was always cheerful, easygoing, approachable, and soft-spoken. He was never rude or harsh. He never laughed loudly, never uttered obscenities, never looked for faults in people, and never flattered anyone."[116]
6. When speaking about the Messenger of Allah ﷺ, ʿĀyesha used to say the following about how the Prophet ﷺ dealt with his wives: "Indeed, he was the most honourable of people, and the most forbearing of people; cheery and always smiling."[117]
7. Anas ibn Mālik has stated: "I was at the service of the Messenger of Allah for ten years, and I swear that in that time he never used

---

كَانَ رَسُولُ اللهِ رَحِيمًا رَقِيقًا حَلِيمًا.

[114] *Ṣaḥīḥ al-Bukhārī*, Vol. 6, Pg. 145 (Book of Marriage), Section on Mildness with Women.

[115] *Musnad Aḥmad*, Vol. 3, Pg. 112; *Ṣaḥīḥ Muslim*, Vol. 7, Pg. 76. The Arabic text of this is as follows:

مَا رَأَيْتُ أَرْحَمَ بِالْعِيَالِ مِنْ رَسُولِ اللهِ.

[116] *Kanz al-ʿUmmāl*, Vol. 7, Pg. 166. The Arabic text of this is as follows:

كَانَ دَائِمُ الْبِشْرِ سَهْلِ الْخَلْقِ لَيْتَ الْجَانِبِ لَيْسَ بِفَظٍّ وَلَا غَلِيظٍ وَلَا سَخَّابٍ وَلَا فَحَّاشٍ وَلَا عَيَّابُ.

[117] Ibid., Pg. 222. The Arabic text of this is as follows:

كَانَ أَكْرَمُ النَّاسِ وَأَلْيَنُ النَّاسِ ضَحَّاكًا بَسَّامًا.

abusive language against me, nor did he ever even say the smallest of bad words to me; and anytime I would perform an action, he never asked me why I did such and such a thing; and whenever I failed to perform a certain action, he never questioned me or asked me why I refrained from performing such and such an action."[118]

8. In regard to physically abusing one's wife, the Messenger of Allah ﷺ said the following: "Do you not have any shame that you physically abuse your wife, just as you hit your servants – you have the nerve to hit her at the beginning of the day, and then at the end of the day [at night] you lie in bed with her!?"[119]

In closing, if the character and morals of the Prophet ﷺ are like this – and much more than this – then we need to seriously think about the actions of those who did not have such morals yet claimed to be the successors *(khulafāʾ)* of the Prophet ﷺ.

---

[118] *Kanz al-ʿUmmāl*, Vol. 7, Pp. 207-208. The Arabic text of this is as follows:
خَدَمْتُ رَسُولَ اللّٰهِ عَشْرَ سِنِينَ لَا وَاللّٰهِ مَا سَبَّنِي بسبّة قَطُّ وَلَا قَالَ لِي: أُفٍّ قَطُّ وَلَا قَالَ لِشَيْءٍ فَعَلْتُهُ لِمَ فَعَلْتَهُ؟ وَلَا لِشَيْءٍ لَمْ أَفْعَلْهُ لِمَ لَا فَعَلْتَهُ؟

[119] *Al-Muṣannaf ʿAbdul Razzāq*, Vol. 9, Pg. 442, Tradition 17,943; *Kanz al-ʿUmmāl*, Vol. 16, Pg. 377; Tradition 44,983. The Arabic text of this is as follows:

أَمَّا يَسْتَحْيِي أَحَدُكُمْ أَنْ يَضْرِبَ امْرَأَتَهُ كَمَا يَضْرِبُ الْعَبْدَ، يَضْرِبُهَا أَوَّلَ النَّهَارِ ثُمَّ يُضَاجِعُهَا آخِرَهِ.

Bibliography

The Noble Quran.

ʿAbdul Barr, Abū ʿUmar Yūsuf ibn ʿAbdullāh ibn Muḥammad ibn, *Al-Istīʿāb fī Maʿrifah al-Aṣḥāb* (Beirut: Dār al-Jīl, 1st Edition, 1412 AH - Edited by ʿAlī Muḥammad al-Bajawī).

ʿAbdul Barr, Abū ʿUmar Yūsuf ibn ʿAbdullāh ibn Muḥammad ibn, *Jāmiʿ al-Bayān al-ʿIlm wa Fadhluhu* (Beirut: Dār al-Kutub al-ʿIlmīyyah, 1398 AH).

Andalūsī, Ibn ʿAbd Rabbah al-, *Al-ʿUqd al-Farīd* (Beirut: Dār al-Kutub al-ʿArabī, 1403 AH).

ʿAsqalānī, Aḥmad ibn ʿAlī ibn Ḥajr al-, *Al-Iṣābah fī Maʿrifah al-Ṣaḥābah* (Beirut, 1st Printing, 1415 AH).

ʿAsqalānī, Aḥmad ibn ʿAlī ibn Ḥajr al-, *Fatḥ al-Bārī fī Sharḥ Ṣaḥīḥ al-Bukhārī* (Beirut: Dār al-Maʿrifah, n.d.).

Balādhurī, Aḥmad ibn Yaḥyā ibn Jābir al-, *Ansāb al-Ashrāf* (Beirut: Dār al-Fikr, 1st Printing, 1417 AH - Researched by Suhail Zukkār).

Bhūtī, Manṣūr ibn Yūnus, *Kashshāf al-Qanāʿ al-* (Beirut - Dār al-Kutub al-ʿIlmīyyah, 1st Printing, 1418 AH - Researched by Abū ʿAbdillāh Muḥammad Ḥasan Ismāʿīl al-Shāfiʿī).

Bukhārī, Abū ʿAbdillāh Muḥammad ibn Ismāʿīl al-, *Ṣaḥīḥ al-Bukhārī* (Beirut: Dār al-Fikr, 1st Edition, 2005 CE - Researched by Ṣiddīqī Jamīl al-Aṭṭār).

Dārimī, ʿAbdullāh ibn ʿAbdul Raḥmān al-, *Sunan al-Dārimī.* (n.d.).

Dhahabī, Shams al-Dīn al-, *Tadhkirat al-Ḥuffāz* (Beirut: Dār Iḥyāʾ al-Turāth al-Arabī, n.d.).

Dhahabī, Shams al-Dīn al-, *Tārīkh al-Islām* (Beirut: Dār al-Kitāb al-ʿArabī, 2nd Printing, 1413 AH - Researched by ʿUmar ʿAbdul Salām).

Dhuhlī, Abū ʿAbdillāh Aḥmad ibn Muḥammad ibn Ḥanbal al-,

Musnad Aḥmad (Beirut: Dār al-Sadir).

Dimashqī, Abūl Fiḍā' 'Imād al-Dīn Ismā'īl ibn 'Umar ibn Kathīr al-Qurayshī al-, *Al-Bidāyah wa al-Nihāyah* (Beirut: Dār al-Fikr, 1st Edition, 1407 AH).

Haythamī, Nūr al-Dīn ʿAlī ibn Abī Bakr ibn Sulaymān Abūl Ḥasan al-, *Majmūʿ al-Zawā'id wa Manba' al-Fawā'id* (Beirut: Dār al-Kutub al-ʿIlmīyyah, 1408 AH).

Ḥibbān, Muḥammad ibn, *Ṣaḥīḥ Ibn Ḥibbān*, (Al-Risālah Foundation, 2nd Edition, 1414 AH - Edited by Shuʿayb al-Arnaout).

Hindī, ʿAla al-Din ʿAlī ibn ʿAbdul Malik Husām al-Dīn al-Muttaqī al-*Kanz al-ʿUmmāl* (Beirut: Mu'assasah al-Risālah, 1409 AH).

Ḥumayrī, Ibn Hishām al-, *Al-Sīrah al-Nabawiyyah,* better known as the *Sīrah of Ibn Hishām* (Beirut: Dār al-Maʿrifa, n.d. - Researched by Muṣṭafā al-Saqā and Others).

Jawzī, ʿAbdul Raḥmān ibn ʿAlī ibn Muḥammad ibn al-, *Al-Muntaḍhim fī Tārīkh al-Ummam al-Mulūk* (Beirut: Dār al-Kutub al-ʿIlmīyyah, 1st Printing, 1412 AH - Researched by Muḥammad ʿAbdul Qādir ʿAṭā).

Jazarī, ʿIzz al-Dīn ibn al-Athīr al-, *Usd al-Ghābah fī Maʿrifah al-Ṣaḥābah* (Beirut: Dār al-Fikr, 1409 AH).

Karam, ʿIzz al-Dīn ʿAlī ibn Abī al-Karam al-, better known as Ibn Athīr, *Al-Kāmil fī al-Tārīkh* (Beirut: Dār Ṣadir, 1384 AH).

Khaldūn, ʿAbdul Raḥmān ibn Muḥammad ibn al-, *Tārīkh Ibn Khaldūn* (Dār al-Fikr, 2nd Edition, 1408 AH - Researched by Khalīl Shahādah).

Muʿtazilī, Ibn Abī al-Ḥadīd al-, *Sharḥ Nahj al-Balāgha* (Beirut: Dār Iḥyā' al-Kutub al-Arabiyyah - Edited by Muḥammad Abul Fadl Ibrāhīm, n.d.).

Nahj al-Balāgha.

Nawawī, Muḥī al-Dīn ibn Sharaf al-, *Al-Majmūʿ fī Sharh al-Muhadhab* (Beirut: Dār al-Fikr, n.d.).

Naysābūrī, Abū ʿAbdillāh Ḥākim al-, *Al-Mustadrak ʿalā al-Ṣaḥīḥḥayn* (Beirut: Dār al-Maʿrifah, 1st Printing, 1406 AH).

Naysābūrī, Muslim ibn Ḥajjāj al-, *Ṣaḥīḥ Muslim* (Beirut: Dār al-Fikr, n.d.).

Qudāmah, ʿAbdullāh ibn al-, *Al-Mughnī* (Beirut: Dār al-Kutub al-ʿArabī, n.d.).

Saʿd, Muḥammad ibn al-, *Al-Ṭabaqāt al-Kubrā* (Beirut: Dār al-Kutub al-ʿIlmīyyah, 1st Printing, 1410 AH - Researched BY Muḥammad ʿAbdul Qādir ʿAṭā).

Ṣanaʿāī, ʿAbdul Razzāq al-, *Al-Muṣannaf* (Manshūrāt al-Majlis al-ʿIlmī, n.d. - Researched by Ḥabīb al-Raḥmān al-Aʿaẓamī).

Shaybah, Ibn Abī al-, *Al-Muṣannaf of Ibn Abī Shaybah* (Beirut: Dār al-Fikr, 1st Printing, 1409 AH - Researched by Saʿīd al-Liḥḥām).

Shirwānī wa al-ʿAbādī al-, *Ḥawashī al-Shirwānī* (Beirut: Dār Iḥyā al-Turāth al-ʿArabī, n.d.).

Shurbaynī, Muḥammad ibn Aḥmad al-, *Mughnī al-Muḥtāj* (Beirut: Dār al-Iḥyāʾ al-Turāth al-ʿArabī, 1388 AH).

Ṭabarānī, Abūl Qāsim Sulaymān ibn Aḥmad ibn Ayyūb ibn Muṭayyir al-Lakhmī al-Shāmī al-, *Al-Muʿjam al-Kabīr* (Beirut: Dār Iḥyāʾ al-Turāth al-Arabī, 2nd Edition, 1404 AH - Edited by Aḥmad ʿAbdul Majīd al-Salafī).

Ṭabarī, Muḥammad ibn Jarīr ibn al-, *Tārīkh al-Ṭabarī* (Beirut: Dār al-Turāth, 2nd Edition, 1387 AH - Edited by Muḥammad Abūl Fadl Ibrahim).

Tirmidhī, Abū ʿIsā al-, *Sunan Tirmidhī* (Beirut: Dār al-Fikr, 1st Printing, 1424 AH - Researched by ʿAbdul Raḥmān Muḥammad

ʿUthmān).

Chapter Five

The Marriage of Umm Kulthūm binte ʿAlī

Introduction

Another controversial issue in the history of Islam that needs to be analyzed in our series is the marriage of Umm Kulthūm ﷺ – the daughter of Imam ʿAlī ﷺ and Lady Fāṭima al-Zahrāʾ ﷺ – with the second caliph, ʿUmar ibn al-Khaṭṭāb.

The reason why this topic is labelled as 'controversial' is because of the unfortunate events that took place after the demise of the Messenger of Allah ﷺ where the Commander of the Faithful, Imam ʿAlī ﷺ, was pushed aside from his rightful position in the caliphate, and the house of Lady Fāṭima al-Zahrāʾ ﷺ was attacked – in addition to many other things that occurred.

Given all that transpired between ʿUmar ibn al-Khaṭṭāb and Imam ʿAlī ﷺ and Lady Fāṭima al-Zahrāʾ ﷺ, the marriage of ʿUmar ibn al-Khaṭṭāb to Umm Kulthūm ﷺ seems to be more of a myth than a reality.

Evidence shows that the second caliph played a fundamental and influential role in the unfortunate and regretful events – namely keeping Imam ʿAlī ﷺ away from the caliphate, attacking the house of Lady Fāṭima al-Zahrāʾ ﷺ, and physically assaulting her. Therefore, a question that has occupied the minds of some Muslims is: If the second caliph was involved in these assaults against Fāṭima al-Zahrāʾ ﷺ and taking away the right of Imam ʿAlī ﷺ that was given to him by Allah ﷻ, then how could a father marry off his daughter to such a person?!

There are some pertinent questions that one must ask:

1. Did the marriage take place at all?
2. If the marriage did take place, then on what basis was it done?
3. How far did it progress?

Some scholars from the Ahlul Sunnah consider the occurrence of such a marriage as sufficient reason for denying the unfortunate events of the attack on the house of Lady Zahrāʾ ﷺ. Simply put, they do not believe that such a confrontation ever occurred and consider the story of her martyrdom that some Muslims speak about as mere fiction.[1]

The authenticity of the raid on the house of Lady Zahrāʾ ﷺ and the threats directed at her and Imam ʿAlī ﷺ are well established as we have previously proven, and there is no room to entertain any doubt with respect to this event.

The threat to set the house of Fāṭima al-Zahrāʾ ﷺ on fire to force the pledge of allegiance is also mentioned in the authentic books of the Ahlul Sunnah, and some even conclude that this threat was indeed implemented.[2]

The scholars that follow the teachings of the Ahlul Bayt ﷺ have also discussed this in detail in their historical and *Ḥadīth* literature, and it is a well-known and accepted fact among the Shīʿa.[3]

Let us delve into our central question for this research piece: Did the daughter of Imam ʿAlī ﷺ and Lady Fāṭima ﷺ marry ʿUmar during his caliphate? If so, then how is this marriage compatible with his controversial, and sometimes violent history?

This question will be examined in several stages:

1. Who is Umm Kulthūm?
2. What are the statements of the Muslim scholars about this

---

[1] The followers of the Wahhābī ideology have been publishing books on this topic and handing them to Iranian pilgrims. Some of the Friday Prayer leaders in Iran who follow the Ahlul Sunnah sect of Islam have also raised this issue in their speeches and completely deny the issue of the martyrdom of Lady Fāṭima al-Zahrāʾ ﷺ – citing the marriage of Umm Kulthūm ﷺ to ʿUmar ibn al-Khaṭṭāb as sufficient proof.

[2] See the chapter in this book, *Fire in the House of Revelation*; and the book, *Attack on the House of Revelation,* written by Āyatullāh Jaʿfar Subḥānī. In this book by the esteemed Shīʿa scholar, he quotes countless references from Sunnī scholars to draw his conclusions.

[3] Majlisī, Muḥammad Bāqir al-, *Biḥār al-Anwār,* Vol. 43. See also *House of Sorrows,* written by Shaykh ʿAbbās al-Qummī, published by Islamic Publishing House (ISBN: 978-0-9809487-2-1).

marriage?
3. What are the historical reflections on this marriage?
4. What is the chain of transmitters *(isnād)* for these narrations in both the Ahlul Sunnah and Shīʿa books?
5. Were there any threats or other factors that necessitated this marriage to take place?

Who is Umm Kulthūm?

Ibn ʿAbdul Barr in *Al-Istīʿāb*, Ibn Athīr in *Usd al-Ghābah*, and Shaykh al-Mufīd in *Al-Irshād*, considered Umm Kulthūm ؑ – along with Ḥasan ؑ, Ḥusayn ؑ, and Zaynab ؑ - to be among the children of Fāṭima al-Zahrāʾ ؑ and Imam ʿAlī ؑ.[4] In addition, Ṭabarī and Ibn Shahrāshūb also consider Moḥsin as one of the children of the couple who was miscarried.[5]

The name of Umm Kulthūm ؑ appears in many sensitive time periods of the life of Imam ʿAlī ؑ until that of Imam Ḥusayn ؑ. Among them is the 19th night of the month of Ramaḍān in 40 AH, when Imam ʿAlī ؑ was struck with a poisonous sword as he prayed in Masjid al-Kūfa. That evening, he was the guest of his daughter, Umm Kulthūm, for *iftār*.[6] When she saw her father's impending

---

[4] *Al-Istīʿāb fī Maʿrifah al-Aṣḥāb,* Vol. 4, Pg. 1893, No. 4057 (description of Lady Fāṭima al-Zahrāʾ ؑ), Vol. 4, Pg. 1954, No. 4204 (Description of Umm Kulthūm). In *Al-Istīʿāb,* it is stated that Umm Kulthūm was born before the death of the Messenger of Allah ﷺ; *Usd al-Ghābah fī Maʿrifah al-Ṣaḥābah,* Vol. 6 Pg. 387, No. 7578; Shaykh Mufīd, *Al-Irshād,* Vol. 1, Pg. 354.

[5] *Tārīkh al-Rusul wa al-Mulūk,* Vol. 5, Pg. 153; Muḥammad ibn ʿAlī ibn Shahrashūb, *Manāqib Āl Abī Ṭālib,* Vol. 3, Pg. 89.

[6] *Biḥār al-Anwār,* Vol. 42, Pg. 226. The Arabic text of this is as follows:

سَهِرَ أَمِيرُ الْمُؤْمِنِينَ فِي اللَّيْلَةِ الَّتِي قُتِلَ فِي صَبِيحَتِهَا وَلَمْ يَخْرُجْ إِلَى الْمَسْجِدِ لِصَلَاةِ اللَّيْلِ عَلَى عَادَتِهِ فَقَالَتْ لَهُ ابْنَتُهُ أُمُّ كُلْثُومٍ رَحْمَةُ اللَّهِ عَلَيْهَا: مَا هٰذَا الَّذِي قَدْ أَسْهَرَك؟ فَقَالَ: إِنِّي مَقْتُولٌ لَوْ قَدْ

martyrdom, she became inconsolable and cried, thus Imam ʿAlī ؑ comforted her.[7]

She also accompanied her brother, Imam Ḥusayn ؑ, during his historic move towards Kūfa, which later concluded with the tragic massacre in Karbalāʾ, on the Day of ʿĀshūrāʾ in 61 AH. When Imam Ḥusayn ؑ came to the tent to bid farewell to the womenfolk, he mentioned Umm Kulthūm, along with Sukayna, Fāṭima, and Zaynab, where he said: "O Sukayna, O Fāṭima, O Zaynab, O Umm Kulthūm, peace be upon you all from me."[8]

Umm Kulthūm's ؑ name is also seen in the list of captives after the tragedy of Karbalāʾ, and historians note that she gave a powerful sermon, addressing the people of Kūfa after her sister, Zaynab al-Kubrā ؑ. In Syria, where Yazīd was "apparently" trying to make amends for his crimes, he addressed Umm Kulthūm ؑ: "Take this property from us in compensation for the problems and hardships [we put you through]." To this, she replied: "O Yazīd, how shameless and thick-headed you are! You kill my brother and my family, then give me this as compensation?!"[9]

When she entered Madina, she recited a eulogy for her brother,

---

أَصْبَحْتُ. فَأَتَاهُ ابْنُ النَّبَّاحِ فَآذَنَهُ بِالصَّلَاةِ فَمَشَى غَيْرَ بَعِيدٍ ثُمَّ رَجَعَ فَقَالَتْ لَهُ أُمُّ كُلْثُومٍ: مُرْ جَعْدَةَ فَلْيُصَلِّ بِالنَّاسِ. قَالَ: نَعَمْ مُرُوا جَعْدَةَ فَلْيُصَلِّ ثُمَّ قَالَ: لَا مَفَرَّ مِنَ الْأَجَلِ. فَخَرَجَ إِلَى الْمَسْجِدِ وَإِذَا هُوَ بِالرَّجُلِ قَدْ سَهِرَ لَيْلَتَهُ كُلَّهَا يَرْصُدُهُ فَلَمَّا بَرَدَ السَّحَرُ نَامَ فَحَرَّكَهُ أَمِيرُ الْمُؤْمِنِينَ بِرِجْلِهِ فَقَالَ لَهُ: الصَّلَاةَ فَقَامَ إِلَيْهِ فَضَرَبَهُ.

[7] *Biḥār al-Anwār*, Vol. 42, Pg. 223.

[8] Ibid., Vol. 45, Pg. 47. The Arabic text of this is as follows:

يَا سُكَيْنَةُ يَا فَاطِمَةُ يَا زَيْنَبُ يَا أُمَ كُلْثُومٍ عَلَيْكُنَّ مِنِّي السَّلَام.

[9] Ibid., Pg. 197. The Arabic text of this is as follows:

يَا يَزِيدُ مَا أَقَلَ حَيَاءَكَ وَأَصْلَبَ وَجْهَكَ تَقْتُلُ أَخِي وَأَهْلَ بَيْتِي وَتُعْطِينِي عِوَضَهُمْ.

Imam Ḥusayn ﷺ in a tearful and sorrowful manner.[10]

According to some historical reports, Umm Kulthūm ﷺ died during the reign of Muʿāwiyah when it was the governorate of Saʿīd ibn al-ʿĀṣ al-Umawī in Madina (before 53 AH).[11]

Both Ibn ʿAbdul Barr and Ibn Ḥajr al-ʿAsqalānī, two prominent Sunnī scholars, consider her death to be at the time of Imam Ḥasan ﷺ. However, if one accepts the presence of Umm Kulthūm ﷺ during the massacre of Karbalāʾ, then her death must have been after the year 61 AH.[12] Therefore, some have speculated that her death took place four months after the return of the captives from Syria.[13]

What Scholars Say about this Marriage

The subject of the marriage of Umm Kulthūm ﷺ with the second caliph has been discussed and investigated by historians from various angles. Some have denied it,[14] while others have accepted its

---

[10] *Biḥār al-Anwār,* Vol. 42, Pg. 197. In other instances, in the incident of Karbalāʾ and before that, the name of Lady Umm Kulthūm ﷺ is seen; but the above cases were a major part of the role and presence of her that have been mentioned.

[11] ʿAbdul Karīm, Sayyid Moḥsin ibn, *Aʿyān al-Shīʿa,* Vol. 3, Pg. 485.

[12] *Al-Istīʿāb fī Maʿrifah al-Aṣḥāb,* Vol. 4, Pg. 1956; *Usd al-Ghābah fī Maʿrifah al-Ṣaḥābah,* Vol. 6 Pg. 387.

[13] *Aʿlām al-Nisāʾ,* Pp. 238–247.

[14] The late Shaykh Bāqir Sharīf al-Qarashī believes that Lady Fāṭima ﷺ did not have a daughter named Umm Kulthūm, and that Zaynab ﷺ was nicknamed Umm Kulthūm, and her husband was ʿAbdullāh ibn Jaʿfar (*Life of Fāṭima al-Zahrāʾ*, Pg. 219). Shaykh Mufīd rejected this marriage of Umm Kulthūm in his book. Although, apart from Zaynab ﷺ, he mentions a girl named Umm Kulthūm ﷺ as Fāṭima's ﷺ daughter *(Al-Masāʾil al-Sariyyah,* Pg. 86). However, in another book, he accepted it *(Al-Masāʾil al-Akbariyyah,* Pp. 61). ʿAllāmah Sayyid Nāṣir Ḥusayn Mūsawī Hindī also rejects this marriage in his book, *Ifhām al-Adāʾ wa al-Khusūm.*

occurrence.

Yaʿqūbī and Ṭabarī considered the marriage to have taken place in the 17th year of Hijrah,[15] and some have even mentioned a child born from this marriage, with Zayd ibn ʿUmar ibn al-Khaṭṭāb[16] or Ruqayyah being the alleged name.[17]

Most Sunnī historians accept the latter opinion and mention it in their historical and *Ḥadīth* books, which will be discussed later. They also refer to it in their jurisprudential books under the discussions of how an *imam* should stand in front of the corpses of men and women during the Burial *(Janāzah)* Prayer.[18]

The famous Shīʿa scholar, Sayyid Murtaḍā, believes that the marriage took place after several threats, but it was not a marriage by consent.[19]

ʿAllāmah Muḥammad Taqī al-Shūstarī in his book, *Qāmūs al-Rijāl,* also accepts the marriage in principle.[20]

Abū Muḥammad al-Nawbakhtī was of the view that Umm Kulthūm ﷺ was far too young for this marriage to have ever taken place, although he believes that the engagement took place –

---

[15] *Tārīkh al-Rusul wa al-Mulūk,* Vol. 4, Pg. 69; *Tārīkh al-Yaʿqūbī,* Vol. 2, Pg. 149.

[16] Ṭūsī, Abū Jafʿar Muḥammad ibn al-, *Tahdhīb al-Aḥkām*, Vol. 9, Pg. 362, Tradition 15.

[17] *Al-Ṭabaqāt al-Kabīr,* Vol. 3, Pg. 14; *Al-Isābah fī Maʿrifah al-Ṣaḥābah,* Vol. 8, Pg. 456; *Al-Istīʿāb fī Maʿrifah al-Aṣḥāb,* Vol. 4, Pg. 1956.

[18] Nawawī, Yaḥya ibn Sharaf al-, *Al-Majmuʿ,* Vol. 5, Pg. 224; Muḥammad ibn Aḥmad al-Shirbānī al-Khātib, *Mughnī al-Muḥtāj,* Vol. 1, Pg. 348; Muḥammad ibn Aḥmad ibn Abī Sahl Abū Bakr al-Sarakhsī, *Al-Mabsūṭ,* Vol. 2, Pg. 65; ʿAbdullāh ibn Aḥmad ibn Muḥammad ibn Qudamah al-Maqdisī, *Al-Mughnī,* Vol. 2, Pg. 395.

[19] Al-Murtaḍā, ʿAlī ibn al-Ḥusayn al-Sharif al-, *Rasāʾil Murtaḍā,* Vol. 3, Pg. 149.

[20] Shushtarī, Muḥammad Taqī, *Qāmūs al-Rijāl,* Vol. 12, Pp. 215–216.

however, before the marriage could be consummated, 'Umar passed away.

Therefore, in total, there are four opinions about this marriage:
1. Fāṭima al-Zahrā' 🌺 did not have a daughter named Umm Kulthūm.
2. She had a daughter by that name, but she did not marry the second caliph.
3. She was engaged, but the marriage was never consummated.
4. The marriage took place, but it was under duress and coercion.

Reflections about this Marriage

Although some scholars have accepted the reality of this marriage in principle, there are others who point to certain contexts and circumstances that lead to interesting considerations.

Ethical Questions Surrounding Some Narrations

Regarding this marriage and its background, there are certain things mentioned in Sunnī books that are very shameful – far from the dignity of a Muslim. The following are a few examples of this:

1. Ibn 'Abdul Barr narrates in his *Al-Istī'āb fī Ma'rifah al-Aṣḥāb*: "'Umar said to 'Alī: 'Give Umm Kulthūm's hand in marriage to me because I want to achieve a nobility that no one has achieved with this union!' 'Alī replied: 'I will send her to you...' Imam 'Alī sent Umm Kulthūm with a cloth to 'Umar and said: 'Tell him on my behalf, this is the cloth I told you about.' When Umm Kulthūm conveyed the message to 'Umar, he said: 'Tell your father, I like it and I am satisfied, may Allah be pleased with you!' Then 'Umar put his hand on Umm Kulthūm's leg and uncovered it. Umm Kulthūm said: 'What are you doing? If you were not the caliph, I would have broken your nose!' Then she returned to her father and said: 'You

sent me to a terrible old man!'"[21]

Noteworthy is the fact that this report is narrated by a respected, well-known Sunnī scholar.

2. In another report documented by the Sunnī scholar, Ibn Ḥajr al-ʿAsqalānī, it is stated that: "Umm Kulthūm was upset and said to ʿUmar: 'If you were not the caliph, I would have struck your eye (in other words, I would have blinded you!)'"[22]

3. Khaṭīb al-Baghdādī documents an even more shameful report in his book: "Following ʿUmar's request, ʿAlī put his daughter's makeup on and sent her to ʿUmar. When ʿUmar saw her, he stood up, held her leg, and said: 'Tell your father that I like it.'" (He repeated this three times). When the girl returned to her father, she said: "ʿUmar called me to himself and when I stood up, he held my leg and said: 'Tell your father for me, I like it!'"[23]

These reports are unpleasant, to say the least. Would such an honourable father like Imam ʿAlī ﷺ send his daughter to a stranger in this way, and after the daughter reports the disturbing treatment, is unbothered by it? Do these scholars think that ʿUmar's "decency," and their self-acclaimed "righteousness of the companions" will not be tarnished by such an action?

Ḥāfiẓ Sibṭ ibn al-Jawzī [d. 654 AH] comments on this report and states: "This is ugly, by Allah, [even] if it was a slave, he should not have done this to her. According to the consensus of the Muslims, it is not permissible to touch a woman that one is not related to (by blood or marriage), so how is this action attributed to ʿUmar?!"[24]

Such reports are neither accepted by the Shīʿa or Sunnī scholars.

---

[21] *Al-Istīʿāb fī Maʿrifah al-Aṣḥāb,* Vol. 4, Pg. 1,955.

[22] *Al-Iṣābah fī Tamyīz al-Ṣahābah,* Vol. 8, Pg. 465.

[23] Shāfiʿī, Aḥmad ibn ʿAlī ibn Thābit al-, Khaṭīb al-, *Tārīkh al-Baghdādī,* Vol. 6, Pg. 180.

[24] Kozoglu, Shams al-Dīn Abū al-Muzaffar Yūsuf ibn al-, *Tadhkirat al-Khawās,* Pg. 321.

However, some have resorted to these slanderous reports to tarnish the dignified image of the Commander of the Faithful, Imam ʿAlī ﷺ.

Umm Kulthūm's Age at the Time of Marriage

As mentioned earlier, Yaʿqūbī and Ṭabarī consider this marriage to have taken place in the 17th year after Hijrah;[25] thus at that time, Umm Kulthūm would have been less than nine years old.

If we accept these reports, how is it acceptable that Imam ʿAlī ﷺ would marry his eight-year-old daughter – with consent – to a 57-year-old man – that is an age difference of approximately 50 years?

Indeed, one of the reasons that Imam ʿAlī ﷺ refused that marriage was because: "She is a child."[26 & 27]

Quick Tempered

ʿUmar's quick and hot temper is well-known and widely documented

---

[25] Ibn Saʿd writes in *Al-Ṭabaqāt al-Kubrā*: "ʿUmar married Umm Kulthūm, while she had not yet reached puberty." (Vol. 8, Pg. 338). Ibn Jawzī in his *Al-Muntaẓam* (Vol. 4, Pg. 237) also writes: "ʿUmar married Umm Kulthūm when she had not reached the age of puberty." Although Al-Dhahabī wrote that she was born in the 6th year after Hijrah (*Siyar Aʿlām al-Nubalā,* Vol. 3, Pg. 500), and as a result, in the 17th year AH, her age would have been 11 years. However, according to the words of her father, Imam ʿAlī ﷺ, who considered her to be a child still, and the reports of other historians who said that she had not yet reached the age of puberty, Al-Dhahabī's narration is incorrect, and she could not have reached 9 years of age (the time of puberty for girls).

[26] *Al-Ṭabaqāt al-Kubrā*, Vol. 8, Pg. 339.

[27] Although the age difference between Prophet Muḥammad ﷺ and some of his wives was very wide, they were proud to be the wives of the Prophet ﷺ. As well, sometimes the proposal of marriage was presented from their side; however, with the marriage in question, Imam ʿAlī ﷺ did not agree with it, and it was ʿUmar who insistently came with the proposal to him.

in various books of the Ahlul Sunnah to the extent that when he became the caliph, the first words he uttered on the pulpit, according to Ibn Saʿd, were: "O Allah, I am hot-tempered, so make me soft and gentle! I am weak, so make me strong! I am stingy, so make me generous."[28] However, these states – according to the *aḥādīth* of the Ahlul Sunnah – persisted in him. Indeed, it was due to this very reason that according to historical reports, some women refused to accept his marriage proposals.

Ṭabarī narrates through ʿĀyesha that ʿUmar proposed to Umm Kulthūm, the daughter of Abū Bakr, while she was still young. ʿĀyesha discussed this marriage proposal with her sister, Umm Kulthūm, who said: "I do not want him!"

ʿĀyesha responded: "Reluctance towards the caliph?"

She replied: "Yes because his life is strict, and he treats women violently."[29]

We can see that even a little girl like Umm Kulthūm, the daughter of Abū Bakr, was aware of his aggressive ways.

According to yet another report, Umm Kulthūm, the daughter of Abū Bakr, said to her sister, ʿĀyesha: "Do you want me to get married to someone whose severity and strictness you are aware of?"

Then, she added: "By Allah, if you do that [force me to marry him], then I will go to the grave of the Prophet of Allah, and shout there."[30]

Additionally, according to Balādhurī, Ṭabarī, and Ibn Athīr, when Yazīd ibn Abū Sufyān passed away, ʿUmar proposed to his wife, Ammābān – the daughter of ʿUtbah – but she refused. ʿUmar is said to have entered the house sullen and angry, slamming the door

---

[28] *Ṭabaqāt al-Kubrā*, Vol. 3, Pg. 208.

[29] *Tārīkh al-Rusul wa al-Mulūk*, Vol. 4, Pg. 199. This matter has also been discussed in *Al-Kāmil fī al-Tārīkh*, Vol. 3, Pg. 54.

[30] *Al-Istīʿāb fī Maʿrifah al-Aṣḥāb*, Vol. 4, Pg. 1807.

behind him.[31]

With all these historical anecdotes, how is it possible that Imām ʿAlī ﷺ would have given his daughter to him with his consent and goodwill?

Motives behind such a Marriage

In his book, the Sunnī author, Ibn Ḥajr al-ʿAsqalānī narrates that ʿUmar asked Imam ʿAlī ﷺ for the hand in marriage of Umm Kulthūm ﷺ.

Imam ʿAlī ﷺ replied: "I have kept my daughters for the children of [my brother] Jaʿfar."

ʿUmar insisted and said: "Marry her to me, O Abal Ḥasan, for by Allah, there is no man on the face of this earth who seeks to achieve through good companionship that which I seek to achieve."

ʿAlī then said: "I have done so."

ʿUmar came to the *Muhājirūn* and said: "Congratulate me!"

They said: "Why?"

He said: "Due to my marriage with the daughter of ʿAlī, and because the Prophet said: 'Every lineage and kinship will be cut off on the Day of Judgement, except for the lineage and kinship with me.' Therefore, I wanted to benefit from this blessing through this marriage."[32]

Ibn Athīr quotes ʿUmar as saying: "I had a family-relationship with the Prophet (because I was his father-in-law), and now I wanted to become the son-in-law of this family (i.e. the Prophet's ﷺ family)."[33]

---

[31] *Ansāb al-Ashrāf*, Vol. 9, Pg. 368; *Tārīkh al-Rusul wa al-Mulūk*, Vol. 4, Pg. 400; *Al-Kāmil fī al-Tārīkh*, Vol. 3, Pg. 55.

[32] *Al-Iṣābah fī Tamyīz al-Ṣahābah*, Vol. 8, Pg. 467; *Al-Istīʿāb fī Maʿrifah al-Aṣḥāb*, Vol. 4, Pg. 1955.

[33] *Usd al-Ghābah fī Maʿrifah al-Ṣaḥābah*, Vol. 6, Pg. 387.

According to Yaʿqūbī's narration, ʿUmar revealed the reason for this request to ʿAlī himself.[34]

We state that it is unlikely that the second caliph expressed this motive, and we do not imagine that such a motive would make him propose to Umm Kulthūm ﷺ. This is because according to Balādhurī's narration in *Ansāb al-Ashrāf*, when Imam ʿAlī ﷺ did not show up to swear allegiance to Abū Bakr, ʿUmar went to that same house – the house of the daughter of the Prophet ﷺ – with fire in his hand. He met Fāṭima ﷺ near the door of the house and when she saw ʿUmar with fire, she said: "O son of al-Khaṭṭāb, do you want to burn my house?!"

ʿUmar replied: "Yes."[35]

According to Ibn Qutayba al-Dīnawarī, the famous Sunnī scholar, ʿUmar ordered firewood to be brought and threatened those who had gathered in the house of Fāṭima ﷺ to come out of the house and pledge allegiance, or else, as he is quoted as saying: "I will set the house on fire."

When he was told: "O Abā Ḥafṣ (ʿUmar's epithet), Fāṭima is inside this house!" He said: "And so?! (Even if Fāṭima is there – so what!)"[36]

Ṭabarī also mentioned the attack on the house of ʿAlī ﷺ and the threat to burn the house down.[37]

How is offending Fāṭima al-Zahrāʾ ﷺ and disrespecting her

---

[34] *Tārīkh al-Yaʿqūbī*, Vol. 2, Pg. 149.

[35] *Ansāb al-Ashrāf*, Vol. 1, Pg. 586; *Al-ʿIqd al-Farīd*, Vol. 4, Pg. 259, has a similar narrative. The Arabic text of this is as follows:

يَابْنَ الْخَطَّابِ! أَتُرَاكَ مُحْرِقًا عَلَىٰ بَابِي.

[36] *Al-Imāmah wa al-Siyāsah*, Vol. 1, Pg. 30. The Arabic text of this is as follows:

يَا أَبَا حَفْصٍ إِنَّ فِيهَا فَاطِمَةَ. فَقَالَ: وَإِنْ.

[37] *Tārīkh al-Rusul wa al-Mulūk*, Vol. 3, Pg. 202.

compatible with marrying her daughter for the purpose of saving one's afterlife? Meaning – how can one dare to hurt the person whose anger and grief is tied to the anger and grief of the Messenger of Allah ﷺ? In this regard, the Prophet ﷺ has been quoted as saying: "Fāṭima is a part of me. Whoever has harmed her has harmed me; and whoever angers her has angered me."[38]

Therefore, **assuming** that there was a marriage, it was certainly **not** for the sake of having a relation with the family of the Prophet ﷺ or seeking the Hereafter. Rather, it was for ulterior motives.

Examining the Chain of Narrators

The books of the Ahlul Sunnah have extensively narrated this story in various ways and different wordings, however, only a portion of the event has been reported. Some researchers have examined the chain of transmitters *(isnād)* of the narrations and have made it clear that **all of them,** in line with their own standards, are weak.[39]

There is also a reference to this matter in *Ṣaḥīḥ al-Bukhārī.*[40]

As it has been noted, many Sunnī scholars consider everything that is mentioned in this book to be correct, but with respect to this incident, contained in the chain of transmission of the *aḥādīth* is an individual named Ibn Shihāb al-Zuhrī. Even though his trustworthiness has been confirmed by Sunnī scholars of *'Ilm Rijāl,* it is clear from the historical reports that he had close proximity to

---

[38] *Musnad Aḥmad,* Vol. 4, Pg. 5; This is like the narration found in *Ṣaḥīḥ al-Bukhārī,* Vol. 6, Pg. 157. The Arabic text of this is as follows:

فَاطِمَةُ بَضْعَةٌ مِنِّي يُؤْذِينِي مَا آذَاهَا، وَيُغْضِبُنِي مَا أَغْضَبَهَا.

[39] See *The Marriage of Umm Kulthūm with 'Umar,* written by Āyatullāh Sayyid ʿAlī Ḥusaynī Mīlānī.

[40] *Ṣaḥīḥ al-Bukhārī, Kitāb al-Jihād wa al-Sīr,* Vol. 3, Pg. 222.

the Umayyads, and was an enemy of the Ahlul Bayt ﷺ.[41] Therefore, there is a possibility of falsification in his narrations, and perhaps it is for this reason that the story of this marriage is not included in *Ṣaḥīḥ Muslim* – even though it is documented in *Ṣaḥīḥ al-Bukhārī*.

In addition to this, *Ṣaḥīḥ al-Bukhārī* has been criticized by fair thinkers and non-biased experts since the author of this book, Muḥammad ibn Ismāʾīl al-Bukhārī, **did not** include *Ghadīr Khumm's mutawātir ḥadīth* in his book. As well, he omitted the *Ḥadīth* of *Thaqalayn* which is also a *mutawātir ḥadīth*, while other authentic books have all included it.

Al-Bukhārī's efforts were always to present the early period of Islam as entirely peaceful and thereby ignore what happened afterwards, most significant of which was the oppression enacted against the Ahlul Bayt ﷺ. His biased behaviour in regards to the Ahlul Bayt ﷺ is clear to all reasonable thinkers to the extent that through a careful study of his multi-volume work of *Ḥadīth*, one will find that he did not quote a single *ḥadīth* from Imam Ḥasan al-Mujtabā ﷺ in his book [the grandson of Prophet Muḥammad ﷺ], nor has he quoted any *ḥadīth* from Imam Jaʿfar al-Ṣādiq ﷺ, nor any of the other Imams and family of the Ahlul Bayt ﷺ – all the way up to Imam Ḥasan al-ʿAskarī ﷺ.

At the same time, he has taken narrations from the likes of ʿImrān ibn Hiṭṭān, one of the leaders of the *Khawārij* movement, and even from the sermons of such individuals and others in the *Khawārij* group. In addition, he also narrates *aḥādīth* from the likes of ʿAmr ibn al-ʿĀs, Marwān ibn al-Ḥakam, Muʿāwiyah ibn Abū Sufyān, and other well-known opponents of Islam.

Also, the author of *Ṣaḥīḥ al-Bukhārī* documents narrations about

---

[41] See: www.valiasr.com; An article investigating the suspicion of 'Umar's marriage with Umm Kulthūm, written by Sayyid Muḥammad Ḥusaynī al-Qazwīnī.

the distortion of the Quran where he quotes from ʿAlqamah with his chain of narrators that: "The Messenger of Allah recited the third verse of Sūrah al-Layl in this way:

وَ ٱلذَّكَرَ وَٱلۡأُنثَىٰٓ

whereas what is in the present Quran is:

﴿وَمَا خَلَقَ ٱلذَّكَرَ وَٱلۡأُنثَىٰٓ﴾

"And by the creation of the male and the female."[42]
He also narrates from Anas ibn Mālik that the "verse:"

قد بلغوا قومنا أن لقينا ربّنا فرضى عنّا ورضينا عنه

---

[42] *Ṣaḥīḥ al-Bukhārī*, Vol. 6, Pg. 84. The Arabic text of this is as follows:

حَدَّثَنَا عُمَرُ حَدَّثَنَا أَبِي حَدَّثَنَا الأَعْمَشُ عَنْ إِبْرَاهِيمَ قَالَ: قَدِمَ أَصْحَابُ عَبْدِ اللهِ عَلَى أَبِي الدَّرْدَاءِ فَطَلَبَهُمْ فَوَجَدَهُمْ فَقَالَ: أَيُّكُمْ يَقْرَأُ عَلَى قِرَاءَةِ عَبْدِ اللهِ؟ قَالَ: كُلُّنَا. قَالَ: فَأَيُّكُمْ يَحْفَظُ وَأَشَارُوا إِلَى عَلْقَمَةَ. قَالَ: كَيْفَ سَمِعْتَهُ يَقْرَأُ ﴿وَاللَّيْلِ إِذَا يَغْشَى﴾. قَالَ عَلْقَمَةُ: وَالذَّكَرِ وَالأُنْثَى. قَالَ: أَشْهَدُ أَنِّي سَمِعْتُ النَّبِيَّ صَلَّى اللهُ عَلَيْهِ وَسَلَّمَ يَقْرَأُ هٰكَذَا، وَهٰؤُلَاءِ يُرِيدُونِي عَلَى أَنْ أَقْرَأَ ﴿وَمَا خَلَقَ الذَّكَرَ وَالأُنْثَى﴾ وَاللهِ لَا أُتَابِعُهُمْ.

The companions of ʿAbdullāh (ibn Maṣʿūd) came to Abū al-Dardāʾ, (and before they arrived at his home), he looked for them and found them. Then he asked them: "Who among you can recite (Quran) like ʿAbdullāh recites it?" They replied: "All of us." He asked: "Who among you knows it by heart?" They pointed at ʿAlqamah. Then he asked ʿAlqamah. "How did you hear ʿAbdullāh ibn Maṣʿūd reciting Sūrah al-Layl?" ʿAlqamah recited: "By the male and the female." Abū al-Dardāʾ said: "I testify that I heard the Prophet reciting it likewise, but these people want me to recite it as: 'And by He Who created the male and the female,' but by Allah, I will not follow them."

was revealed about the martyrs of *Biʾr Maʿūna*,[43] however, the verse

---

[43] The event known as *Sariyya Biʾr Maʿūna* refers to a historical occurrence in which a group of people who were sent by Prophet Muḥammad ﷺ to the tribes of Banū Salīm and Banū ʿĀmir were attacked by polytheists around *Biʾr Maʿūna* (The Maʿūna Well). In this event, all the representatives of the Prophet ﷺ were martyred except for two people, after which the Prophet ﷺ cursed the perpetrators of this killing in his *Fajr* prayer for several days.

Biʾr Maʿūna was in south-east area of Madina in the Najd region and is the region where the two tribes of Banū ʿĀmir and Banū Salīm resided.

In the month of Ṣafar, in the 4th year after the migration, four months after the Battle of Uḥud, Abū Barāʾ ʿĀmir ibn Mālik, the chief of the Banū ʿĀmir tribe who lived in Najd, went to meet the Prophet ﷺ in Madina, and offered him some gifts; however, the Prophet ﷺ said that he ﷺ would not accept any gift from the polytheists, and rather, presented Islam to him. Abū Barāʾ expressed his tendency towards accepting Islam and asked the Prophet ﷺ to send some of his companions to his tribe to invite them to Islam and learn more about its teachings.

The Prophet ﷺ was suspicious about the people of Najd and considered it possible that they may kill his representatives, however, Abū Barāʾ promised to protect them. Thus, the Prophet ﷺ sent some young men among the *Anṣār* to Najd – who were also reciters of the Quran – led by Mundhir ibn ʿUmrūr al-Sāʿidī, known as *al-Muʿniq li Yamūt* (lit. The one who is rushing towards death). The exact number of people in this group is not known; however, it has been noted in the historical texts that it was either 30, 40, or 70 people. The exact names of these people are also not known, and only the names of some of them have been recorded.

The representatives of the Prophet ﷺ stayed near *Biʾr Maʿūna*, and one of them, named Ḥarām ibn Milḥān took the letter of the Prophet ﷺ to ʿĀmir ibn Ṭufayl, who was among the chiefs of Banū ʿĀmir and the nephew of Abū Barāʾ.

Without even reading the letter, ʿĀmir ibn Ṭufayl ordered the killing of Ḥarām ibn Milḥān and asked his tribesmen to fight the companions of the Prophet ﷺ, however, Abū Barāʾ prevented it, and the tribe of Banū ʿĀmir

was later abrogated and removed from the Quran.[44]

---

avoided breaking the promise of Abū Barā'. Then, with the help of some people from Banū Salīm, including 'Uṣayya, Raghil, and Dhakwān, 'Āmir ibn Ṭufayl attacked the Muslims at *Bi'r Ma'ūna.*

The fight ended with all the representatives of the Prophet ﷺ except one being killed. The polytheists decided to spare the life of Mundhir ibn 'Umrū, however, he fought until he was killed. Thus, it was only Ka'b ibn Zayd from the Banū Najjār tribe who was wounded but hid among the killed ones and remained alive.

Two of the Muslim representatives, Ḥārith ibn al-Ṣimma and 'Umrū ibn Umayya ibn Ḥārith al-Ḍamrī, who had taken camels for grazing arrived in *Bi'r Ma'ūna.* Ḥārith ibn Ṣimma too was killed while fighting against the polytheists; but since 'Umrū ibn Umayya was from the Mudrī tribe – the same tribe as 'Āmir ibn Ṭufayl – 'Āmir released him.

On his return, 'Umrū ibn Umayya killed two people from the Banū 'Āmir tribe who were given safety by the Prophet ﷺ. When hearing about all of this, the Prophet ﷺ asked for help from the Banū Naḍīr tribe who were allied with Banū 'Āmir to pay the blood money, however, the Banū Naḍīr also plotted against the Prophet ﷺ, and this event led to the Battle of Banū Naḍīr.

When the Prophet ﷺ was informed about the killing at *Bi'r Ma'ūna,* he considered it the result of the request of Abū Barā', and for 15 or 40 days, he cursed the perpetrators of this killing in his morning prayers.

In addition, in a poem written by Ḥasān ibn Thābit, he considered the *Bi'r Ma'ūna* event a plot of trickery enacted by of 'Āmir ibn Ṭufayl.

In some sources, it is quoted from 'Āmir ibn Ṭufayl that he said: "One of the men among the Muslims was killed, and I saw his body raised from the ground and it was floating between the earth and the sky." It is reported that this was the body of 'Āmir ibn Fuhayra, however, researchers such as the late Sayyid Ja'far Murtaḍā al-Āmilī who studied the paradoxes in these reports, believe that this story was made-up for certain purposes. (Tr.)

[44] *Ṣaḥīḥ al-Bukhārī,* Vol. 3, Pg. 207. [It should be noted that this is **not** a verse of the Quran, however, in the most important and authentic book of

He even quotes from ʿUmar ibn al-Khaṭṭāb that: "The verse about stoning *(al-rajm)* was also in the Quran and we used to recite it,[45] however, it is not found in the Quran any longer."

Therefore, an objective scholar cannot trust everything that Bukhārī has narrated.

Back to the issue of this marriage, in the Shīʿa Imāmiyyah books

---

Ḥadīth of the Ahlul Sunnah, they deem this to be revelation which came to Prophet Muḥammad ﷺ – which Allah ﷻ later abrogated from the Quran. (Tr.)]

[45] *Ṣaḥīḥ al-Bukhārī*, Vol. 8, Pg. 26. The Arabic text of this is as follows:

حَدَّثَنَا مُحَمَّدُ بْنُ بَشَّارٍ حَدَّثَنَا ابْنُ أَبِي عَدِيٍّ وَسَهْلُ بْنُ يُوسُفَ عَنْ سَعِيدٍ عَنْ قَتَادَةَ، عَنْ أَنَسٍ رضى الله عنه أَنَّ النَّبِيَّ صَلَّى اللَّهُ عَلَيْهِ وَسَلَّمَ أَتَاهُ رِعْلٌ وَذَكْوَانُ وَعُصَيَّةُ وَبَنُو لِحْيَانَ، فَزَعَمُوا أَنَّهُمْ قَدْ أَسْلَمُوا، وَاسْتَمَدُّوهُ عَلَى قَوْمِهِمْ، فَأَمَدَّهُمُ النَّبِيُّ صَلَّى اللَّهُ عَلَيْهِ وَسَلَّمَ بِسَبْعِينَ مِنَ الأَنْصَارِ قَالَ أَنَسٌ كُنَّا نُسَمِّيهِمُ الْقُرَّاءَ، يَحْطِبُونَ بِالنَّهَارِ وَيُصَلُّونَ بِاللَّيْلِ، فَانْطَلَقُوا بِهِمْ حَتَّى بَلَغُوا بِئْرَ مَعُونَةَ غَدَرُوا بِهِمْ وَقَتَلُوهُمْ، فَقَنَتَ شَهْرًا يَدْعُو عَلَى رِعْلٍ وَذَكْوَانَ وَبَنِي لِحْيَانَ. قَالَ قَتَادَةُ وَحَدَّثَنَا أَنَسٌ أَنَّهُمْ قَرَءُوا بِهِمْ قُرْآنًا أَلاَ بَلِّغُوا عَنَّا قَوْمَنَا بِأَنَّا قَدْ لَقِينَا رَبَّنَا فَرَضِيَ عَنَّا وَأَرْضَانَا. ثُمَّ رُفِعَ ذَلِكَ بَعْدُ.

"The people of the tribes of Rʿil, Dhakwān, ʿUṣayya, and Bani Liḥyān came to the Prophet ﷺ and claimed that they had embraced Islam, and they requested him to support them with some men to fight their own people. The Prophet ﷺ supported them with 70 men from the *Anṣār* whom we used to call *al-Qurrā'* (i.e. Scholars) who (out of piety) used to cut wood during the day and pray all night. So, those people took the (70) men until they reached a place called *Bi'r Maʿūna* where they betrayed and martyred them. So, the Prophet ﷺ invoked evil on the tribe of Riʿl, Dhakwān, and Bani Liḥyān for one month in his prayers." It was narrated by Qatadā: "Anas told us that they (i.e. the Muslims) used to recite a Quranic verse concerning those martyrs which was: 'O Allah! Let our people be informed on our behalf that we have met our Lord Who has got pleased with us and made us pleased,' however, this verse was later cancelled."

of *Ḥadīth*, this marriage is narrated as follows: Shaykh Kulaynī in *Al-Kāfī* narrates from Muʿāwiyah ibn ʿAmmār that he asked Imam Jaʿfar al-Ṣādiq ﷺ regarding a woman whose husband has passed away, that while she is observing the *ʿiddah* (a waiting period that a Muslim woman must observe after the death of her husband, or after a divorce), is she required to remain in the same house, or can she go anywhere she wants? Imam Jaʿfar al-Ṣādiq ﷺ replied: "She can go anywhere she wants." Then he added: "After the death of ʿUmar, ʿAlī came and took Umm Kulthūm (ʿUmar's wife) back home."[46]

Sulaymān ibn Khālid also reports a similar narration from Imam Jaʿfar al-Ṣādiq ﷺ,[47] however, it is not clear whether this Umm Kulthūm was the child of Imam ʿAlī ﷺ with Lady Fāṭima al-Zahrāʾ ﷺ, or his concubine, or a daughter who grew up under his guardianship.

At any rate, assuming the acceptance of these two narrations,[48] the reason for this marriage is mentioned in two other narrations of *Al-Kāfī*, which will be examined later.

Threats

Regardless of the details mentioned, and if in principle this marriage is accepted, it does not indicate the existence of a good relationship between Imam ʿAlī ﷺ and the second caliph.

---

[46] Kulaynī, Muḥammad ibn Yaʿqūb al-, *Furūʿ al-Kāfī,* Vol. 6, Pg. 115, Tradition 1. The Arabic of this is as follows:

إِنَّ عَلِيًّا لَمَّا تُوُفِّيَ عُمَرُ أَتَى أُمَّ كُلْثُومٍ فَانْطَلَقَ بِهَا إِلَى بَيْتِهِ.

[47] *Furūʿ al-Kāfī,* Vol. 6, Pg. 115, Tradition 2.

[48] If this marriage is accepted to have taken place, it could not have happened in the 17th year after Hijrah as Umm Kulthūm ﷺ. Another possibility is that since the second caliph died in the 23rd year after Hijrah, so the marriage may have taken place a year before ʿUmar's death, when Umm Kulthūm ﷺ was about 16 years old.

Reports that have been narrated from both the Shīʿa and Sunnī books show that the second caliph used threats to accomplish his desires due to his position as the caliph of the Muslim nation.

Of course, Imam ʿAlī ﷺ was a man known to have tolerated a lot of injustice for the goal of preserving Islam and the legacy of the final Prophet ﷺ. He was a noble man who did not engage in unnecessary conflict,[49] just as his master and predecessor, the Messenger of Allah ﷺ, showed patience and tolerance against the opposition.[50]

Certainly, Umm Kulthūm's ﷺ marriage was not more important than leadership after the death of the Prophet of Islam ﷺ. After resistance and opposition, when the people present at Ṣaqīfah were determined to seize the caliphate at any cost and keep it away from the Ahlul Bayt ﷺ, Imam ʿAlī ﷺ had no choice but to turn to patience and steadfastness. Indeed, he did not even hesitate to give advice to the caliphs at that time for the sake of Islam.

Imam ʿAlī ﷺ said the following about withdrawing from the caliphate after the conflicts: "I put a curtain against the caliphate and kept myself detached (from it)."[51] Furthermore, he patiently suffered injustices, as he eloquently recalls: "So, I adopted patience as if there was pricking in the eye and suffocation in the throat. I watched the

---

[49] It is enough to look around us and see how many dignified, noble, and modest people put aside their own rights under certain conditions so that family, society, and environment do not get involved in internal issues.

[50] To learn more about this sad story, refer to the Chapter in this book on *The Event of the Pen and Paper.*

[51] *Nahj al-Balāgha*, Sermon No. 3; Ibrāhīm ibn Muḥammad al-Thaqafī al-Kūfī, *Al-Ghārāt*, Vol. 2, Pg. 768. The Arabic text of this is as follows:

فَسَدَلْتُ دُونَهَا ثَوْبًا وَطَوَيْتُ عَنْهَا كَشْحًا.

plundering of my inheritance..."[52]

Additionally, in letter 62 of *Nahj al-Balāgha*, Imam ʿAlī ﷺ first talks about the usurpation of the caliphate, and the fact that the commandments of the Messenger of Allah ﷺ were ignored. Then, he explained the reason for his cooperation with the caliphs, and he ﷺ says: "I swear to Allah! It never occurred to me or ever crossed my mind that after the demise of the Prophet, the Arabs would usurp the mantle of successorship from his family (and place it somewhere else) and keep me away from it. The thing that upset me was the gathering of the people around so-and-so as they pledged allegiance to him. I folded my hands (in observation) until I saw with my own eyes that a group of Muslims returned (to the Age of Ignorance) and wanted to destroy the religion of Muḥammad. It was here that I was afraid that if I do not help Islam and its people, I will have to witness the destruction and division in Islam, which would be a bigger tragedy for me than abandoning the caliphate and government."[53]

Many historians have mentioned the apostasy of many tribes during that time, and the rise of a group of Jews, Christians, and hypocrites after the demise of the Messenger of Allah ﷺ. In this situation, Imam ʿAlī ﷺ concluded that internal conflict would have

---

[52] *Nahj al-Balāgha*, Sermon No. 3. The Arabic text of this is as follows:

فَصَبَرْتُ وَفِي الْعَيْنِ قَذًى وَفِي الْحَلْقِ شَجًا أَرَى تُرَاثِي نَهْبًا.

[53] The Arabic text of this letter is as follows:

فَوَاللَّهِ مَا كَانَ يُلْقَى فِي رُوعِي وَلَا يَخْطُرُ بِبَالِي أَنَّ الْعَرَبَ تُزْعِجُ هٰذَا الْأَمْرَ مِنْ بَعْدِهِ صَلَّى اللهُ عَلَيْهِ وَآلِهِ وَسَلَّمَ عَنْ أَهْلِ بَيْتِهِ وَلَا أَنَّهُمْ مُنَحُّوهُ عَنِّي مِنْ بَعْدِهِ فَمَا رَاعَنِي إِلَّا انْثِيَالُ النَّاسِ عَلَى فُلَانٍ يُبَايِعُونَهُ فَأَمْسَكْتُ [بِيَدِي] يَدِي حَتَّى رَأَيْتُ رَاجِعَةَ النَّاسِ قَدْ رَجَعَتْ عَنِ الْإِسْلَامِ يَدْعُونَ إِلَى مَحْقِ دَيْنِ مُحَمَّدٍ صَلَّى اللهُ عَلَيْهِ وَآلِهِ وَسَلَّمَ فَخَشِيتُ إِنْ لَمْ أَنْصُرِ الْإِسْلَامَ وَأَهْلَهُ أَنْ أَرَى فِيهِ ثَلْمًا أَوْ هَدْمًا تَكُونُ الْمُصِيبَةُ بِهِ عَلَيَّ أَعْظَمَ مِنْ فَوْتِ وِلَايَتِكُم.

put Islam and the traditions of the Noble Prophet ﷺ in greater danger, thus he remained patient and did not revolt against them.

He has also been quoted as saying: "When the Prophet died, the Arabs returned to the Era of Ignorance *(Jāhiliyyah)*, and the Jews and Christians raised their heads [hoping to destroy Islam], while the hypocrites revealed themselves and entered the scene, and the Muslims became like a shepherd-less flock caught in the desert on a cold and rainy winter night."[54]

In addition, Imam 'Alī ؑ was patient upon the attack on his house and the insults towards Lady Fāṭima al-Zahrā' ؑ, the beloved daughter of the Prophet ﷺ and the leader of the women of the worlds.[55]

It is crystal clear that Imam 'Alī ؑ laid down his entire life with sincerity during the time of the Messenger of Allah ﷺ. He made exhausting and effective efforts in helping the progress of Islam. He was always ready to sacrifice his own blood and everything for the Messenger of Allah ﷺ to preserve that precious heritage. He suffered immensely, but remained patient, and gave up his own rights for the betterment of the Muslims and the survival of Islam.

Imam 'Alī ؑ was also patient during the usurpation of Fadak by tolerating the greed and jealousy of the oppressive group, leaving everything to Allah ﷻ. He said the following on one occasion: "Of

---

[54] *Al-Sīrah al-Nabawiyyah*, Vol. 2, Pg. 665; *Tārīkh al-Rusul wa al-Mulūk*, Vol. 3, Pg. 225; For more information about the apostasy of different Arab tribes after the death of the Messenger of Allah ﷺ refer to: *Al-Bidāyah wa al-Nihāyah*, Vol. 6, Pg. 312. The Arabic text of this is as follows:

لما تُوفى رسول الله، ارتدت العرب، واشرأبت اليهوديه والنصرانيه، ونجم النفاق، وصار المسلمون كالغنم المطيره في الليله الشاتيه.

[55] Read about the attack on the house of Lady Fāṭima al-Zahrā' ؑ - Chapter Three in this book.

course, all that we had in our possession under this sky was Fadak, but a group of people were greedy for it, and the other party withheld themselves from it. Allah is, after all, the best Arbiter."[56]

Now, let us discuss the threats that preceded Umm Kulthūm's ﷷ marriage.

According to Ibn Jawzī's narration, when ʿUmar requested the hand of Umm Kulthūm ﷷ in marriage, Imām ʿAlī ﷷ replied that she is a child (not yet mature for marriage), to which ʿUmar (angrily) said: "By Allah! That is not true. You are seeking to avoid me."[57]

From this narration, ʿUmar's displeasure with the rejection of Imam ʿAlī ﷷ is obvious.

In *Muʿjam al-Kabīr* of Ṭabarānī, and *Majmūʿ al-Zawāʾid* of Abul Ḥasan al-Ḥaythamī, both being famous Sunnī scholars, it is documented that Imam ʿAlī ﷷ consulted with ʿAqīl (his brother), ʿAbbās (his uncle), and Imam Ḥusayn ﷷ about the request of the second caliph, then replied to ʿAqīl's advice by saying: "By Allah! His words were not out of goodwill, but the scourge of his life has forced him to do what you see."[58]

In the Shīʿa *Ḥadīth* sources, this threat is profoundly expressed. It is documented in a report that Hishām ibn Sālim al-Jawālīqī al-Juʿfī

---

[56] *Nahj al-Balāgha*, Letter 45. The Arabic text of this is as follows:

بَلَى كَانَتْ فِي أَيْدِينَا فَدَكٌ مِنْ كُلِّ مَا أَظَلَّتْهُ السَّمَاءُ فَشَحَّتْ عَلَيْهَا نُفُوسُ قَوْمٍ وَسَخَتْ عَنْهَا نُفُوسُ آخَرِينَ، وَنِعْمَ الْحَكَمُ اللّٰهُ.

[57] *Kitāb al-Muntaẓam*, Vol. 4, Pg. 238. The Arabic text of this is as follows:

إِنَّکَ وَاللّٰهَ مَا بِکَ ذٰلِکَ، وَلٰکِنْ قَدْ عَلِمْنَا مَا بِکَ.

[58] *Muʿjam al-Kabīr*, Vol. 3, Pp. 44–45; *Majmuʿ al-Zawāʿid*, Vol. 4, Pg. 271. The Arabic text of this is as follows:

والله ما ذاك من نصيحه، ولكن دره عمر أحرجته الى ماترى.

narrates from Imam Jaʿfar al-Ṣādiq that "When ʿUmar came to make the marriage proposal, the Commander of the Faithful, ʿAlī, told him: 'She is a child.'

Thereupon, ʿUmar met ʿAbbās (the uncle of Prophet Muḥammad) and told him: 'What is wrong with me? Do I have any defects?'

ʿAbbās said: 'Why do you say that?'

ʿUmar replied: 'I asked your nephew for his daughter's hand in marriage, but he turned me down. I swear by Allah! I will fill the well of Zamzam with earth, I will destroy every honour that you have, and I will set up two witnesses to testify that he stole, so that I can cut off his right hand!'

ʿAbbās thereupon came to ʿAlī and informed him about what had transpired. He asked ʿAlī to put the matter in his hands, and ʿAlī complied."[59] Thereby, ʿAbbās arranged and married Umm Kulthūm to ʿUmar.[60]

Imam Jaʿfar al-Ṣādiq summed up all these threats in a short and meaningful sentence as follows: "She (Umm Kulthūm) was an honour who was usurped from us."[61]

The threats of the second caliph to attack the house of Lady Fāṭima al-Zahrāʾ that he carried out makes us believe that he would have carried out this threat mentioned above as well against

---

[59] *Furūʿ al-Kāfī*, Vol. 5, Pg. 346, Tradition 2. The Arabic text of this is as follows:

أَمَا وَاللهِ لَأَغُورَنَّ زَمْزَمَ وَلَا أَدَعُ لَكُمْ مَكْرُمَةً إِلَّا هَدَمْتُهَا وَلَأُقِيمَنَّ عَلَيْهِ شَاهِدَيْنِ أَنَّهُ سَرَقَ وَلَأَقْطَعَنَّ يَمِينَهُ...

[60] *Biḥār al-Anwār*, Vol. 5, Pg. 346, Tradition 1.
[61] *Furūʿ al-Kāfī*, Vol. 5, Pg. 346, Tradition 1. The Arabic text of this is as follows:

إِنَّ ذَلِكَ فَرَجٌ غُصِبْنَاهُ.

Imam ʿAlī ☙.

Ibn Abī Shaybah narrates from Zayd ibn Aslam, on the authority of his father Aslam, in an authentic tradition that: "After the death of the Prophet when the pledge of allegiance was taken for Abū Bakr, ʿAlī and Zubayr ibn ʿAwwām would visit Fāṭima al-Zahrāʾ – the daughter of the Messenger of Allah – and consult with her about their work. This news reached ʿUmar ibn al-Khaṭṭāb. So, he came and attacked Fāṭima and said: '…I swear to Allah! If these few people continue their work, your sanctity (with us) will not prevent me from setting the house on fire!'"

In the following report, Aslam narrates that after ʿUmar went out, Fāṭima ☙ said to them (ʿAlī, Zubayr, and the others): "Do you know that ʿUmar came to me and swore by Allah that if you return (to my house and consult), then he would burn down the house? I swear to Allah that he will do what he has sworn!"[62]

This is the testification of Lady Fāṭima al-Zahrāʾ ☙ who informed them about ʿUmar's threat and temperament and believed that he would carry out his threat! This threat of ʿUmar and the testimony of Lady Fāṭima al-Zahrāʾ ☙ have also been documented by ʿAlī Muttaqī al-Hindī[63] and al-Dehlawī,[64] who considered it to be authentic upon the criteria of the two Shaykhs, Bukhārī and Muslim.[65]

---

[62] *Ibn Abī Shaybah, Al-Muṣannaf,* Vol. 8, Pg. 572, Tradition 4.
[63] *Kanz al-ʿUmmāl,* Vol. 5, Pg. 651, Tradition 14,138.
[64] Dehlawī, Shāh Walīullāh, *Izālat al-Khafā ʿan Khilāfat al-Khulafāʾ,* Vol. 2, Pp. 29 and 179.
[65] "Upon the conditions of the two Shaykhs" that is, the conditions that Al-Bukhārī and Muslim consider valid for the authenticity of this tradition in their respective *Ṣaḥīḥ* books. In his book, Āyatullāh Jaʿfar Subḥānī has examined the authentic sources of this tradition according to the standards of the Ahlul Sunnah scholars in the Science of *Rijāl and* has clearly

Therefore, ʿUmar could easily carry out his threat here, especially since he was the "official caliph" at that time and had a lot more authority. As a result, **if** such a marriage had taken place, then Imam ʿAlī ﷺ gave consent out of compulsion, necessity, and duress; and it is natural that in such a case, the union was never a sign of love, affection, or true consensus.

There are several other cases whereby the second caliph applied strict measures to other Muslims as well, and they had to tolerate it to protect the value and principles of the religion and avoid internal conflicts. Sufficient for us is the following example.

Muslim ibn al-Ḥajjāj documents in his *Ṣaḥīh Muslim* that Saʿīd ibn ʿAbdul Raḥmān ibn Abzā came to ʿUmar and said: "I have seminal discharges, and I cannot find water (to perform *ghusl).*"

He (ʿUmar) replied: "Do not perform *ṣalāt* then."

ʿAmmār (ibn Yāsir) replied: "Do you remember, O the Commander of the Faithful (ʿUmar), when you and I were in a military detachment, and we had seminal discharges and could not find water, and you (ʿUmar) did not perform the *ṣalāt.* As for me, I rolled myself in dust and performed the *ṣalāt.*

Then, (when we returned and asked) the Prophet said: "It was enough for you to strike the soil with your hands and then blow (off the excess)? and wipe your face and palms."

ʿUmar responded: "Fear Allah, O ʿAmmār!"

Therefore, he (ʿAmmār) replied: "If you so like, then I will not narrate this."[66]

In this case, ʿAmmār shortened the story of the incident and did

---

explained the authenticity of this tradition. Refer to the Chapter found in this book entitled: *Fire in the House of Revelation.*

[66] *Ṣaḥīḥ Muslim,* Chapter on *Tayammum,* Vol. 1, Pg. 193. The Arabic text of this is as follows:

فَقَالَ عُمَرُ: إِتَّقِ اللّٰهَ يَا عَمَّارُ. قَالَ: إِنْ شِئْتَ لَمْ أُحَدِّثْ بِهِ.

not insist on the ruling, even though he was right. In addition to the words of the Messenger of Allah ﷺ, the Quran also specifies that in such a case, one must perform *tayammum*.[67]

ʿUmar ibn al-Khaṭṭāb also forbade narrating the *aḥādīth* of the Messenger of Allah ﷺ, and in this regard, he dealt with the companions very severely. He imprisoned some people who narrated them and beat others. Yet, they tolerated it and did not rise to militancy or conflict (as they realized that this would have been very detrimental to Islam if they spoke up).

The Sunnī scholar, Shams al-Dīn al-Dhahabī narrates that ʿUmar imprisoned three great companions: ʿAbdullāh ibn Maṣʿūd, Abūl Dardāʾ, and Abū Maṣʿūd al-Anṣārī for narrating several *aḥādīth* of the Messenger of Allah.[68]

Al-Ḥākim al-Naysābūrī also narrates that ʿUmar exiled ʿAbdullāh ibn Maṣʿūd, Abul Dardāʾ, and Abū Dharr al-Ghifārī from Madina because they were quoting *aḥādīth*, and such imprisonments, exiles, and bans continued until the death of ʿUmar.[69]

Abū Hurayrah also stated that if he had narrated any *aḥādīth* during the time of ʿUmar, then he would have beaten him with his whip. Abū Hurayrah says: "If I reported a (single) narration at the time of ʿUmar like what I have narrated to you [after the death of

---

[67] Quran, Sūrah al-Nisāʾ (4), Verse 43:

﴿...وَإِن كُنتُم مَّرْضَىٰٓ أَوْ عَلَىٰ سَفَرٍ أَوْ جَآءَ أَحَدٌ مِّنكُم مِّنَ ٱلْغَآئِطِ أَوْ لَٰمَسْتُمُ ٱلنِّسَآءَ فَلَمْ تَجِدُوا۟
مَآءً فَتَيَمَّمُوا۟ صَعِيدًا طَيِّبًا فَٱمْسَحُوا۟ بِوُجُوهِكُمْ وَأَيْدِيكُمْ...﴾

"And if you are ill, or on a journey, or one of you comes after answering the call of nature, or you have been in contact with women (by sexual relations), and you find no water, then perform *tayammum* (dry ablution) with clean earth and rub therewith your faces and hands."

[68] *Tadhkirat al-Ḥuffaẓ,* Vol. 1, Pg. 7.

[69] *Al-Mustadrak ʿalā al-Ṣaḥīḥayn,* Vol. 1, Pg. 110.

ʿUmar], then he would have flogged me with his whip."[70]

In any case, Imam ʿAlī ﷺ and his companions had to be patient amidst the harshness and strictness of the second caliph so that the position of caliphate would remain respected [and Islam would not be abolished]. The reason for this was that any conflict would have ended in favour of the hypocrites and the sworn enemies of Islam, and serious damage would have been done to the whole of Islam, just like what happened after the murder of the third caliph, ʿUthmān ibn al-ʿAffān.

Therefore, the second caliph's purported marriage with Umm Kulthūm could **never** be an indication of the existence of affection between him and Imām ʿAlī ﷺ.

We can better understand this by reflecting on the Noble Quran and how it relates to the words of Prophet Lūṭ ﷺ that he said in front of the disbelieving people who rushed to his house because of his guests: "[Lūṭ] said: 'These are my daughters – if you would be doers [of lawful marriage].'"[71]

Consequently, if a marriage takes place under special conditions, and an Imam like the Commander of the Faithful ʿAlī ﷺ consents to this matter due to duress, then this is due to a different situation, and it is never a sign of affection or friendship.

---

[70] *Tadhkirat al-Ḥuffaẓ*, Vol. 1, Pg. 7. Ibn ʿAbdul Barr also narrates a similar statement in his *Jāmiʿ al-Bayān al-ʿIlm wa Faḍlihi,* Vol. 2, Pg. 121. The Arabic of the statement of Abū Hurayrah is:

لَوْ كُنْتُ أُحَدِّثُ فِي زَمَانِ عُمَرَ مِثْلَ مَا أُحَدِّثُكُمْ لَضَرَبَنِي بِمِخْفَقَتِه.

Many cases of violence and harshness of the second caliph, and the imposed tolerance of the Muslims and companions have been mentioned in history. This will be talked about separately.

[71] Quran, Sūrah al-Ḥijr (15), Verse 71:

﴿قَالَ هَٰٓؤُلَآءِ بَنَاتِيٓ إِن كُنتُمۡ فَٰعِلِينَ ۝٧١﴾

This reveals another angle of the oppression against Imam ʿAlī (ʿa). In the same way that the first Imam (ʿa) said in response to Muʿāwiyah ibn Abū Sufyān who insulted him by saying that: "You were the one who was dragged to pledge allegiance like a harnessed camel," Imam ʿAlī (ʿa) replied: "You say: 'They tied me like a camel and dragged me to pledge allegiance.' I swear by Allah! You wanted to condemn me, but you have unwillingly praised me. You wanted to disgrace me, but you have been disgraced."[72]

Then he (Imam ʿAlī (ʿa)) drew the position of the oppressed in the continuation of this reply that being oppressed and tolerating it for a more important purpose is not a problem, nor is it disgraceful; rather it is an honour and virtue. What is a defect is that a Muslim doubts one's religion. The Imam (ʿa) continued in his letter (to Muʿāwiyah) by saying: "It is not a deficiency for a Muslim to be oppressed, as long as the person does not doubt one's religion and does not doubt the certainty (of one's religion)."[73]

Of course, if the Imam (ʿa) was oppressed in this incident and was forced to agree to this marriage, then the fault was not on him – rather, it was on those who put him in such a situation. The oppressed Imam (ʿa) was once again forced to avoid conflict and strive for a more important purpose by taking care of the seedling of Islam, so he swallowed this proposal like a poisonous liquid. He was patient and bore the oppression yet again.

---

[72] The Arabic text of this is as follows:

وَقُلْتَ إِنِّي كُنْتُ أُقَادُ كَمَا يُقَادُ الْجَمَلُ الْمَخْشُوشُ حَتَّى أُبَايِعَ وَلَعَمْرُ اللّٰهِ لَقَدْ أَرَدْتَ أَنْ تَذُمَّ فَمَدَحْتَ وَأَنْ تَفْضَحَ فَافْتَضَحْتَ.

[73] *Nahj al-Balāgha*, Letter 28. The Arabic text of this is as follows:

وَمَا عَلَى الْمُسْلِمِ مِنْ غَضَاضَةٍ فِي أَنْ يَكُونَ مَظْلُومًا، مَا لَمْ يَكُنْ شَاكًّا فِي دِينِهِ، وَلَا مُرْتَابًا بِيَقِينِهِ.

Conclusion

Umm Kulthūm was the daughter of Imām ʿAlī ﷺ and Lady Fāṭima al-Zahrā' ﷺ. Her marriage was recognized by both Sunnī and Shīʿa historians as having occurred with the second caliph. The scholars of the school of Ahlul Bayt ﷺ believe that ʿUmar ibn al-Khaṭṭāb played a central role in removing Imam ʿAlī ﷺ from the caliphate, and in the attack against the house of Lady Fāṭima al-Zahrā' ﷺ.

Therefore, a question is raised: Did such a marriage ever take place?

If it did, then can it be concluded that there was a good relationship between Imam ʿAlī ﷺ and ʿUmar? Or was necessity, expediency, or even compulsion more likely the reasons for accepting such a marriage?

Some scholars deny the existence of a daughter named Umm Kulthūm by Lady Fāṭima al-Zahrā' ﷺ, while other scholars do not accept her marriage to ʿUmar. Other scholars accept marriage in principle but reject the consummation of it.

Another group of them consider the marriage to have taken place out of force and coercion.

A few, in addition to accepting the marriage, mention a child or two from the union of Umm Kulthūm and ʿUmar.

While examining the reports of Sunnī scholars in this regard, we have mentioned some reflections about it that cast doubt on the marriage itself.

In any case, if this marriage occurred, we do not consider it a sign of love between Imam ʿAlī ﷺ and the second caliph. The restraint and tolerance of the pious Imam ﷺ, as well as his focus on more important issues such as preventing internal strife and the weakening of Islam, are reasons why Imam ʿAlī ﷺ **may** have consented to this marriage.

If this is the case, then this marriage is another page from the notebook of the oppressions meted out against Imam ʿAlī ﷺ and his noble family.

Bibliography

The Noble Quran.

ʿAbdul Barr, Abū ʿUmar Yūsuf ibn ʿAbdullāh ibn Muḥammad ibn, *Al-Istīʿāb fī Maʿrifah al-Aṣḥāb* (Beirut: Dār al-Jīl, 1st Edition, 1412 AH - Edited by ʿAlī Muḥammad al-Bajawī).

ʿAbdul Barr, Yūsuf ibn ʿAbdullāh ibn Muḥammad ibn, *Jamiʾ Bayan al-ʿIlm wa Faḍlihi* (Beirut: Dār al-Kutub al-ʿIlmīyyah, 1st Edition, 1397 AH).

ʿAbdul Rabbih, Aḥmad ibn Muḥammad ibn, *al-ʿIqd al-Farīd* (Beirut: Dār al-Kitāb al-Arabī, 1406 AH).

ʿAsqalānī, Aḥmad ibn Nūrud Dīn ʿAlī ibn Muḥammad ibn Ḥajar al-, *Al-Iṣābah fī Tamyīz al-Ṣahābah* (Beirut: Dār al-Kutub al-ʿIlmīyyah, 1415 AH - Edited by ʿĀdil Aḥmad ʿAbdul Mawjūd).

Balādhurī, Aḥmad ibn Yaḥyā ibn Jābir al-, *Ansāb al-Ashrāf* (Beirut: Dār al-Fikr, 1st Edition, 1417 AH - Edited by Saḥīl Zakār).

Baṣrī, Abū Muḥammad ʿAbdul Malik ibn Hishām ibn Ayyūb al-Ḥimyarī al-Muʿāfirī al-, *Al-Sīrah al-Nabawiyyah* (Beirut: Dār al-Maʿrifah, n.d. - Edited by Mustafa al-Saqā and others).

Bukhārī, Abū ʿAbdillāh Muḥammad ibn Ismāʿīl al-, *Ṣaḥīḥ al-Bukhārī* (Beirut: Dār al-Fikr, 1st Edition, 2005 - Researched by Ṣiddīqī Jamīl al-Aṭṭār).

Dakhīl, ʿAlī Muḥammad ʿAlī, *Aʿlām al-Nisāʾ* (Beirut: Dār al-Islāmiyyah, 3rd Edition, 1412 AH).

Dehlawī, Shāh Walīullāh, *Izālat al-Khafāʾ ʿan Khilāfat al-Khulafāʾ* (Pakistan, n.d.).

Dhahabī, Shams al-Dīn al-, *Siyar Aʾlam al-Nubalā* (Beirut: Muʾassasah al-Risālah, 9th Edition, 1413 AH - Edited by Shuayb al-Arnaut).

Dhahabī, Shams al-Dīn al-, *Tadhkirat al-Ḥuffāz* (Beirut: Dār Iḥyāʾ al-Turāth al-Arabī).

Dhuhlī, Abū ʿAbdillāh Aḥmad ibn Muḥammad ibn Ḥanbal al-, *Musnad Aḥmad* (Beirut: Dār al-Sādir).

Dimashqī, Abūl Fiḍāʾ ʿImād al-Dīn Ismāʾīl ibn ʿUmar ibn Kathīr al-Qurayshī al-, *Al-Bidāyah wa al-Nihāyah* (Beirut: Dār al-Fikr, 1st Edition, 1407 AH).

Dīnawarī, Abū Muḥammad ʿAbdullāh ibn Muslim ibn Qutayba al-, *Al-Imāmah wa al-Siyāsah* (Beirut: Dār al-Aḍwāʾ, 1st Edition, 1410 AH - Edited by ʿAlī Basharī).

Haythamī, Nūr al-Dīn ʿAlī ibn Abī Bakr ibn Sulaymān Abūl Ḥasan al-, *Majmūʿ al-Zawāʾid wa Manbaʾ al-Fawāʾid* (Beirut: Dār al-Kutub al-ʿIlmīyyah, 1408 AH).

Hindī, ʿAla al-Din ʿAlī ibn ʿAbdul Malik Husām al-Dīn al-Muttaqī al-, *Kanz al-ʿUmmāl* (Beirut: Muʾassasah al-Risālah, 1409 AH).

Hindī, Sayyid Nāṣir Ḥusayn Mūsawī, *Ifhām al-Adāʾ wa al-Khusūm* (Tehran: Maktab Naynawā - Edited by Dr. Muḥammad Ḥādi Amīni).

Ibn Qudāmah Abū Muḥammad ʿAbdullāh ibn Aḥmad ibn Muḥammad al-Maqdisī, *Al-Mughnī* (Beirut: Dār al-Kitāb al-Arabi).

Ibn Saʿd, Abū ʿAbdullāh Muḥammad, *Kitāb al-Ṭabaqāt al-Kabīr* (Beirut: Dār al-Kutub al-ʿIlmiyyah, 1st Edition, 1410 AH - Edited by Mustafa ʿAbdul Qādr ʿAṭa).

Jawzī, ʿAbdul Raḥmān ibn ʿAlī ibn Muḥammad Abul Farash ibn al-, *Al-Muntazam fī Tārīkh al-Mulūk wa al-Umam* (Beirut: Dār al-Kutub al-ʿIlmīyyah, 1st Edition, 1412 AH - Edited by Muḥammad ʿAbdul Qādir ʿAṭā).

Jawzī, Sibṭ ibn al-, *Tadhkirat al-Khawāṣ minal Umma fī Dhikr Khaṣāʾiṣ al-Aʾimmah* (Beirut: Muʾassasah Ahlul Bayt, 1401 AH).

Jazarī, ʿAlī ʿIzz al-Dīn ibn al-Athīr al-, *Al-Kāmil fi Tārīkh* (Beirut: Dār Ṣādr, 1385 AH).

Jazarī, ʿAlī ʿIzz al-Dīn Ibn al-Athīr al-, *Usd al-Ghābah fī Maʿrifah al-Ṣaḥābah* (Beirut: Dār al-Fikr, 1409 AH).

Khaṭīb, Muḥammad Shirbīnī al-, *Mughnī al-Muḥtāj* (Beirut: Dār Iḥyāʾ al-Turāth al-Arabī, 1377 AH).

Kūfī, Abū Bakr ibn Abī Shaybah al-, *Al-Muṣannaf* (Beirut: Dār al-Fikr, 1st Edition, 1409 AH - Edited by Saʿīd al-Lahām).

Kūfī, Ibrāhīm ibn Muḥammad al-Thaqafī al-, *Al-Ghārāt* (n.d., Edited by Sayyid Jalāl al-Dīn Huseini).

Majlisī, Muḥammad Bāqir ibn Muḥammad Taqī ibn Maqṣūd ʿAlī al-, *Biḥār al-Anwār al-Jāmiʿat li-Durar Akhbār al-Aʾimmah al-Aṭhār* (Beirut: Muʾassasah al-Wafāʾ, 2nd Edition, 1403 AH).

Māzandarānī, Abū ʿAbdullāh Muḥammad ibn ʿAlī ibn Shahrāshūb al-Sarawī al-, *Manāqib Āl Abī Ṭālib* (Najaf: Matbuʾ al-Ḥaydariyyah, 1376 AH).

Mīlānī, Āyatullāh Sayyid Ḥusaynī, *Marriage of Umm Kulthūm with ʿUmar* (Qum: Markaz Ḥaqāʾīq Islāmī, 2nd Edition, 1386 AH).

Nahj al-Balāgha (with research and annotation of Ṣubḥī Ṣāliḥ).

Nawawī, Abū Zakariyyā Yaḥyā ibn Sharaf al-, *Al-Majmūʿ Sharh al-Muhadhab* (Beirut: Dār al-Fikr).

Naysābūrī, Abūl Ḥusayn ʿAsākir al-Dīn Muslim ibn al-Ḥajjāj, *Ṣaḥīḥ Muslim* (Beirut: Dār al-Fikr).

Nishābūrī, Abū ʿAbdullāh Muḥammad ibn ʿAbdullāh al-Ḥakim al-, *Al-Mustadrak ʿala al-Ṣaḥīḥhayn* (n.d. - Edited by Yūsuf ʿAbdul Raḥmān al-Marʿashī).

Nuʿmān, Abū ʿAbdullāh Muḥammad ibn Muḥammad ibn al- (Shaykh

Mufīd), *Al-Irshād* (Qum: Mu'assasah Āl al-Bayt, 2nd Edition, 1414 AH).

Nuʿmān, Abū ʿAbdullāh Muḥammad ibn Muḥammad ibn al- (Shaykh Mufīd), *Al-Masā'il al-Sar'wiyah* (Beirut: Dār al-Mufīd, 2nd Edition, 1414 AH).

Nuʿmān, Abū ʿAbdullāh Muḥammad ibn Muḥammad ibn al- (Shaykh Mufīd), *Al-Masā'il al-Ukbariyyah* (Beirut: Dār al- Mufīd, 2nd Edition, 1414 AH - Edited by ʿAlī Akbar Ilaḥi Khurāsānī).

Qarashī, Shaykh Bāqir Sharīf al-, *Ḥayāt Sayyida al-Nisā' Fāṭima al-Zahrā'* (Qum: Dār al-Dhakhā'ir al-Islāmīyyah, 1st Edition, 1427 AH).

Rāzī, Abū Jaʿfar Muḥammad ibn Yaʿqūb ibn Isḥāq al-Kulaynī al-, *Kitāb al-Kāfī* (Beirut: Dār Sab - Dār al-ʿĀrif, 4th Edition, 1401 AH).

Sarakhsī, Muḥammad ibn Aḥmad ibn Abī Sahl Abū Bakr al-, *Kitāb al-Mabsūṭ* (Beirut: Dār al-Maʿrifah, 1406 AH).

Sayyid Murtaḍā, *Rasā'il al-Murtaḍā* (Qum: Dār al-Quran al-Karīm, 1405 AH - Edited by Sayyid Aḥmad Huseini).

Shāfiʿī, Abū Bakr Aḥmad ibn ʿAlī ibn Thābit ibn Aḥmad ibn Mahdī al-, *Tārīkh al-Baghdādī* (Beirut: Dār al-Kutub al-ʿIlmīyyah, 1st Edition, 1417 AH - Edited by Mustafa ʿAbdul Qādir ʿAṭā).

Shushtarī, ʿAllāmah Muḥammad Taqī al-, *Qāmūs al-Rijāl* (Qum: Publications of Qum Seminary, 1st Edition, 1425 AH).

Subḥānī, Jaʿfar, *Attack on the House of Revelation* (Qum, Islamic Publication Office, 2nd Edition, 1383 AH).

Ṭabarānī, Abūl Qāsim Sulaymān ibn Aḥmad ibn Ayyūb ibn Muṭayyir al-Lakhmī al-Shāmī al-, *Al-Muʿjam al-Kabīr* (Beirut: Dār Iḥyā' al-Turāth al-Arabī, 2nd Edition, 1404 AH - Edited by Aḥmad ʿAbdul Majīd al-Salafī).

Ṭabarī, Abū Jaʿfar Muḥammad ibn Jarīr ibn Yazīd al-, *Tārīkh al-*

Ṭabarī (Beirut: Dār al-Turāth, 2nd Edition, 1387 AH - Edited by Muḥammad Abūl Fadhl Ibrahīm).

Ṭūsī, Abū Ja'far Muḥammad ibn al-Ḥasan al-, *Tahdhīb al-Aḥkām fī Sharḥ al-Muqni'ah* (Tehran: Dār al-Kutub al-Islāmīyah, 1365 AH).

Ya'qūbī, Abūl 'Abbās Aḥmad ibn Abī Ya'qūb ibn Gha'far ibn Wahb ibn Waḍīḥ al-Ya'qūbī, *Tārīkh al-Ya'qūbī* (Beirut: Dār Ṣādr).

www.valiasr.com.

Chapter Six

The Six-Person Shūrā Devised to Elect a Caliph

Introduction

The establishment of a six-member *"Shūrā,"* sometimes referred to as *"The Council,"* by the second caliph, ʿUmar ibn al-Khaṭṭāb, stands as a controversial issue in the history of Islam.

Its purpose was simple: to select the future caliph from among its chosen members. Notably, this event remains remarkable for its uniqueness as it had no precedent in Islamic history, nor was it ever replicated afterwards.

The question arises as to the criteria used, and the motivations that influenced ʿUmar ibn al-Khaṭṭāb's decision for creating such a complex system to put his successor in place. After all, the first caliph was selected by a small, select group of people; the second caliph was appointed by the first caliph; yet now, the third caliph was going to be placed in his position through a six-member council?!

In contrast to the Shīʿa belief which holds that Prophet Muḥammad ﷺ appointed Imām ʿAlī ﵇ as the leader of the Islamic nation after himself – **as per the direct command of Allah** ﷻ – ʿUmar ibn al-Khaṭṭāb's actions diverged significantly from his predecessor. According to the viewpoint of the Ahlul Sunnah, ʿUmar ibn al-Khaṭṭāb entrusted the selection of the caliphate to a hand-picked group of people, thus abstaining from choosing a specific individual to rule the Muslim nation after himself.

Furthermore, ʿUmar ibn al-Khaṭṭāb's approach differed from that of the first caliph, who personally designated ʿUmar as his successor and introduced him to the people as such. Thus, the second caliph's behaviour contrasted with that of his predecessor.

In short, ʿUmar ibn al-Khaṭṭāb created a novel approach, one that defied any prior conventions.

The decree of ʿUmar ibn al-Khaṭṭāb was clear: A directive was issued to assemble six specific individuals within a house, placing an armed group to oversee them, to choose a caliph from among themselves within a three-day timeframe. If they could not come up with a conclusive outcome, then they were all to be killed!

This unconventional "solution" to choose the third caliph poses intriguing questions, prompting inquisitive minds to seek a reasonable explanation.

To comprehensively explore the dimensions and intricacies of this significant historical event, we will once again delve into it by referencing the authoritative books of prominent scholars of the Muslim community from among the Ahlul Sunnah.

Our examination will encompass the following focal points:

1. The edict of ʿUmar ibn al-Khaṭṭāb.
2. The passing away of ʿUmar ibn al-Khaṭṭāb, and the formation of The Council *(Shūrā)*.
3. Reactions and responses.
4. Analysis and a detailed examination.

The Edict of ʿUmar ibn al-Khaṭṭāb

As ʿUmar ibn al-Khaṭṭāb lay gravely injured after being attacked, and nearing the end of his life, those who were around him begged him: "O Commander of the Faithful *(Amīr al-Muʾminīn)!* It would be beneficial if you could designate a successor (caliph) after you!"

In response, he pondered: "Whom should I select as the caliph? If Abū ʿUbaydah ibn al-Jarrāḥ were still among us, then I would have unhesitatingly appointed him; and if I was then questioned by the Almighty regarding my choice, I would have proudly affirmed: 'I directly heard from the Prophet himself, who extolled Abū ʿUbaydah as a trustworthy pillar of this nation.'"

He went on to say: "Had Sālim, the liberated slave of Ḥudhayfah, been among us, I would have entrusted him with the position of caliph; and if I was then questioned by my Lord regarding the wisdom behind my choice, I would have firmly stated: 'I received the teachings of Your Prophet, who declared that Sālim is greatly beloved by Allah.'"[1]

When someone suggested to ʿUmar: "Choose ʿAbdullāh ibn ʿUmar (his own son) as the successor," ʿUmar vehemently rejected the idea and exclaimed: "May Allah take your life! You have completely disregarded Divine guidance in this matter. How can I appoint someone who is incapable of even divorcing his own wife? (In other words, he is weak and indecisive)."

ʿUmar then continued: "I will reflect on this matter. If I were to appoint a caliph, it would not be problematic, as even the one who was superior to me (referring to Abū Bakr) followed this course of action. However, if I refrain from designating a caliph (granting freedom to the people to choose for themselves) again, then the one who was superior to me (referring to the Prophet ﷺ) acted similarly. Nevertheless, rest assured that Allah will protect His religion from harm."

After some time, they approached ʿUmar once again and urged him to decide. He responded: "With these words, I have reached the conclusion to consider someone who surpasses all of you and has the ability to guide you towards the truth,"[2] and he specifically pointed towards Imam ʿAlī ﷺ to indicate his choice.

Then he continued: "However, I do not wish to impose the burden of caliphate upon you (or to single out a specific individual). Nonetheless, I urge you to consider this group, for the Prophet has

---

[1] Abū ʿUbaydah al-Jarrāḥ and Sālim are individuals that Prophet Muḥammad ﷺ had established the pact of brotherhood between. (See *Al-Ṭabaqāt al-Kubrā*, Vol. 3, Pg. 65.) They were alongside ʿUmar during the Event at Saqīfah of Banū Sāʿida.

[2] The Arabic text of this is as follows:

قَدْ كُنْتُ أَجْمَعْتُ بَعْدَ مَقَالَتِي أَنْ أُوَلِّي أَمْرَكُمْ رَجُلًا هُوَ أَحْرَاكُم أَنْ يَحْمِلَكُمْ عَلَى الْحَقِّ وَ أَشَارَ إِلَى عَلِيٍّ.

said: 'They are the people of Paradise,'[3] and among them are these six individuals: ʿAlī [ibn Abī Ṭālib], ʿUthmān [ibn al-ʿAffān], ʿAbdul Raḥmān ibn ʿAwf, Saʿd ibn Abī Waqqāṣ, Zubayr ibn al-ʿAwwām, and Ṭalḥa ibn ʿUbaydullāh. Choose one person from among them and extend your cooperation and support (to them) when they appoint a leader."

ʿAbbās, the uncle of the Prophet ﷺ, advised Imam ʿAlī ؑ: "Do not engage in this *Shūrā* with them."

Imam ʿAlī ؑ replied: "I dislike any dissension and division."

ʿAbbās warned him: "In that case, you will witness what displeases you."

In the morning, ʿUmar summoned ʿAlī ؑ, ʿUthmān, Saʿd, ʿAbdul Raḥmān ibn ʿAwf, and Zubayr, while Ṭalḥa was absent. He addressed them, saying: "After careful consideration, I have recognized you as the esteemed personalities of the community. Therefore, the caliph should emerge from among you. You were the individuals whom the Messenger of Allah was pleased with before he departed from this world. If you remain united and harmonious, I have no concerns for you regarding the people. However, I fear for you if you engage in disputes, as it will sow discord among the people."

He then instructed them to proceed and engage in consultation. They departed and began their discussions, gradually raising their voices. ʿUmar said: "Now, it is time for me to step in and express my thoughts. When I depart from this world, you will have three days to engage in consultation. During these three days, Ṣuhayb will lead the people in prayer. On the fourth day, no decision should be made except for selecting a leader. ʿAbdullāh ibn ʿUmar (the son of ʿUmar

---

[3] This is a reference to the fabricated *ḥadīth* in which Prophet Muḥammad ﷺ was reported to have given ten "companions" the glad tidings that they were going to Paradise. For more information on this fabrication and its analysis refer to: http://al-mubin.org/the-ten-promised-paradise/

ibn al-Khaṭṭāb) will be present in your discussions, although he has no authority in the matter of the caliph. Ṭalḥa is your partner, and if he joins during the three days, then include him in the process. If he does not come, then proceed without him.

Then ʿUmar ibn al-Khaṭṭāb continued: "I believe that either ʿAlī or ʿUthmān will assume the responsibility of caliph. If ʿUthmān becomes the leader, he possesses a gentle demeanour; and if ʿAlī is chosen, he may be spirited, but he is more deserving than anyone else to guide the people on the path of truth. If they choose Saʿd, he is indeed worthy of this position; and if Saʿd is not selected, then the chosen leader should seek his assistance. Let us also acknowledge the intellect and wisdom of ʿAbdul Raḥmān ibn ʿAwf, may Allah protect and guide him! Please pay attention to his valuable insights."[4]

Other Points to Consider

According to Dīnawarī's narration of this event, ʿUmar also mentioned that if Abū ʿUbaydah ibn al-Jarrāḥ or Sālim were alive, he would have appointed them as caliph. ʿUmar then remembered Khālid ibn al-Walīd and noted: "Had Khālid ibn al-Walīd been alive, I would have appointed him as the leader of the Muslims, as he was honoured by the Prophet as the Sword of Allah *(Sayfullāh).*"[5]

ʿAbdullāh ibn ʿUmar narrates that ʿUmar addressed the *Shūrā*, stating: "If they were to appoint ʿAlī as their guardian and leader *(walī)*, then he would lead them on the righteous path, even if a sword is placed upon his neck."

I asked him: "You acknowledge this, yet you hesitate to designate

---

[4] *Tārīkh al-Rusul wa al-Mulūk*, Vol. 4, Pp. 227-229 (summarized).

[5] *Al-Imāmah wa al-Siyāsah*, Vol. 1, Pg. 42. However, what is correct is that Abū Bakr called him *Sayfullāh* – the Sword of Allah – this was not done by the Messenger of Allah ﷺ. (See *Al-Ishtiqāq*, Pg. 149; *Sharḥ Nahj al-Balāgha*, Vol. 16, Pp. 168-159.)

him as the leader *(walī)*?"

ʿUmar replied: "If I were to select him as the caliph, then I would be following the precedence of someone more deserving and superior to me (Abū Bakr). If I refrain from suggesting anyone, then it would not pose a problem, for even a superior person (the Messenger of Allah) did not explicitly name a successor."[6]

According to the account of Ibn Abī al-Ḥadīd, Ṭalḥa was also present in Madina, and ʿUmar summoned the six individuals, declaring: "The Prophet left this world with his satisfaction towards the six of you. I intend to establish a *Shūrā* among you to choose a caliph from within your ranks."

Then he addressed them: "I am aware that each of you desires to assume the caliphate after me."

They remained silent, so ʿUmar reiterated his statement. It was at this point that Zubayr responded: "We are not inferior to you, neither in our devotion to the faith, nor in our close connection to the Messenger of Allah."[7]

Then ʿUmar proceeded to offer his criticisms to each of the six individuals. He addressed Zubayr, saying: "Your actions are inconsistent, as one day you display humane qualities, and another day you are influenced by Satan."

Then he said to Ṭalḥa: "It is said that the Prophet was displeased with you because of a statement you made after the revelation of the

---

[6] *Al-Mustadrak ʿalā al-Ṣaḥīḥḥayn,* Vol. 3, Pg. 95; *Al-Kāmil* of Ibn ʿAdī, Vol. 5, Pg. 37; *Mizān al-Iʿtidāl,* Vol. 3, Pg. 210.

[7] Ibn Abī al-Ḥadīd, after quoting this statement of Zubayr, says that ʿUthmān al-Jāḥiẓ, one of the great scholars of Ahlul Sunnah, exclaimed: "By Allah, I swear that if Zubayr had not been certain of ʿUmar's death, he would never have uttered such words." (*Sharḥ Nahj al-Balāgha,* Vol. 1, Pg. 185.)

verse on *ḥijāb*."[8]

He addressed Saʿd ibn Abī Waqqāṣ, stating: "You are a brave warrior (but lack the qualities required for leadership). The tribe of Banī Zuhrah (referring to Saʿd's tribe) is in one place, but the caliph and the affairs of the people are in another!"

When addressing ʿAbdul Raḥmān ibn ʿAwf, he acknowledged: "Even if half of the faith of the Muslims were to be measured against your faith, yours would still surpass theirs. However, the position of caliph does not suit a weak individual."

ʿUmar then directed his attention to Imam ʿAlī (ع) and remarked: "Your only fault lies in your playful nature. However, if you were to assume leadership over the people, you would guide them firmly on the path of truth and illuminate their way with righteousness."

Lastly, addressing ʿUthmān, ʿUmar ibn al-Khaṭṭāb stated: "It appears that the Quraysh have bestowed upon you the caliphate, but you have shown favouritism towards the Banū Umayyah by entrusting them with the public treasury. Beware, for a group of Arabian wolves will strike you down in your own bed."[9]

It is truly astonishing how ʿUthmān, despite this significant flaw highlighted by ʿUmar, was chosen for the caliphate, while Imam ʿAlī (ع), with what ʿUmar deemed as a "minor issue" of 'playfulness,' was sidelined: such a stark contrast between their qualifications is

---

[8] This statement refers to Verse 53 of Sūrah al-Aḥzāb. (فَاسْأَلُوهُنَّ مِن وَرَاءِ حِجَابٍ) which states: "When you ask [his] womenfolk for something, do so from behind a curtain." This refers to the wives of the Prophet ﷺ. Ṭalḥa said: "The Prophet wants to veil them from us today, but tomorrow, when he is no longer in this world, we will marry them." After this statement, Allah revealed the next part of this same verse which says: "You do not have the right to marry them after him." (*Tafsīr Ṭalḥa*, Vol. 6, Pg. 403; *Al-Durr al-Manthūr*, Vol. 5, Pg. 25; *Maʿālim al-Tanzīl*, Vol. 3, Pg. 659; *Mafātīḥ al-Ghayb*, Vol. 25, Pg. 180.)

[9] *Sharḥ Nahj al-Balāgha*, Vol. 1, Pg. 186 (summarized).

noteworthy!

ʿAbdullāh ibn ʿUmar says that ʿUthmān, Imam ʿAlī ﷺ, Zubayr, ʿAbdul Raḥmān ibn ʿAwf, and Saʿd came to ʿUmar. He looked at them and said: "I nominated you for the sake of caliphate over the people. People will not fall into conflict except through you."

Then he added: "People will choose one of you three: ʿUthmān, ʿAbdul Raḥmān, or ʿAlī." Then he looked at ʿUthmān and said: "If you attain the caliphate, do not favour your relatives and kin over the people."

Then he turned to ʿAbdul Raḥmān and said: "You too, shall you attain the caliphate, do not exert control over your relatives and kinfolk."

Finally, he turned to ʿAlī and said: "If you attain the caliphate, do not impose Banū Hāshim upon the people."[10]

According to a narration of Dīnawarī, ʿUmar criticized ʿAbdul Raḥmān ibn ʿAwf by saying: "You are the Pharaoh of this nation."

Regarding Ṭalḥa, he said: "Ṭalḥa is arrogant and conceited, and if he becomes the caliph, he will place the caliph's ring on the finger of his wife (indicating that he is submissive to his wife)."[11]

The Method of Choosing a Caliph

After finalizing the members of the *Shūrā*, ʿUmar ibn al-Khaṭṭāb instructed Abū Ṭalḥa al-Anṣārī, saying: "Gather fifty armed men and escort the members of the *Shūrā* to a designated room, where they will proceed with selecting a caliph among themselves."

He further emphasized: "Their decision must be binding. If five individuals reach a unanimous agreement on a candidate for the caliphate, and one dissents, then execute the dissenting individual.

---

[10] *Al-Ṭabaqāt al-Kubrā,* Vol. 3, Pg. 262; *Tārīkh al-Islam,* Vol. 3, Pp. 281-282; Ibn Asākir, *Tārīkh Madīna Dimashq,* Vol. 44, Pg. 438.

[11] *Al-Imāmah wa al-Siyāsah,* Vol. 1, Pg. 43.

If four individuals reach a consensus, while two oppose, behead the two dissenters.

In the case of three individuals standing on one side and three on the other, appoint ʿAbdullāh ibn ʿUmar as the arbitrator. Whichever group he aligns with, their decision will be accepted.

If they do not accept his opinion, then side with those three individuals who are with ʿAbdul Raḥmān ibn ʿAwf, and if the other three individuals oppose, then kill them!"[12]

According to the account provided by Balādhurī, he instructed Abū Ṭalḥa al-Anṣārī: "They have no more than three days to select a caliph. During this period, Suhayb will lead the congregation in prayer. If Ṭalḥa joins the gathering, then include him in the decision-making process; otherwise, let the five individuals themselves determine the course of the caliphate."[13]

Foresight of Imam ʿAlī ﷺ

Based on the narration of Balādhurī, Imam ʿAlī ﷺ, upon hearing the statement of ʿUmar which said: "In the case of a tie, then side with those three individuals who are with ʿAbdul Raḥmān ibn ʿAwf," expressed dissatisfaction and said: "I swear by Allah! The caliphate has been taken away from our family!"[14]

ʿAbbās asked him: "How can you say such a thing?" Imam ʿAlī ﷺ replied: "Saʿd ibn Abī Waqqāṣ will not oppose his cousin's son,

---

[12] *Al-Mustadrak ʿalā al-Ṣaḥīḥḥayn,* Vol. 4, Pg. 230 (with slight summarization); Also refer to: *Tajārib al-Umam,* Vol. 1, Pg. 418; *Kāmil ibn Athīr,* Vol. 3, Pg. 67. *Al-Imāmah wa al-Siyāsah,* Vol. 1, Pg. 43; *Ansāb al-Ashrāf,* Vol. 5, Pg. 500; *Kanz al-ʿUmmāl,* Vol. 5, Pg. 743.

[13] *Ansāb al-Ashrāf,* Vol. 5, Pg. 504.

[14] The Arabic text of this is as follows:

وَاللّٰهِ لَقَدْ ذَهَبَ الْأَمْرُ مِنَّا.

ʿAbdul Raḥmān,[15] who is also the brother-in-law[16] of ʿUthmān, and thus, they will not oppose each other; so even if Ṭalḥa and Zubayr are with me (due to the presence of ʿAbdul Raḥmān on the other side), it will not benefit our cause."[17]

Death of ʿUmar and the Shūrā

After ʿUmar passed away and was buried, the members of the *Shūrā* gathered in a house, and Abū Ṭalḥa al-Anṣārī looked after them. At that time, Ṭalḥa was not present in Madina.

ʿAbdul Raḥmān ibn ʿAwf asked the other members of the *Shūrā:* "Who among you is willing to step aside so that the most deserving among us can attain the caliphate?" No one answered, so he continued: "I myself will step aside."

After some discussions, Zubayr was asked to vote for someone. He said: "I step aside in favour of ʿAlī."

Then ʿAbdul Raḥmān asked Saʿd ibn Abī Waqqāṣ to give his right to him, and after some discussions, Saʿd agreed to this. As a result, ʿAbdul Raḥmān, who now had two votes (his own vote and Saʿd's vote), engaged in discussions with ʿUthmān and Imam ʿAlī ﷺ to convince one of them to withdraw. He had lengthy conversations with Imam ʿAlī ﷺ, then engaged in prolonged negotiations and consultations with ʿUthmān.

In the morning, after the *Fajr* prayer, ʿAbdul Raḥmān sent for the *Muhājirūn*, notable individuals in Islam, various leaders of the *Anṣār*, and the commanders of the armies. With the *masjid* full of people, ʿAbdul Raḥmān addressed the attendees and said: "The people in the cities want to return to their hometowns, but before that, they want

---

[15] ʿAbdul Raḥmān and Saʿd were both from the tribe of Banī Zuhrah.

[16] He was married to Umm Kulthūm, the sister of ʿUthmān ibn al-ʿAffān.

[17] *Ansāb al-Ashrāf,* Vol. 5, Pg. 505; *Tārīkh al-Rusul wa al-Mulūk,* Vol. 4, Pp. 229-230 (also narrates the same incident, but in a more detailed manner).

to know who their caliph is."

Among them was Saʿīd ibn Zayd[18] who said: "We consider you worthy of the caliphate."

ʿAbdul Raḥmān replied: "Just say this much."

ʿAmmār said: "If you do not want the Muslims to be divided, then pledge allegiance to ʿAlī."[19]

Miqdād ibn al-Aswad said: "You have spoken the truth, ʿAmmār. If you pledge allegiance to ʿAlī, then we will say: 'We hear and we obey!'"[20]

Ibn Abīl Sarḥ[21] said: "If you do not want the Qurąysh to be

---

[18] Saʿīd ibn Zayd was the nephew of ʿUmar ibn al-Khaṭṭāb, and the husband of his sister. He embraced Islam before ʿUmar. He passed away in the year 50 or 51 AH. See: *Al-Istīʿāb fī Maʿrifah al-Aṣḥāb*, Vol. 2, Pg. 415.

[19] The Arabic text of this is as follows:

إن أردت ألّا يختلف المسلمون فبايع عليًّا.

[20] The Arabic text of this is as follows:

صَدَقَ عَمَّارُ إِنْ بَايَعْتَ عَلِيًّا قُلْنَا: سَمِعْنَا وَأَطَعْنَا.

[21] ʿAbdullāh ibn Saʿd ibn Abīl Sarḥ was the foster brother of Uthmān, and he was a staunch enemy of the Prophet ﷺ who often used to mock him. Due to his actions, the Prophet ﷺ considered shedding his blood. During the time of the final Messenger ﷺ, he fled Madina out of fear and later came to Mecca – seeking refuge with ʿUthmān. ʿUthmān concealed him, and at an opportune moment, he brought him before Prophet Muḥammad ﷺ – interceding on his behalf.

The Prophet ﷺ, after a period of silence, granted him forgiveness. However, after his departure, the Messenger ﷺ said: "My silence was to give someone else the chance to rise and strike him."

He outwardly embraced Islam but later apostatized. He once again pretended to embrace Islam during the caliphate of ʿUthmān. ʿUthmān then appointed him as the governor of Egypt, and his tyranny led to the revolt

divided, then pledge allegiance to ʿUthmān."[22]

ʿAbdullāh ibn Abī Rabīʿah[23] said: "Indeed, if you pledge allegiance to ʿUthmān, then we will say: 'We hear and we obey!'"[24]

ʿAmmār ibn Yāsir said to Ibn Abīl Sarḥ: "When did you start advising the Muslims?!"[25]

There was a conversation between the Banū Hāshim and the Banū Umayyah, and ʿAmmār ibn Yāsir expressed his support for Imam ʿAlī ﷺ. However, some of the Quraysh began to attack him, so Saʿd ibn Abī Waqqāṣ said to ʿAbdul Raḥmān: "Finish the matter before people get involved in turmoil and chaos."

ʿAbdul Raḥmān first called upon Imam ʿAlī ﷺ and said: "You have the covenant and pledge of Allah to follow the Book of Allah, the *Sunnah* of His Messenger, and the conduct *(sīrah)* of the two caliphs

---

of the Egyptians against ʿUthmān. (See: *Usd al-Ghābah fī Maʿrifah al-Ṣaḥābah,* Vol. 3, Pp. 153-156; *Ansāb al-Ashrāf,* Vol. 5, Pg. 512; *Tārīkh al-Rusul wa al-Mulūk,* Vol. 4, Pg. 367.)

[22] The Arabic text of this is as follows:

إِنْ أَرَدْتَ أَلَّا تَخْتَلِفُ قُرَيش فَبَايِعْ عُثْمَانُ.

[23] ʿAbdullāh ibn Abī Rabīʿah al-Qurashī was one of the leaders of the Quraysh who embraced Islam on the Day of the Conquest of Mecca. On that day, he sought refuge with Umm Hānī, the sister of Imam ʿAlī ﷺ. Imam ʿAlī ﷺ intended to kill him, but Umm Hānī prevented him from doing so. (See: *Al-Istīʿāb fī Maʿrifah al-Aṣḥāb,* Vol. 3, Pp. 896-897; *Usd al-Ghābah fī Maʿrifah al-Ṣaḥābah,* Vol. 3, Pp. 128-129.)

[24] The Arabic text of this is as follows:

صدق إن بايعت عثمان قُلْنَا: سَمِعْنَا وَأَطَعْنَا.

[25] The Arabic text of this is as follows:

متى كنت تنصح المسلمين.

(meaning Abū Bakr and ʿUmar) who came after him."[26]

Imam ʿAlī ﷺ responded: "I hope that (in addition to acting according to the Book of Allah and the *Sunnah* of the Messenger of Allah ﷺ) I can also exert my own independent judgement, and act based on my knowledge and abilities (not the practices of the two previous caliphs)."[27]

ʿAbdul Raḥmān then called upon ʿUthmān and conveyed the exact words to him, to which ʿUthmān responded: "Yes, I will act accordingly." ʿAbdul Raḥmān then pledged allegiance to him.[28]

According to another account, Imam ʿAlī ﷺ straightforwardly replied to ʿAbdul Raḥmān: "Indeed, I will act according to the Book of Allah, the *Sunnah* of His Messenger, and my own judgement."[29] ʿAbdul Raḥmān then turned to ʿUthmān, who stated his acceptance. ʿAbdul Raḥmān repeated this request three times, and each time Imam ʿAlī ﷺ responded with the same answer. Therefore, ʿAbdul Raḥmān joined hands with ʿUthmān, and said: "Peace be upon you, O Commander of the Faithful."[30]

---

[26] The Arabic text of this is as follows:

عليك عهد الله وميثاقه لتعملنّ بكتاب اللهِ وسنّة رسوله وسيرة الخليفتَيْن من بعده.

[27] The Arabic text of this is as follows:

أرجوا أن أفعل وأعمل بـمبلغ عملي وطاقتي.

[28] *Tārīkh al-Rusul wa al-Mulūk,* Vol. 4, Pp. 230-234; *Al-Kāmil fī al-Tārīkh,* Vol. 3, Pp. 68-71; *Al-ʿIqd al-Farīd,* Vol. 4, Pp. 278-279 (summarized); Also see: *Tārīkh al-Islam,* Vol. 3, Pg. 305; *Tārīkh al-Madina,* Vol. 3, Pp. 929-930.

[29] The Arabic text of this is as follows:

بَلْ عَلَىٰ كِتَابِ اللهِ وَسُنَّةَ رَسُولِهِ وَاجْتِهَادِ رَأْيِي.

[30] *Sharḥ Nahj al-Balāgha,* Vol. 1, Pg.188. The Arabic text of this is as follows:

In the book, *Tārīkh al-Yaʿqūbī*, a more precise interpretation is provided. According to his account, Imam ʿAlī responded to ʿAbdul Raḥmān by saying: "I will follow the Book of Allah, and the *Sunnah* of His Prophet to the best of my ability."[31]

However, in response, ʿUthmān said to ʿAbdul Raḥmān: "I will follow the Book of Allah, the *Sunnah* of His Prophet, and the practices *(sīrah)* of Abū Bakr and ʿUmar."[32]

This request was repeated twice, with Imam ʿAlī and ʿUthmān giving the same response each time. On the third occasion, Imam ʿAlī said: "With the Book of Allah, and the *Sunnah* of His Prophet, there is no need for anyone else's practices. But you are trying to distance the caliphate away from me."[33]

Then, ʿAbdul Raḥmān turned to ʿUthmān, and repeated the same statement, to which ʿUthmān accepted, and as a result, pledged allegiance to him.[34]

According to another narration, it is believed that Ṭalḥa was also present at the council meeting.

ʿAbdul Raḥmān ibn ʿAwf said to the members of the council: "You should entrust your affairs to three individuals."

Zubayr said: "I have given my vote to ʿAlī."

اَلسَّلَامُ عَلَيْكَ يَا أَمِيرَ الْمُؤْمِنِينَ.

[31] The Arabic text of this is as follows:

أَسِيرُ فِيكُمْ بِكِتَابِ اللَّهِ وَ سُنَّةِ نَبِيِّهِ مَا إِسْتَطَعْتُ.

[32] The Arabic text of this is as follows:

لَكُمْ أَنْ أَسِيرَ فِيكُمْ بِكِتَابِ اللَّهِ وَسُنَّةِ نَبِيِّهِ وَسِيرَةِ أَبِي بَكْرٍ وَ عُمَرٍ.

[33] The Arabic text of this is as follows:

إِنَّ كِتَابَ اللَّهِ وَسُنَّةَ نَبِيِّهِ لَا يَحْتَاجُ مَعَهُمَا إِلَى إِجِيرِي أَحَدٍ أَنْتَ مُجْتَهِدٌ أَنْ تَزْوِي هَذَا الْأَمْرُ عَنِّي.

[34] *Tārīkh al-Yaʿqūbī*, Vol. 2, Pg. 162.

Saʿd said: "I have given my right to ʿAbdul Raḥmān."

Ṭalḥa said: "I have given my share to ʿUthmān."

ʿAbdul Raḥmān then continued: "I am withdrawing from the caliphate. Which one of you two is willing to withdraw?" Both Imam ʿAlī ﷺ and ʿUthmān remained silent.

ʿAbdul Raḥmān held a private conversation with both and agreed that he would appoint one of them as the caliph and the other would obey. Then, he used the same trick and pledged allegiance to ʿUthmān.[35]

Reactions and Responses

By choosing ʿUthmān, the nobles of Quraysh and Banī Umayyah were pleased because ʿUthmān belonged to the same tribe.[36]

During the time of the Prophet ﷺ and throughout his own period after having converted to Islam, ʿUthmān had never killed any of the pagans or enemies of the Prophet ﷺ. As a result, various Quraysh factions had no animosities with him. In fact, it is reported that when ʿAbdul Raḥmān consulted with the elites and nobles about the caliphate, he learned that most of them preferred ʿUthmān.[37]

The effects of this satisfaction were later evident in the words of Abū Sufyān. One day, he candidly said to ʿUthmān: "The leadership has come to you after Banū Taym (referring to Abū Bakr) and the Banū Wādī (referring to ʿUmar). Now, handle it like a ball and put its pegs in the Banū Umayyah (his tribe). (Know that) It is only a matter of ruling (not an Islamic caliphate), and I do not know anything

---

[35] *Tārīkh al-Islam,* Vol. 3, Pg. 280; *Al-Muntaẓam,* Vol. 4, Pg. 331.

[36] ʿUthmān ibn ʿAffān ibn Abīl ʿĀṣ ibn Umayyah ibn ʿAbd Shams.

[37] *Tārīkh al-Islam,* Vol. 3, Pg. 305.

about Paradise or Hellfire [if they even exist]."[38]

Mughīrah ibn Shuʿbah, who was known for his enmity towards the Ahlul Bayt ﷺ also said to ʿAbdul Raḥmān: "You did a good thing by pledging allegiance to ʿUthmān." Then he said to ʿUthmān: "We would not have been satisfied if ʿAbdul Raḥmān had pledged allegiance to anyone else."[39]

On the other hand, Imam ʿAlī ﷺ and the sincere Muslims, such as Miqdād, were dissatisfied with this choice. In this respect, Ṭabarī writes: "After ʿAbdul Raḥmān pledged allegiance to ʿUthmān, ʿAlī addressed him and said: 'This is not the first time you have shown your opposition to us. But I will exercise patience, and may Allah help me against your actions. By Allah, you did not pledge allegiance to ʿUthmān except to hand it over to yourself (after him).'[40]

When ʿAbdul Raḥmān heard these words, he threatened ʿAlī and said: 'Do not put yourself on a path against me (do not become the

---

[38] *Sharḥ Nahj al-Balāgha,* Vol. 16, Pg. 136; *Al-Istīʿāb fī Maʿrifah al-Aṣḥāb,* Vol. 4, Pg. 1679 (Note: The provided text mentions that ʿUthmān reacted sharply to his ugly statement). The Arabic text of this is as follows:

صارتْ إليك بعد تيم وعديّ فأدرها كالكرة واجعل أوتادها بني أمية فإنما هو الملك ولا أدري ما جنّة ولا نار.

[39] *Tārīkh al-Rusul wa al-Mulūk,* Vol. 4, Pg. 234; *Al-Kāmil fī al-Tārīkh,* Vol. 3, Pg. 72. The Arabic text of this is as follows:

لو بايع عبد الرحمٰن غيرك ما رضينا.

[40] The Arabic text of this is as follows:

حبوته حبو دهر ليس هذا أوّل يوم تظاهرتم فيه علينا فصبر جميل والله المستعان على ما تصفون واللهِ ما ولّيت عثمان إلّا ليردّ الأمر إليك.

cause of your own death).'[41]

Miqdād also said after this incident: 'I have never seen such mistreatment towards any family after their Prophet.'[42]

ʿAbdul Raḥmān also warned him to be cautious and not to incite discord."[43]

According to another narration, after ʿAbdul Raḥmān's decision and his allegiance to ʿUthmān, Imam ʿAlī ﷺ said: "It was deception, and what a hideous deception!"[44]

Balādhurī writes: "The members of the *Shūrā* pledged allegiance to ʿUthmān, but ʿAlī did not pledge his allegiance. So ʿAbdul Raḥmān addressed ʿAlī and said: 'Pledge allegiance, or I will strike your neck.'"[45]

After that, Imam ʿAlī ﷺ left the session, and the members of the *Shūrā* followed him and threatened him, saying: "Pledge allegiance, or we will fight you."[46]

---

[41] The Arabic text of this is as follows:

لا تجعل على نفسك سبيلًا.

[42] The Arabic text of this is as follows:

ما رأيت مثل ما أوتي إلى أهل هذا البيت بعد نبيّهم.

[43] *Tārīkh al-Rusul wa al-Mulūk,* Vol. 4, Pg. 233; *Tārīkh al-Madina,* Vol. 3, Pg. 930.

[44] *Tārīkh al-Rusul wa al-Mulūk,* Vol. 4, Pg. 239; *Tārīkh al-Islam,* Vol. 3, Pg. 306; *Tajārib al-Umam,* Vol. 1, Pg. 421; *Ansāb al-Ashrāf,* Vol. 5, Pg. 508. The Arabic text of this is as follows:

خدعة وأيّما خدعة.

[45] The Arabic text of this is as follows:

بايع وإلّا ضربت عنقك.

[46] The Arabic text of this is as follows:

In response to these threats, Imam ʿAlī ﷺ returned and pledged allegiance to ʿUthmān.[47]

Imam ʿAlī's ﷺ Account of the Shūrā

In regard to the *Shūrā*, Imam ʿAlī ﷺ said the following: "(This situation continued) until he (the second caliph) followed his own path, and at that time (on the verge of his demise), he placed the caliphate in a council *(Shūrā)* through consultation, in which, according to his perception, I was also one of them."[48]

He then adds: "By Allah, when did any doubt arise regarding my superiority over the first (Abū Bakr) to the extent that they would consider me equal to this council *(Shūrā* members)?"[49]

He continues by recounting his participation and entry into the *Shūrā*, saying: "But I (for the sake of Islamic interests) accompanied them and joined the *Shūrā*. When they descended, I descended, and when they flew, I flew."[50]

Imam ʿAlī ﷺ then confidentially revealed the outcome of the *Shūrā* by saying: "One of them harboured resentment against me, while the other prioritized his kinship, among other reasons that I

بايع وإلّا جاهدناك.

[47] *Ansāb al-Ashrāf*, Vol. 5, Pg. 508.

[48] The Arabic text of this is as follows:

حتّى إذا مضى لسبيله جعلها في جماعة زعم أني أحدهم.

[49] The Arabic text of this is as follows:

فَيَا لَلّٰهِ لَهُمْ وَلِلشُّورَى مَتَى اعْتَرَضَ الرَّيْبُ فِيَّ مَعَ الْأَوَّلِ مِنْهُمْ حَتَّى صِرْتُ أُقْرَنُ بِهَذِهِ النَّظَائِرِ.

[50] The Arabic text of this is as follows:

لٰكني أسفقت إذ أسفّوا وطرت إذا طاورا.

prefer not to mention."[51]

Some people said that the person who harboured resentment against ʿAlī ؑ was Ṭalḥa, but others believe that Ṭalḥa was not present in that gathering, and it was Saʿd ibn Abī Waqqāṣ who was meant.[52] As for the person who inclined towards ʿUthmān due to their kinship, it was ʿAbdul Raḥmān ibn ʿAwf, because as mentioned earlier, ʿAbdul Raḥmān was married to ʿUthmān's sister, Umm Kulthūm.

The phrase "مع هن هن" is an allusion to unpleasant matters that cannot be explicitly mentioned,[53] or it may refer to the motive behind ʿAbdul Raḥmān's vote. It is said that Imam ʿAlī ؑ had told him that his vote for ʿUthmān was to ensure that ʿUthmān would entrust the caliphate to him after his passing away.

Prioritizing the Interests of the Muslims

Imam ʿAlī ؑ did not attain the caliphate in the incident of the six-member *Shūrā* and ended up having to pledge allegiance to ʿUthmān after expressing his objections. However, it was not because he considered ʿUthmān worthy of that position, but rather Imam ʿAlī ؑ once again chose the path of cooperation to prevent turmoil and avoid internal conflicts, like what happened after the death of Prophet Muḥammad ﷺ.

In Sermon 74 of *Nahj al-Balāgha,* Imam ʿAlī ؑ reflects on this matter very well. The account and significance of this sermon is as follows.

Ibn Abī al-Ḥadīd al-Muʿtazilī writes: "After the pledge of

---

[51] *Nahj al-Balāgha,* Sermon 3. The Arabic text of this is as follows:

فَصَغَا رَجُلٌ مِنْهُمْ لِضِغْنِهِ وَمَالَ الْآخَرُ لِصِهْرِهِ مَعَ هَنٍ وَهَنٍ.

[52] *Sharḥ Nahj al-Balāgha,* Vol. 1, Pg. 189.

[53] Ibid., Pg. 184.

allegiance of ʿAbdul Raḥmān ibn ʿAwf to ʿUthmān, ʿAlī refrained from pledging allegiance and said: 'I swear by Allah, is there anyone among you who, on the day when the Messenger of Allah established the brotherhood among the Muslims, has a covenant of brotherhood with him as I did?' They all replied: 'No.' Then he asked: 'Is there anyone among you other than me whom the Prophet said about: 'Of whomsoever I am the Master *(Mawla)*, ʿAlī is also his Master *(Mawla)*?'[54] They replied: 'No.'

He continued: 'Is there anyone among you who, according to the Prophet's words: 'You are to me like (the status of) Hārūn to Mūsā, except that there is no Prophet after me?'[55] They all replied: 'No.'

He further questioned: 'Is there anyone among you who was entrusted with conveying the verse of *barāʾah* (disavowal), and the Prophet of Allah said about him: 'This verse should not be conveyed except by me or a man from me?'' They all replied: 'No.'

ʿAlī continued: 'Do you know that the companions of the Prophet fled from the battlefield multiple times, but I never fled?' They answered: 'Yes.'

Then he asked: 'Which of us is closest to the Prophet in kinship?' They replied: 'It is you.'

At this point, ʿAbdul Raḥmān ibn ʿAwf interrupted ʿAlī and said: 'O ʿAlī, people were not satisfied with anyone other than ʿUthmān, so do not trouble yourself or put yourself in danger (of the sword).'

Afterward, ʿAbdul Raḥmān turned to the group of fifty people, led by Abū Ṭalḥa al-Anṣārī, and said: 'O Abū Ṭalḥa, what instructions did ʿUmar give you?' He replied: 'He instructed me to kill anyone

---

[54] The Arabic text of this is as follows:

مَنْ كُنْتُ مَوْلَاهُ فَهٰذَا مَوْلَاهُ.

[55] The Arabic text of this is as follows:

أَنْتَ مِنِّي بِمَنْزِلَةِ هَارُونَ مِنْ مُوسَى إِلَّا أَنَّهُ لَا نَبِيَّ بَعْدِي.

who causes discord among the Muslims.'

'Abdul Raḥmān then turned to 'Alī and said: 'Now, give your allegiance, or else we will execute 'Umar's command regarding you.'

'Alī responded: 'You know that I am the most rightful for the caliphate, but you hindered me because you do not see your own interests aligned with mine. However, I swear by Allah that I will remain silent so long as the Muslims are in harmony, and injustice is only inflicted upon me. Through this path, I will seek rewards and favours from Allah and remain indifferent to the material wealth and decorations that you all compete for.' Then 'Alī stretched out his hand and pledged his allegiance."[56]

Imam 'Alī was not willing to use any means necessary to attain the caliphate, even though it was his rightful position. He endured great injustices upon himself to prevent further discord among the Muslims, and to avoid the complete destruction of Islam. However, on the other hand, he reaffirmed his rightful claim in history by refusing to give his initial allegiance and protested with the members of the *Shūrā* and those who took away his rights after the death of the Prophet. On the other hand, he also exposed the violence of some of the companions and their animosity towards him for future generations to be informed about.

---

[56] *Sharḥ Nahj al-Balāgha*, Commentary of Sermon 74, Vol. 6, Pp. 167-168. During the entire period of the caliphate of 'Uthmān, Imam 'Alī continuously reminded him when he saw him acting against the religious rulings of Islam; and Imam 'Alī also spoke out when people such as Abū Dharr and Ajḥāf al-'Ummāl were exiled from Madina – while at the same time, trying to walk the fine line to ensure that the unity of the Muslims was not destroyed. The Arabic text of this is as follows:

لَقَدْ عَلِمْتُمْ أَنِّي أَحَقُّ النَّاسِ بِهَا مِنْ غَيْرِي وَ وَاللهِ لَأُسْلِمَنَّ مَا سَلِمَتْ أُمُورُ الْمُسْلِمِينَ وَلَمْ يَكُنْ فِيهَا جَوْرٌ إِلَّا عَلَيَّ خَاصَّةً الْتِمَاسًا لِأَجْرِ ذٰلِكَ وَفَضْلِهِ وَزُهْدًا فِيمَا تَنَافَسْتُمُوهُ مِنْ زُخْرُفِهِ وَزِبْرِجِه.

Ṭalḥa's Position

According to Ṭabarī and Ibn Athīr, on the day when allegiance was given to 'Uthmān, Ṭalḥa entered Madina. He was told to pledge allegiance to 'Uthmān, to which he asked: "Are all the people of Quraysh satisfied?"

They replied: "Yes."

Then Ṭalḥa went to 'Uthmān and asked him: "Have the people pledged their allegiance to you?"

'Uthmān answered: "Yes."

So Ṭalḥa said: "Then I will not turn away from what the people have chosen."

After that, he pledged allegiance to 'Uthmān.[57]

However, Balādhurī writes that Ṭalḥa had gone to the Sarat[58] regions to attend to his properties, and after 'Umar's injury, a messenger was quickly sent to inform him about the situation. Ṭalḥa hurried and came back to Madina, but by the time he arrived, the people had already pledged allegiance to 'Uthmān. Upon seeing this, Ṭalḥa stayed at home and did not come out, saying: "You should not have chosen on my behalf, you rushed without my presence and made decisions on your own, while I was attending to my own businesses."[59]

Upon learning about this incident, 'Abdul Raḥmān went to Ṭalḥa, acknowledged his position in Islam, and persuaded him to avoid

---

[57] *Tārīkh al-Rusul wa al-Mulūk*, Vol. 4, Pg. 234; *Al-Kāmil fī al-Tārīkh*, Vol. 3, Pg. 72.

[58] A place between Mecca and Yemen (See: *Al-Sīrah al-Nabawiyyah*, Vol. 4, Pg. 621); it is also said to be a place in the region of Ṭā'if (See: *Tāj al-'Urūs*, Vol. 7, Pg. 248 under the word *'ayr).*

[59] The Arabic text of this is as follows:

مثلي لا يفتأت عليه ولقد عجلتم وأنا على أمري.

creating divisions (and compelled him to pledge allegiance).[60]

Analysis and Examination

With an understanding of the history of the *Shūrā,* and the way it led to ʿUthmān's appointment; several notable points can be observed:

1. The second caliph, on his deathbed, expressed that if Sālim, the freed slave of Ḥudhayfah, were still alive, he would have chosen him for the caliphate. This is even though he and Abū Bakr explicitly stated on the Day of Saqīfah that the caliphate should come from the Quraysh and the close relatives of the Prophet ﷺ. That is why Saʿd ibn ʿUbādah was kept away from the caliphate at that time.[61] However, in this situation, ʿUmar desired that Sālim was alive so that he could unquestionably hand over the caliphate to him, even though historians and genealogists assert that Sālim was from the people of Fars.[62]
2. In addition, the virtues extolled about Abū ʿUbaydah ibn Jarrāḥ and Sālim in ʿUmar's statement were less significant than that of Imam ʿAlī ﷺ. Imam ʿAlī ﷺ possessed way greater virtues, but ʿUmar was not willing to acknowledge this right and present him with the caliphate.
3. Furthermore, if the criteria were past experiences and worthiness, then regardless of tribal affiliations, ʿAmmār ibn Yāsir was among the great fighters and early followers of

---

[60] *Ansāb al-Ashrāf,* Vol. 5, Pg. 505.

[61] *Tārīkh al-Rusul wa al-Mulūk,* Vol. 3, Pg. 221; *Ṣaḥīḥ Bukhārī,* Vol. 8, Pg. 27. For more information, refer to the Chapter on *The Legitimacy of the Event at Ṣaqīfah.*

[62] *Usd al-Ghābah fī Maʿrifah al-Ṣaḥābah,* Vol. 2, Pg. 155; *Al-Istīʿāb fī Maʿrifah al-Aṣḥāb,* Vol. 2, Pg. 567; *Al-Ṭabaqāt al-Kubrā,* Vol. 3, Pg. 62. For more information, refer to the Chapter on *The Legitimacy of the Event at Ṣaqīfah.*

Islam, and his parents were brutally tortured and among the first ones martyred for the sake of Islam. So why was he never mentioned?

It seems that the prominence of these two individuals (Abū 'Ubaydah ibn Jarrāḥ and Sālim), and their association with the caliph during the Event at Saqīfah incident is noteworthy.[63]

'Umar even considered Khālid ibn al-Walīd worthy of the caliphate, despite Khālid not being among the early followers of Islam. Khālid's involvement in the unjust killing of Mālik ibn Nuwayrah, and having sexual relations with his wife on the same night that her husband was murdered during the reign of Abū Bakr, had angered 'Umar to such an extent that he believed Khālid should be stoned to death; however, Abū Bakr did not agree with this.[64] Yet, after all of this, he regarded Khālid as deserving of the caliphate!

Although 'Umar believed that Imam 'Alī was worthy of the caliphate, and he believed that if Imam 'Alī were to become caliph, then he would have guided people to the truth, he still refrained from introducing Imam 'Alī for various reasons. At times, he used the excuse that he did not want to impose the caliphate on the people; while at other times, he cited Imam 'Alī's 'playful nature' as a reason for not nominating him.

If a person makes a favourable judgement, then one can say that since the second caliph had a strong and harsh temperament, he could not appreciate someone with a gentle and playful nature. However, Imam 'Alī was kind and affectionate towards Muslims and believers, but he was firm and resolute against aggressors and oppressors. This spirit was evident in Imam 'Alī during the time

---

[63] For more information, refer to the Chapter on *The Legitimacy of the Event at Ṣaqīfah*.

[64] *Al-Kāmil fī al-Tārīkh*, Vol. 2, Pg. 359 *Al-Bidāyah wa al-Nihāyah*, Pg. 323. *Tārīkh al-Rusul wa al-Mulūk*, Vol. 3, Pg. 280.

of the Prophet ﷺ, and throughout his five-year reign as the caliph after the death of ʿUthmān, as his character always embodied the principles outlined in the Quran.

Furthermore, the excuses for not imposing the caliphate on the people are not consistent for the following reasons:

1. ʿUmar himself imposed the caliphate of Abū Bakr on the people during the Saqīfah.
2. The masses were interested in Imam ʿAlī ؑ and welcomed his caliphate.

So, what was the basis for forming such a specific *Shūrā*?

Suppose it was based on the command of Allah ﷻ to consult in matters of action.[65] In that case, after consulting with the elders and the people, the second caliph could have introduced someone as the caliph, rather than entrusting it to a limited *Shūrā*.

In fact, the actions of the second caliph do not reflect the process of engaging in a consultation at all! Instead, it is the formation of an 'Appointment Committee' to appoint someone from among themselves a caliph – such that you kill the one who does not agree with the others – and differs drastically from the intended consultation process outlined in Islam.

On the other hand, such formations are neither based on public opinion, nor the consultation of knowledgeable leaders from among the community. Otherwise, the elders from the *Muhājirūn* and *Anṣār* should have been consulted, and the scope would not have been

---

[65] Quran, Sūrah al-Shūrā (42), Verse 38:

﴿...وَأَمْرُهُمْ شُورَىٰ بَيْنَهُمْ...﴾

"...and whose affairs are by consultation among themselves..."

Sūrah Āle ʿImrān (3), Verse 159:

﴿...وَشَاوِرْهُمْ فِي الْأَمْرِ...﴾

"...and take counsel with them in the affairs (of public concern)..."

limited to just six individuals who were chosen for biased reasons.

Moreover, the selection of some of these individuals seems to be influenced more by tribal and ethnic affiliations, rather than their worthiness. It appears that the second caliph chose individuals from influential Qurayshī tribes such as the Banū Hāshim, Banū Umayyah, and Banū Zuhra for this *Shūrā*. However, historical accounts also indicate that the second caliph himself pointed out certain flaws in some of the *Shūrā* members, which revealed their managerial weaknesses and lack of competence for leadership.

For example, regarding Zubayr, he said: "One day, you are a human, and another day, you are devilish."

He considered Saʿd ibn Abī Waqqāṣ as someone fond of fighting and not worthy of the caliphate.

Concerning ʿAbdul Raḥmān, he remarked that the caliphate should not reach a weak person like him.

He saw ʿUthmān as someone who favoured the Banū Umayyah over the people [which happened] and eventually lead to their oppression and triggered a widespread rebellion.

As for Ṭalḥa, he introduced him as someone under the influence of his wife!

The evidence of these statements exists in historical records, and we have mentioned most of them above.

In addition, the command of the caliph to hold all six individuals accountable, and the permission to kill the minority in case of disagreement or opposing the majority has no legitimate or religious basis.

In the case that the *Shūrā* members could not agree on the selection of a caliph, an alternative and suitable mechanism could have been envisaged instead of issuing an order to kill six companions of the Prophet ﷺ!

Furthermore, if some of the members did not agree with the chosen caliph and refused to pay allegiance, then why were they targeted for harm? Not pledging allegiance is different from openly opposing the caliphate.

During the caliphate of Imam ʿAlī ﷺ, individuals such as Saʿd ibn Abī Waqqāṣ, ʿAbdullāh ibn ʿUmar, Ḥasān ibn Thābit, Zayd ibn Thābit, and others did not pledge allegiance to him, however, Imam ʿAlī ﷺ respected their freedom of choice, and did not threaten or force them to do so.[66]

ʿUmar ibn al-Khaṭṭāb, while addressing the members of the *Shūrā*, told them: "You are the ones whom the Prophet was pleased with." However, when it came to Ṭalḥa, he said: "You are the one whom the Prophet was dissatisfied with because of the statement you made about the *ḥijāb* verse, and he passed away while being displeased with you." It is obvious that his initial statement contradicted his latter statement; and if the Prophet ﷺ was displeased with one of them, then why were they placed on the deciding committee for the next caliph?

The decision to grant ʿAbdul Raḥmān ibn ʿAwf a veto in case of a tie also raises further questions. Despite lacking the same level of experience, virtues, and worthiness as Imam ʿAlī ﷺ, why was he given this privilege? If past records and contributions to *jihād,* and so many other distinguishing factors determine such rights, then Imam ʿAlī ﷺ surpasses him in all these aspects.

The way the members of this *Shūrā* were chosen raises concerns about Imam ʿAlī's ﷺ exclusion from the caliphate as well, just as the Imam ﷺ himself acknowledged.

The presence of Saʿd ibn Abī Waqqāṣ and ʿAbdul Raḥmān ibn ʿAwf who both belonged to the same tribe and were allies with each other made Imam ʿAlī's ﷺ exclusion predictable. Furthermore, the

[66] *Tārīkh al-Rusul wa al-Mulūk*, Vol. 4, Pp. 429-430. *Al-Kāmil fī al-Tārīkh*, Vol. 3, Pg. 191.

Prophet ﷺ had established a bond of brotherhood[67] between 'Uthmān and 'Abdul Raḥmān, and 'Abdul Raḥmān was 'Uthmān's brother-in-law.

Ṭalḥa, who also hailed from the Banū Taym tribe, the same tribe as the first caliph, was additionally connected to Abū Bakr through marriage. His wife, Umm Kulthūm, was Abū Bakr's daughter, and 'Āyesha's sister.[68] Given the tribal dynamics that influenced the events at Saqīfah, it was evident that Ṭalḥa would not have leaned towards Imam 'Alī ؑ in this *Shūrā*. Therefore, only Zubayr, whose mother, Ṣafīyyah, was from the Banū Hāshim and Imam 'Alī's ؑ cousin, would have potentially shown some inclinations towards the Imam ؑ.

In addition to all of this, 'Abbās, the uncle of the Prophet ﷺ, had urged Imam 'Alī ؑ not to participate in the *Shūrā* knowing that they had no intention of granting him the caliphate.

Thus, the arrangement of these individuals was deliberately orchestrated by 'Umar ibn al-Khaṭṭāb to pave the way for 'Uthmān ibn al-'Affān to assume the role of the caliph. What is more interesting is that the second caliph himself foresaw the caliphate of 'Uthmān.

According to Ibn Sa'd's account in his book, *Al-Ṭabaqāt*, Sa'īd ibn 'Āṣ narrates: "During the caliphate of 'Umar, I approached him and requested an increase in the land of my house. The next day, 'Umar visited my house, drew a line with his foot, and added some land to my property. I said: 'O Commander of the Faithful, please grant me some more land as I have a big family.' He replied: 'For now, this amount is sufficient for you, but I confide in you that soon after me, someone will come to power who will honour your kinship and will

---

[67] *Mustadrak 'alā al-Ṣaḥīḥḥayn*, Vol. 13, Pg. 14; *Al-Ṭabaqāt al-Kubrā*, Vol. 3, Pg. 174.
[68] *Al-Iṣābah*, Vol. 3, Pg. 432; *Al-Muntaẓam*, Vol. 5, Pg. 111.

fulfill your desires.'[69]

Saʿīd continued: 'I patiently waited during ʿUmar's reign until ʿUthmān was chosen by the *Shūrā* and became the caliph. He fulfilled my kinship and showed me great kindness, fulfilling my requests.'

ʿUthmān's kindness to Saʿīd ibn ʿĀṣ was evident when he appointed him as the governor of Kufa after the removal of Walīd ibn ʿUqbah."[70]

It is no wonder that the second caliph anticipated the rise of ʿUthmān and tactically secured his position as the next caliph. Numerous narrations indicate that Abū Bakr called upon ʿUthmān during his illness to draft a testament regarding the caliphate, and he told ʿUthmān: "Write: 'In the Name of Allah, the All-Beneficent, the All-Merciful. This is a testament that Abū Bakr is making to the Muslims.'"

Abū Bakr lost consciousness at that point, so ʿUthmān wrote these words by himself: "I have appointed ʿUmar ibn al-Khaṭṭāb as your caliph, and I could not have chosen anyone better for you."[71]

After ʿUthmān wrote these statements, Abū Bakr regained consciousness and said: "Read (meaning tell me what you have written)," so he read what he had written. Abū Bakr then said: "I imagine that you were hasty (in writing the caliphate in ʿUmar's name) because you feared that if I died, then people would become divided." ʿUthmān replied: "Yes, that is correct." Then Abū Bakr

---

[69] The Arabic text of this is as follows:

سيلي الأمر بعدي من يصل رحمك ويقضي حاجتك.

[70] *Al-Ṭabaqāt al-Kubrā*, Vol. 5, Pg. 23 (summarized).

[71] The Arabic text of this is as follows:

أما بعد فإني قد استخلفت عليكم عمر بن الخطاب ولم آلكم خيراً.

prayed for him.[72]

While the second caliph refrained from explicitly mentioning 'Uthmān's name to avoid accusations of favouritism, he compensated for this by demonstrating his favour and kindness towards 'Uthmān, in the 23rd year after Hijrah, where he put into action his understanding of the verse: "Is the requital of goodness anything but goodness?"[73]

Thus, despite his Divinely inspired knowledge that the caliphate would not come to him, Imam 'Alī ﷺ chose to participate in this *Shūrā*.

This decision can be attributed to two key factors.

Firstly: He considered himself deserving of the leadership and caliphate of the Muslim nation. Therefore, he deemed it necessary to attend the gathering to assert his rightful position through logical arguments. Failure to participate could have led to speculations that he did not see himself worthy of the position and hence abstained from joining.

Since Imam 'Alī ﷺ did attend, had they appointed him as the caliph, then it would have been evident that a person like him, who believed himself more deserving of the succession of the Prophet ﷺ, should have been entrusted with leadership from the very moment that the Prophet ﷺ departed from this world.

However, he had been kept away from his rightful position for so many years, thus, he seized this opportunity to strive for the exalted position of leading the people so that he could make things better for the nation. His efforts and participation affirmed his legitimacy for

---

[72] *Tārīkh al-Rusul wa al-Mulūk*, Vol. 3, Pg. 439; *Al-Kāmil fī al-Tārīkh*, Vol. 2, Pg. 425; *Ansāb al-Ashrāf*, Vol. 10, Pp. 88-89; *Tārīkh Islām*, Vol. 3, Pg. 117; *Al-Ṭabaqāt al-Kubrā*, Vol. 3, Pg. 149; *Kanz al-'Ummāl*, Vol. 5, Pg. 676.

[73] Quran, Sūrah al-Raḥmān (55), Verse 60:

﴿هَلْ جَزَآءُ ٱلْإِحْسَـٰنِ إِلَّا ٱلْإِحْسَـٰنُ ۝٦٠﴾

that position, and he exposed the tactics and schemes of those selected members of that *Shūrā* who aimed to deprive him of his rightful position once again.

This significant point deserves recognition in history, and the judgement of future generations.

Secondly: The presence of Imam ʿAlī ؈ in that gathering can be attributed to his strong belief in the significance of unity and cohesion within the Muslim community.

He recognized that the well-being of Islam, the unity of Muslims, and the integration of society were crucial elements. To prevent division and discord, and to actively contribute to the unity of the Muslim nation, he chose not to isolate himself or adopt an oppositional or confrontational stance. Instead, he decided to participate in the *Shūrā*, demonstrating his commitment to fostering unity and working towards the collective welfare of the Muslim community.

An intriguing aspect to consider is the divergence among the people in their support of ʿUthmān and Imam ʿAlī ؈. For example, we came across individuals such as ʿAmmār ibn Yāsir and Miqdād,[74] who were devoted believers, esteemed companions of Prophet Muḥammad ﷺ, and valiant participants in the Battle of Badr, choosing to align themselves with Imam ʿAlī ؈.

Conversely, there were those who opposed the Prophet ﷺ until the very end, coerced and forced into accepting Islam, and even involved in shedding the blood of the companions of the Prophet ﷺ. Surprisingly, these individuals became firm supporters of ʿUthmān.

This group, estranged from social positions and harbouring enmity towards Islam and the Prophet ﷺ, found something in Imam ʿAlī ؈ that they opposed, while recognizing certain features in

---

[74] This is Miqdād ibn ʿAmrū al-Baḥrānī – better known as Miqdād ibn al-Aswad. (Tr.)

'Uthmān that compelled them to rally behind him.

As time unfolded, history shed light on these matters, revealing the biases and ulterior motives of the Quraysh aristocracy during 'Uthmān's caliphate, and their opposition and conflicts with Imam 'Alī during his caliphate.

Renowned scholar, Shaykh Muḥammad 'Abduh (d. 1905), a prominent figure among the Ahlul Sunnah and an eminent commentator of *Nahj al-Balāgha*, writes in his explanation of Imam 'Alī's Sermon 74 in *Nahj al-Balāgha* as follows: "The allegiance to 'Uthmān became a battleground between the tribal government of Quraysh who had launched the most severe wars against Islam; and the masses of people who had embraced Islam with enthusiasm and fervour. Those who prepared the ground for 'Uthmān's caliphate, and those who supported his allegiance were individuals who perceived the caliphate merely as a rulership for the Quraysh and nothing more. It never crossed their calculations that the caliph should be a leader of Islam who supports the oppressed and defends the deprived."

He then adds: "The discussions which took place among the people outside the house where the gathering for determining the caliph was held clearly testify that the masses were in favour of 'Alī, while only this group of Quraysh, who had previously fought against the Prophet, were against 'Alī."

In a concise statement, he writes: "With the same bias and animosity that they fought Muḥammad, they fought 'Alī. They opposed and struggled against him with the same motives of 'fanaticism' and 'hatred.'"[75]

Shaykh Muḥammad 'Abduh then narrates those conversations

---

[75] The Arabic text of this is as follows:

وبنفس العصبية والحقد اللّذين حاربوا بهما محمدًا حاربوا بهما عليًّا.

(which we mentioned earlier from Ṭabarī) and concludes: "However, in the end, ʿAbdul Raḥmān of the Quraysh pledged allegiance to ʿUthmān, and when ʿAmmār expressed his dissatisfaction and left, the entire Quraysh community insulted and drove him away, showcasing their collective rejection of his viewpoint."[76]

The cunningness of ʿAbdul Raḥmān ibn ʿAwf's scheme to deprive Imam ʿAlī ☙ of the caliphate and transfer it to ʿUthmān cannot be underestimated. To absolve himself and demonstrate his supposed impartiality to the people, he summoned Imam ʿAlī ☙ and proposed a conditional allegiance that he knew Imam ʿAlī ☙ would not accept.

This allegiance required adherence to the practices of the previous two caliphs, Abū Bakr and ʿUmar, while also following the teachings of the Book of Allah and the traditions of the Prophet ﷺ. ʿAbdul Raḥmān was very aware that Imam ʿAlī ☙ often criticized the actions of the previous caliphs during their reign. Moreover, he himself acknowledged that Imam ʿAlī ☙ was appointed by the Prophet ﷺ, and considered him highly virtuous and knowledgeable, to the extent that he was the ultimate authority in matters of scholarship and problem-solving for the previous caliphs. According to the esteemed *Sunnah* left by Prophet Muḥammad ﷺ, it was impossible to find a more qualified and capable individual than Imam ʿAlī ☙ for the position.

ʿAbdul Raḥmān also knew that Imam ʿAlī ☙ was a man of truth and great integrity who would not resort to deception in his pursuit of the caliphate; meaning that ʿAlī ☙ would not pledge to follow the path of Abū Bakr and ʿUmar; and once in power, he would act in accordance with his own judgements that were based on justice and fairness.

Thus, ʿAbdul Raḥmān put the condition forward that the next caliph **must** follow the dictates of his predecessors, knowing very

---

[76] ʿAbduh, Muḥammad, *Sharḥ Nahj al-Balāgha*, Pg. 176.

well that he would receive a negative response from ʿAlī ﷺ. ʿAbdul Raḥmān then turned to ʿUthmān and presented him with the same conditions, anticipating a positive response. It was at this moment that Imam ʿAlī ﷺ openly denounced this plan as a deception.

In addition, two other noteworthy points should be mentioned:

Firstly: Despite the claims made by ʿUthmān that he would follow in the footsteps of Abū Bakr and ʿUmar, historical records reveal that he never truly did. One notable example was his favourable treatment of the Banū Umayyah, specifically Ibn Abīl Āṣ and his son Marwān. These individuals were previously banished by the Prophet ﷺ and were denied entry into Madina by Abū Bakr and ʿUmar. However, ʿUthmān not only allowed them to enter Madina, but he showered them with privileges and even appointed Marwān as his chief advisor.[77]

Additionally, ʿUthmān deviated from the established precedents by using the Public Treasury *(Baytul Māl)* for the personal benefits of his relatives, and to promote individuals from his own kin to positions of power.[78]

Secondly: Imam ʿAlī ﷺ believed that ʿAbdul Raḥmān pledged allegiance to ʿUthmān with the intention of ensuring his own succession after ʿUthmān's reign. Upon witnessing this, Imam ʿAlī ﷺ remarked: "Surely, Allah is involved in the affairs of every day."[79] This statement emphasizes the belief that Allah ﷻ will not allow individuals to achieve their desires without facing challenges and obstacles along the way.

---

[77] *Usd al-Ghābah fī Maʿrifah al-Ṣaḥābah*, Vol. 1, Pg. 515; *Ansāb al-Ashrāf*, Vol. 5, Pp. 513-513; *Tārīkh Yaʿqūbī*, Vol. 2, Pg. 164; *Sharḥ Nahj al-Balāgha*, Vol. 6, Pp. 148-150.

[78] *Ansāb al-Ashrāf*, Vol. 5, Pp. 541-542 and 580; *Sharḥ Nahj al-Balāgha*, Vol. 1, Pp. 198-199.

[79] *Tārīkh al-Rusul wa al-Mulūk*, Vol. 4, Pg. 233; *Al-Kāmil fī al-Tārīkh*, Vol. 3, Pg. 71.

It is interesting to note that after some time, a dispute arose between ʿAbdul Raḥmān and ʿUthmān.

Ibn ʿAbd Rabbih writes: "ʿUthmān appointed inappropriate (inexperienced) young individuals from his own family to govern the cities, and he granted them superiority over the esteemed companions. Objections were raised against ʿAbdul Raḥmān, stating that this outcome resulted from his decision. ʿAbdul Raḥmān replied: 'I did not expect it to turn out this way.' He then went to ʿUthmān, reproached him, and said: 'I entrusted the caliphate to you on the condition that you follow the practices of Abū Bakr and ʿUmar among us. However, you have opposed their practices, showed favouritism to your own family, and exerted control over the Muslims.'

ʿUthmān responded: 'ʿUmar severed ties with his relatives for the sake of Allah's governance, and I also show kindness to them for the sake of Allah (in order words, both actions are for the sake of Allah)!'

ʿAbdul Raḥmān became upset and said: 'I am making a covenant with Allah never to speak with you again.'

He indeed kept his word and did not speak to ʿUthmān until the time of his death. Even when he was ill, and ʿUthmān came to visit him, ʿAbdul Raḥmān turned his face towards the wall and did not speak to him."[80]

According to reports from Balādhurī, ʿAbdul Raḥmān left a will stating that ʿUthmān should not perform his funeral prayer after his death. Therefore, after ʿAbdul Raḥmān's death, Zubayr led the funeral prayer for him, while some say it was Saʿd ibn Abī Waqqāṣ who performed the prayer.[81]

Once again, we find from historical accounts that Imam ʿAlī ﷺ did not willingly, nor eagerly, pledge allegiance to the third caliph.

---

[80] *ʿAqd al-Farīd*, Vol. 4, Pg. 280; *Ansāb al-Ashrāf*, Vol. 5, Pp. 546-547.

[81] *Ansāb al-Ashrāf*, Vol. 5, Pg. 547.

Instead, his allegiance was coerced under the shadow of threats, and he had to accept it to maintain the unity of the Muslim community.

Thus, Imam ʿAlī ﷺ, who embodied the essence of the *Ḥadīth* of *Thaqalayn*, viewed ʿUthmān's caliphate as lacking legitimacy, as it was obtained through deceit and coercion. Therefore, one can conclude that the consequences of the *Shūrā* and the selection of ʿUthmān are significant aspects that warrant a thorough examination of Islam's historical narrative.

The first consensus regarding the second caliph's decision is considering the five members themselves equal to Imam ʿAlī ﷺ and deserving of assuming the caliphate. Subsequently, the remaining individuals from this group, known as the members of the *Shūrā* of six, gained prominence within the Islamic society.

During Imam ʿAlī's ﷺ caliphate, Muʿāwiyah ibn Abū Sufyān wrote a letter to Zubayr, urging him to come to Syria, where he and the people of Syria would pledge allegiance to him as the caliph.[82]

Some historical sources mention that Muʿāwiyah wrote to Zubayr, stating: "I have pledged allegiance to you, and after you, to Ṭalḥa. Therefore, do not let Iraq slip away."[83]

Once again, it is disheartening to witness how the *Shūrā* that led to ʿUthmān's selection further bolstered the influence of the Banū Umayyah. These individuals were once ardent adversaries of the Prophet ﷺ, yet their apparent conversion to Islam after the conquest of Mecca granted them this sudden power.

Marwān ibn al-Ḥakam assumed the role of ʿUthmān's chief advisor, and Muʿāwiyah's hold on Syria reached unprecedented

---

[82] *Ansāb al-Ashrāf*, Vol. 2, Pg. 257.

[83] *Al-Bada' wa al-Tārīkh*, Vol. 5, Pg. 211. Yaʿqūbī relates another letter which Muʿāwiyah wrote to Saʿd ibn Abīl Waqqās, in which, in addition to instigating him to revolt against Imam ʿAlī ﷺ, he also refers to Saʿd being present in the six-person consultation committee along with Ṭalḥa and Zubayr. (See *Tārīkh Yaʿqūbī*, Vol. 2, Pg. 187.)

heights.

Shockingly, individuals like ʿAbdullāh ibn ʿAmr and ʿAbdullāh ibn Abīl Sarḥ – who actively fought against Islam, and whom the Prophet ﷺ had declared permissible the shedding of their blood – were now appointed as governors of Muslim regions.

Even Walīd ibn ʿUqbah, who has been referred to in Verse 6 of Sūrah al-Ḥujurāt (49),[84] was now entrusted with a governorship position.

Meanwhile, esteemed companions such as Abū Dharr al-Ghifārī and his family were unjustly exiled, enduring harsh conditions that ultimately led to their death.[85] Distinguished figures like ʿAbdullāh ibn Masʿūd faced continuous harassment, insults, and even physical abuse.[86]

Despite having foreseen and knowing very well that ʿUthmān, as a caliph, would prioritize his own relatives' interests over the welfare of the people, the second caliph devised a scheme that eventually gave ʿUthmān a full hold on power and leadership.

The consequences of strengthening the Umayyad front due to the appointment of ʿUthmān as the third caliph were detrimental in the Battles of Jamal and Ṣiffīn, which ultimately weakened Imam ʿAlī's ﵇ Islamic government – when the people finally accepted him as

---

[84] The Arabic text of this is as follows:

﴿يَٰٓأَيُّهَا ٱلَّذِينَ ءَامَنُوٓاْ إِن جَآءَكُمۡ فَاسِقُۢ بِنَبَإٖ فَتَبَيَّنُوٓاْ أَن تُصِيبُواْ قَوۡمَۢا بِجَهَٰلَةٖ فَتُصۡبِحُواْ عَلَىٰ مَا فَعَلۡتُمۡ نَٰدِمِينَ ٦﴾

O you who believe! If some transgressor brings you news (that requires acting), verify it carefully (before you believe and act upon it), lest you harm a people in ignorance and then become regretful for what you have done.

[85] *Usd al-Ghābah fī Maʿrifah al-Ṣaḥābah*, Vol. 1, Pg. 357; *Ansāb al-Ashrāf*, Vol. 5, Pp. 542-544; *Tārīkh Yaʿqūbī*, Vol. 2, Pp. 172-173.

[86] *Ansāb al-Ashrāf*, Vol. 5, Pp. 524-525; *Tārīkh Yaʿqūbī*, Vol. 2, Pp. 171-172.

their fourth caliph. In the Battle of Jamal, figures like Marwān ibn al-Ḥakam, and other Umayyads played a significant role, and Muʿāwiyah instigated Ṭalḥa and Zubayr to join the conflict on the opposite side of Imam ʿAlī ﷺ.

Similarly, the Battle of Ṣiffīn arose from Muʿāwiyah's rebellion and his opposition to Imam ʿAlī ﷺ. It was during this battle that the Khawārij emerged; and thereafter, the Battle of Nahrawān took place; and the emergence of this group tragically culminated in the assassination of Imam ʿAlī ﷺ by Ibn Muljam, a believer and follower of the Khawārij movement.

The martyrdom of Imam ʿAlī ﷺ and the betrayal of some of the so-called 'companions' of Imam Ḥasan ﷺ paved the way for Muʿāwiyah's aggressive campaigns, allowing him to seize power and establish the Umayyad rule. Among the devastating consequences of this rule was the succession of Yazīd ibn Muʿāwiyah, which then led to the tragic events of Karbalāʾ, and the martyrdom of Imām Ḥusayn ﷺ, along with his loyal companions and family members. The injustices by this tyrant Yazīd continued, even after the heart wrenching day of ʿĀshūrāʾ, including the brutal attack on Madina and its inhabitants, along with the burning of the Kaʿbah in Mecca thereafter.

Let us trace the historical trajectory of Karbalāʾ and ʿĀshūrāʾ. In this case, we find that it ultimately leads back to the *Shūrā* of six, which resulted in ʿUthmān's caliphate and the subsequent reinforcement of the Umayyad front.

Even today, the profound impact of these events can be seen in the annals of Islamic history, as their effects continue to reverberate.

The *Shūrā* of six had immediate consequences: The rise of ʿUthmān as the caliph and his subsequent rule over the masses, along with the placement of many unworthy individuals from the Banū Umayyah in places of leadership.

However, the long-term effects of this decision continued to impact Islam and the Muslim community. These effects include the weakening of the Ahlul Bayt ﷺ faction; the rebellion against the Commander of the Faithful, Imam ʿAlī ﷺ; the ascendancy of the descendants of Abū Sufyān and the Marwānids who exerted control over the lives and wealth of the people; and the open disregard for Islamic values which continues until today in parts of the Muslim world.

During Muʿāwiyah's era, various detrimental developments occurred, such as the fabrication of *aḥādīth*,[87] numerous religious innovations, public slander against Imam ʿAlī ﷺ delivered from the pulpits, the turning away of the people from Imam Ḥasan ﷺ and the Ahlul Bayt ﷺ, the destructive cultural impact of their governance, the emergence of divisions and conflicts within the Muslim community, and the proliferation of different sects.

These enduring consequences, and so many more, were the direct result of the *Shūrā* of six; and the burden of that ill-advised decision of the second caliph continues to weigh heavily on the Muslim nation throughout the generations. A thorough examination of these consequences warrants the authorship of an independent book.

In conclusion, we would like to invoke the words of Ibn Abī al-Ḥadīd al-Muʿtazilī, who aptly stated the following regarding the *Shūrā* of six: "Indeed, it is the root cause of every discord that has transpired and will persist until the end of time; and it is the underlying reason for every turmoil that has unfolded and will emerge until the culmination of this world. That cause can be attributed to none other than the *Shūrā* itself."[88]

---

[87] To understand more about the role of Muʿāwiyah in the forgery of *aḥādīth* and his attempts to cover the merits of the Ahlul Bayt ﷺ refer to the book, *Sharḥ Nahj al-Balāgha*, Vol. 4, Pg. 73 and Vol. 11, Pp. 44-46.

[88] *Sharḥ Nahj al-Balāgha*, Vol. 11, Pg. 11. The Arabic text of this is as follows:

Conclusion

In this discussion, we delved into the topic of the *Shūrā* of six which the second caliph, ʿUmar ibn al-Khaṭṭāb, established with the purpose of selecting the next caliph. This matter raises concerns since the actions of the second caliph deviated from the established norms. They were **not** in line with the practices of Prophet Muḥammad ﷺ, nor the precedents set by the first caliph. Moreover, it completely contradicted the concept of consultation in Islam and the Prophet's ﷺ practices, as that would have required the second caliph to explicitly nominate someone as the next caliph after consulting with prominent figures in the community.

Another pertinent question is why ʿUmar ibn al-Khaṭṭāb was solely responsible for assigning the caliphate to a six-member council when other prominent individuals could have been included in the decision-making process.

On the other hand, according to reputable scholars from the Ahlul Sunnah, it becomes apparent that ʿUmar ibn al-Khaṭṭāb **purposefully** selected the *Shūrā* members in such a calculated way that it would deprive Imam ʿAlī ﵇ of his right to leadership, ensuring that the caliphate would pass on to ʿUthmān. Not only did ʿAbbās, the uncle of Prophet Muḥammad ﷺ, and Imam ʿAlī ﵇ themselves foresee this outcome, but ʿUmar even had already previously conveyed this news to Saʿīd ibn ʿĀṣ!

By devising such a plan, ʿUmar ibn al-Khaṭṭāb rewarded ʿUthmān's 'loyalty,' and seemingly absolved himself from accusations of bias against himself.

Another question that emerges is the religious justification behind ʿUmar ibn al-Khaṭṭāb's command to murder all six individuals if they failed to determine the next caliph within three

---

فإن ذلك كان سبب كلّ فتنة وقعت وتقع إلى أن تنقضي الدنيا.

days, as well as the killing of the dissenting minority. We believe that such a command originated from the second caliph's volatile temperament that he consistently demonstrated during his reign, and it lacked rational or religious basis.

The prominence given to ʿAbdul Raḥmān's vote over other opinions in the case of a tie, and the ambiguity surrounding this matter raises further concerns, suggesting that it might have been a strategy to fortify the ʿUthmānic faction.

ʿAbdul Raḥmān's policy and maneuvering to deprive Imam ʿAlī ؑ of his right, and the favouring of ʿUthmān completed the plan of the second caliph. He imposed a condition upon Imam ʿAlī ؑ to pledge a specific allegiance that he knew the Imam ؑ would not accept due to his integrity and upholding of the truth. This is because Imam ʿAlī ؑ was not only the most knowledgeable among them, and the best versed in the Book of Allah ﷻ and the traditions of the Prophet ﷺ, but he also criticized the conduct of the two previous caliphs whenever they went against the rulings of Islam.

Thus, he could not accept the condition of following their path. ʿAbdul Raḥmān knew that Imam ʿAlī ؑ stood firmly on the principles and values of the truth and was unwilling to make false promises that he would not uphold, like many worldly politicians do, to attain the caliphate. He also understood that Imam ʿAlī ؑ would not deviate from his course after attaining power. Thus, ʿAbdul Raḥmān employed a shrewd strategy that would prevent Imam ʿAlī ؑ from attaining the caliphate.

Moreover, our discussion also addressed the issue of Imam ʿAlī's ؑ participation in the *Shūrā*. It was highlighted that the first Imam ؑ, recognizing his worthiness for the position, deemed it necessary to attend the session and present his arguments to assert his legitimacy. Additionally, another motive for his involvement in the *Shūrā* was to contribute to the unity of the Muslim community.

In another section, we scrutinized the characteristics of the supporters of ʿUthmān and Imam ʿAlī ﷷ.

The majority of ʿUthmān's supporters hailed from the Quraysh and the aristocracy. They were individuals who had previously harboured animosity towards the Prophet ﷺ and Islam, embracing the faith only out of fear or personal interests. They viewed the caliphate as a means of governance and authority, rather than a platform for promoting religion, establishing truth and justice, and spreading the teachings of the Quran.

Conversely, Imam ʿAlī's ﷷ supporters were individuals who had endured great sufferings and severe oppression and were deeply rooted in the principles of Islam. They saw the caliphate as an opportunity to serve the marginalized people and advance the cause of the Almighty Creator.

In conclusion, one of the significant consequences of the *Shūrā* of six was the consolidation of the Umayyad front during ʿUthmān's reign. This decision's short-term and long-term effects were examined, unveiling the subsequent unrest in the Islamic world which originated from that era.

The Islamic nation still bears the scars of that ill-advised *Shūrā* and its misguided selection, as well as the dire consequences of the initial oppression that took place in the history of Islam, namely the Event at Saqīfah.

Bibliography

The Noble Quran.

ʿAbduh, Shaykh Muḥammad, *Sharḥ Nahj al-Balāgha* (Maktab al-Iʿlāmī al-Islāmī, 1st Edition, 1411 AH).

ʿAbdul Barr, Abū ʿUmar Yūsuf ibn ʿAbdullāh ibn Muḥammad ibn, *Al-Istīʿāb fī Maʿrifah al-Aṣḥāb* (Beirut: Dār al-Jīl, 1st Edition, 1412 AH - Edited by ʿAlī Muḥammad al-Bajawī).

ʿAdī, ʿAbdullāh ibn, *Al-Kāmil* (Beirut: Dār al-Fikr, 3rd Edition - Edited by Yaḥyā Muktadar Ghazawī).

Andalūsī, Ibn ʿAbd Rabbih, *Al-ʿIqd al-Farīd* (Beirut: Dār al-Kutub al-Arabi, 1403 AH).

ʿAsqalānī, Aḥmad ibn Nūrud Dīn ʿAlī ibn Muḥammad ibn Ḥajr al-, *Al-Iṣābah fī Tamyīz al-Ṣahābah* (Beirut: Dār al-Kutub al-ʿIlmīyyah, 1415 AH - Edited by ʿĀdil Aḥmad ʿAbdul Mawjūd).

Athīr, ʿIzz al-Dīn Ibn al-, *Al-Kāmil fī al-Tārīkh* (Beirut: Dār al-Ṣadr, 1385 AH).

Baghawī, Al-Ḥusayn ibn Masʿūd al-, *Maʿālim al-Tanzīl* (Beirut: Dār Iḥyāʾ al-Turāth al-Arabi, 1420 AH).

Balādhurī, Aḥmad ibn Yaḥyā ibn Jābir al-, *Ansāb al-Ashrāf* (Beirut: Dār al-Fikr, 1417 AH - Researched by Suhail Zukkār).

Bukhārī, Muḥammad ibn Ismāʾīl al-, *Ṣaḥīḥ al-Bukhārī* (Beirut: Dār al-Jīl).

Dhahabī, Muḥammad ibn Aḥmad ibn ʿUthmān al-, *Mizān al-Iʿtidāl* (Beirut: Dār al-Maʿrifah - Edited by ʿAlī Muḥammad al-Bajawī).

Dhahabī, Shams al-Dīn al-, *Tārīkh al-Islām* (Beirut: Dār al-Kutub al-Arabi, 2nd Edition - Edited by ʿUmar ʿAbdul Salām).

Dimashqī, Abūl Fiḍāʾ ʿImād al-Dīn Ismāʾīl ibn ʿUmar ibn Kathīr al-Qurayshī al-, *Al-Bidāyah wa al-Nihāyah* (Beirut: Dār al-Fikr, 1st

Edition, 1407 AH).

Dimashqī, Ibn Kathīr al-, *Al-Sīrah al-Nabawiyyah,* also known as *Sīrah Ibn Kathīr* (Beirut: Dār al-Maʿrifah - Edited by Muṣṭafā ʿAbdul Waḥīd).

Dimashqī, Ibn Kathīr al-, *Tafsīr Ibn Kathīr (Tafsīr al-Quran al-ʿAẓīm)* (Beirut: Dār al-Kutub al-ʿIlmīyyah, 1419 AH).

Dīnawarī, Abū Muḥammad ʿAbdullāh ibn Muslim ibn Qutayba al-, *Al-Imāmah wa al-Siyāsah* (Beirut: Dār al-Aḍwā, 1410 AH - Edited by ʿAlī Shiri).

Hindī, ʿAla al-Din ʿAlī ibn ʿAbdul Malik Husām al-Dīn al-Muttaqī al-, *Kanz al-ʿUmmāl* (Beirut: Muʾassasah al-Risālah, 1409 AH).

Ibn ʿAsākir, *Tārīkh Dimashq* (Beirut: 1415 AH).

Ibn Duraid, *Al-Istiqāq* (Baghdad: Maktabat al-Muthannā, 1399 AH).

Jawzī, ʿAbdul Raḥmān ibn ʿAlī ibn Muḥammad Abūl Farash ibn al-, *Al-Muntazam fi Tārīkh al-Rusul wa al-Mulūk* (Beirut: Dār al-Kutub al-ʿIlmīyyah, 1st Edition, 1412 AH - Edited by Muḥammad ʿAbdul Qādir ʿAtā).

Jazarī, ʿIzz al-Dīn Ibn al-Athīr al-, *Usd al-Ghābah fī Maʿrifah al-Ṣaḥābah* (Beirut: Dār al-Fikr, 1409 AH).

Maqdīsī, Muṭahhar ibn Ṭāhir al-, *Al-Badʿ wa al-Tārīkh* (Port Said: Maktabat al-Thaqāfah al-Dīnīyah).

Muḥammad, Abū ʿAlī Aḥmad ibn, *Tajārib al-Umam* (Tehran: Nashr Soroush, 2nd Edition, 1379 AH - Edited by Abul Qāsim Imām).

Muʿtazilī, Ibn Abī al-Ḥadīd al-, *Sharḥ Nahj al-Balāgha* (Beirut: Dār Iḥyāʾ al-Kutub al-Arabiyya, n.d. - Edited by Muḥammad Abul Fadl Ibrāhīm).

Nahj al-Balāgha.

Naysābūrī, Abū ʿAbdillāh Ḥākim al-, *Al-Mustadrak ʿalā al-Ṣaḥīḥḥayn* (Beirut: Dār al-Maʿrifah, 1st Printing, 1406 AH).

Nimir, ʿUmar ibn Sabba, *Tārīkh al-Madina* (Beirut: Dār al-Fikr, 1410 AH - Edited by Fahīm Muḥammad Shaltūt).

Rāzī, Fakhr al-Dīn al-, *Mafātīḥ al-Ghayb (Tafsīr al-Kabīr)* (Beirut: Dār Iḥyāʾ al-Turāth al-Arabi, 1420 AH).

Saʿd, Muḥammad ibn, *Al-Ṭabaqāt al-Kubrā* (Beirut: Dār al-Kutub al-ʿIlmīyyah, 1st Edition, 1410 AH - Edited by Muḥammad ʿAbdul Qādir ʿAṭā).

Suyūṭī, Jalāl al-Dīn al-, *Al-Durr al-Manthūr* (Qum: Kitābkhāneh Āyatullāh Marʿashī, 1404 AH).

Ṭabarī, Muḥammad ibn Jarīr ibn al-, *Tārīkh al-Ṭabarī* (Beirut: Dār al-Turāth, 2nd Edition, 1387 AH - Edited by Muḥammad Abūl Fadl Ibrāhīm).

Yaʿqūb, Aḥmad ibn Abī, *Tārīkh al-Yaʿqūbī* (Beirut: Dār al-Ṣadr).

Zabīdī, Muḥammad Murtaḍā al-, *Tāj al-Arūs* (Beirut: Dār al-Fikr, 1414 AH).

Conclusion by the Publisher

The Last Word

The Muslim nation *(ummah)* today is afflicted by numerous "fires" – from devastating wars, famines, natural calamities, and political upheavals. Amidst these daunting challenges, some may question the relevance of delving into the past, dismissing history as an irrelevant pursuit. However, it is precisely during these turbulent times that understanding our roots becomes imperative, for it is in the crucible of our history that our collective identity was forged.

The 25 years following the passing away of Prophet Muḥammad ﷺ were a defining period for the nascent Muslim community in Madina. That era witnessed the succession of what was much later in history referred to as the "Rightly Guided Caliphs," the expansion of Islamic territories, and turmoil reared by certain individuals related to governance, jurisprudence, and the careful preservation of the teachings of the faith of al-Islam.

The decisions made and the precedents set during that formative stage of development continue to resonate profoundly within the Muslim world today. Only by understanding this foundational period can we truly comprehend the essence of our identity as Muslims and chart a path towards the future we aspire to build – one that recognizes the clear and blatant blunders made by people who had no religious, nor legal right to shape the direction of the Muslim community. This will facilitate the path to accepting the second of the two weighty things that Prophet Muḥammad ﷺ ordered all Muslims to follow – his Ahlul Bayt عليهم السلام – the selected, immaculate members of his family.

The Muslims today face numerous challenges – many, if not all of which are rooted in historical events and decisions made in the first two decades after the demise of the final Messenger of Allah ﷺ. To address these issues effectively, Muslims must engage in a critical examination of six pivotal episodes that were covered in this book:

1. The Event of the Pen and Paper.
2. The Legitimacy of the Event at Ṣaqīfah.

3. Fire in the House of Revelation.
4. An Analysis of the Life of ʿUmar ibn al-Khaṭṭāb.
5. The Marriage of Umm Kulthūm binte ʿAlī.
6. The Six-Person *Shūrā* Devised to Select a Caliph.

Understanding these events is crucial for comprehending the present predicament of the nation *(ummah)* and paving the way for a more unified and just future.

The Event of the Pen and Paper

The Event of the Pen and Paper occurred in the final days of the life of Prophet Muḥammad ﷺ when he requested writing materials to document his last will. The subsequent refusal and arguments among his companions illustrate a moment of profound disrespect towards the final Messenger ﷺ and disunity amongst the Muslim community. This incident is not merely a historical anecdote, but a critical reflection on the importance of leadership clarity and the catastrophic effects of dissent among key figures. The Prophet's ﷺ intention was to prevent future discord, yet the refusal to honour his request led to disputes that have echoed through Islamic history for centuries. Imagine where the 1.8 billion Muslims would be today had those "companions" of Prophet Muḥammad ﷺ heeded his request for a pen and paper to dictate invaluable advice that would safeguard the nation from falling into disarray and confusion.

The Legitimacy of the Event at Ṣaqīfah

The swift and secretive gathering at the Ṣaqīfah of Banū Sāʿida to appoint Abū Bakr as the first caliph is a cornerstone of Islamic political history. This event raises fundamental questions about legitimacy, representation, and the processes through which leaders are chosen. The exclusion of key figures, notably the Prophet's ﷺ family, from this decision-making process highlights the contentious nature of early Islamic governance. By critically examining the Event at Ṣaqīfah, Muslims can gain insight into the origins of political fragmentation within the nation *(ummah)*, and to what level some people will go to solidify their own strangle grip on power of the Muslim nation.

Fire in the House of Revelation

The attack on the house of Lady Fāṭima al-Zahrā' ﷺ, the beloved daughter of Prophet Muḥammad ﷺ, is one of the most tragic and controversial episodes in Islamic history. This event, involving prominent figures such as ʿUmar ibn al-Khaṭṭāb, represents a profound breach of the sanctity of the household of revelation. A candid exploration of this event is essential for addressing historical grievances and fostering reconciliation. Recognizing the gravity of this breach helps highlight the importance of respecting the family of Prophet Muḥammad ﷺ as more than just blood relations. Rather, they serve as clear reminders of the "red line" that Muslims of the past and present must never cross.

An Analysis of the Life of ʿUmar ibn al-Khaṭṭāb

ʿUmar ibn al-Khaṭṭāb's tenure as the second caliph was marked by what some may deem to be "significant achievements," and without a doubt, controversial decisions. His leadership saw the expansion of the Islamic empire and the implementation of administrative reforms. However, his policies and actions, particularly towards the family of the Prophet ﷺ, as well as notable companions, especially in matters of succession, have been subjects of intense debate. A balanced analysis of ʿUmar's life is crucial for understanding why Muslim communities are where they are today – with so many groups claiming Islam and presenting a face of Islam that is furthest from the true picture that the Quran and the lifestyle of Prophet Muḥammad ﷺ brought for humanity.

The Marriage of Umm Kulthūm binte ʿAlī to ʿUmar

The marriage of Umm Kulthūm, daughter of Imam ʿAlī عليه السلام and Lady Fāṭima al-Zahrāʾ عليها السلام, to ʿUmar ibn al-Khaṭṭāb is a topic fraught with differing accounts and interpretations. This union is often cited as evidence of political alliances between the Commander of the Faithful, Imam ʿAlī عليه السلام, and the second caliph, ʿUmar ibn al-Khaṭṭāb. The circumstances and significance of this marriage [if it even took place] provide important insights into the interplay of politics, social norms, and familial relations in early Islam. Understanding this event is crucial for appreciating the complex dynamics of early Islamic society which Imam ʿAlī عليه السلام fought so hard to maintain.

The Six-Person Shūrā of ʿUmar Devised to Select a Caliph

ʿUmar's formation of a six-person Council *(Shūrā)* to choose his successor reflects a twisted and warped attempt to balance power and prevent unilateral decisions. However, the resultant selection process, which led to the appointment of ʿUthmān, was marred by tension and clear signs of bias. This event illustrates the inherent evils of implementing a "democratic process" and overruling the Divine commandments of Allah ﷻ, and what can happen when familial alliances come head-to-head with religious piety.

Final Thoughts

In conclusion, these six historical episodes are not merely relics of the past but are foundational to understanding the current state of the Muslim nation *(ummah)*. Each event underscore's critical themes of leadership, legitimacy, unity, and justice that resonate deeply with contemporary challenges. By rigorously and unbiasedly studying these events, Muslims can gain a deeper understanding of their heritage, learn from past mistakes, and strive towards a more unified and just future.

By confronting these historical episodes with honesty and courage, Muslims can hope to overcome the challenges facing the world today. These events offer invaluable lessons that can guide contemporary discourse on governance, leadership, and community cohesion. The need for introspection and informed discourse has never been more urgent. Only through a comprehensive and honest examination of our history can we pave the way for a more united, just, and prosperous future for the Muslim nation.

We pray that this book, authored by one of the foremost authorities in the Shīʿa world, serves as a bridge amongst the various groups of Muslims to critically, and without any biases, study their true history, and recognize the wrongs done to the family of Prophet Muḥammad ﷺ.

Our Other Publications

Other Publications Available[1]

1. *A Land Most Goodly: The Story of Yemen in the Quran and in the Times of Prophet Muḥammad and Imam ʿAlī ibn Abī Ṭālib*, by Jaffer Ladak
2. *A Star Amongst the Stars: The Life and Times of the Great Companion: Jabir ibn Abdullah al-Ansari*, by Jaffer Ladak*
3. *Alif, Baa, Taa of Kerbala*, by Saleem Bhimji and Arifa Hudda
4. *Arbāʿīn of Imam Ḥusayn*, compiled and translated by Saleem Bhimji
5. *Daily Devotions*, compiled and translated by Saleem Bhimji*
6. *Deficient? A Review of Sermon 80 from Nahj al-Balāgha*, by Āyatullāh al-ʿUẓmā Shaykh Nāṣir Makārim Shīrāzī and translated by Saleem Bhimji
7. *Exegesis of the 29th Juz of the Quran a Translation of Tafsīr Nemunah*, by Āyatullāh al-ʿUẓmā Shaykh Nāṣir Makārim Shīrāzī and translated by Saleem Bhimji*
8. *Foundations of Islamic Unity* a translation of *Al-Fuṣūl al-Muhimmah fī Taʾlīf al-Ummah*, by ʿAbd al-Ḥusayn Sharaf al-Dīn al-Mūsawī al-ʿĀmilī and translated by Batool Ispahany*
9. *Fountain of Paradise: Fāṭima az-Zahrāʾ in the Noble Quran*, by Āyatullāh al-ʿUẓmā Shaykh Nāṣir Makārim Shīrāzī, compiled and translated by Saleem Bhimji*
10. *God and god of Science*, by Syed Hasan Raza Jafri*
11. *House of Sorrows*, by Shaykh ʿAbbās al-Qummī and translated by Aejaz Ali Turab Husayn Husayni*

---

[1] The following is a list of all the original writings and translations from the Islamic Publishing House. As many of these titles are out of stock, we are slowly re-releasing all our works via Print-on-Demand through various online services. You can find all the titles with a "*" after the name at **https://mybook.to/pH0x**. If you cannot find any of the above titles online, feel free to email us at **iph@iph.ca**.

12. *Iʿtikāf: The Spiritual Retreat – The Philosophy, Spiritual Mysteries and Practical Rulings*, compiled and translated by Saleem Bhimji*
13. *Inspirational Insights*, by Mohammed Khaku
14. *Islam and Religious Pluralism*, by Āyatullāh Murtaḍā Muṭahharī and translated by Sayyid Sulayman Ali Hasan
15. *Journey to Eternity – A Handbook of Supplications for the Soul*, compiled and translated by Saleem Bhimji and Arifa Hudda*
16. *Living The Quran Through The Living Quran: Sūrah al-Fātiḥa (1)*, by Shaykh Muḥsin Qarāʾatī, translated by Saleem Bhimji*
17. *Living The Quran Through The Living Quran: Sūrah Yāsīn (36)*, by Shaykh Muḥsin Qarāʾatī, translated by Saleem Bhimji*
18. *Living The Quran Through The Living Quran: Sūrah Qāf (50)*, by Shaykh Muḥsin Qarāʾatī, translated by Saleem Bhimji*
19. *Living The Quran Through The Living Quran: Sūrah al-Najm (53)*, by Shaykh Muḥsin Qarāʾatī, translated by Saleem Bhimji*
20. *Living The Quran Through The Living Quran: Sūrah al-Wāqiʿah (56)*, by Shaykh Muḥsin Qarāʾatī, translated by Saleem Bhimji*
21. *Living The Quran Through The Living Quran: Sūrah al-Mujādilah (58)*, by Shaykh Muḥsin Qarāʾatī, translated by Saleem Bhimji*
22. *Love and Hate for Allah's Sake*, by Mujtaba Saburi, translated by Saleem Bhimji*
23. *Love for the Family*, compiled and translated by Yasin T. Al-Jibouri, Saleem Bhimji, and others*
24. *Moral Management*, by Abbas Rahimi, translated by Saleem Bhimji*
25. *Morals of the Masumeen*, by Arifa Hudda
26. *Prayers of the Final Prophet – A Collection of Supplications of Prophet Muḥammad*, by ʿAllāmah Sayyid Muḥammad Ḥusayn Ṭabāʾṭabāʾī, translated by Tahir Ridha-Jaffer*
27. *Propaganda and Piety: The Umayyad Rewriting of Syria [From Historical Syria to Apocalyptic Syria]*, written by Shaykh Rasul Jafariyan, translated by Saleem Bhimji*

28. *Prospering Through a Cost of Living Crisis,* by Jaffer Ladak*
29. *Ramaḍān Reflections,* compiled by A Group of Muslim Scholars, translated by Saleem Bhimji*
30. *Ṣalāt al-Āyāt,* by Saleem Bhimji
31. *Ṣalāt al-Ghufaylah: Salvation through Patience & Perseverance,* written by Saleem Bhimji*
32. *Secrets of the Ḥajj,* by Āyatullāh al-ʿUẓmā Shaykh Ḥusayn Mazāherī, translated by Saleem Bhimji
33. *Shadows of Dissent,* by Āyatullāh Nāṣir Makārim Shīrāzī, translated by Saleem Bhimji and a Group of Translators
34. *Sunan an-Nabī,* by ʿAllāmah Sayyid Muḥammad Ḥusayn Ṭabāʾṭabāʾī, translated by Tahir Ridha-Jaffer
35. *Tears from Heaven's Flowers: An Anthology of English Poetry about the Ahlulbayt,* by Abrahim al-Zubeidi*
36. *The Day the Germs Caused Fitnah,* by Umm Maryam*
37. *The Firmest Armament: Commentary on Āyatul Kursī (The Verse of the Throne),* by Sayyid Nasrullah Burujerdi, translated by Saleem Bhimji*
38. *The Last Luminary and Ways to Delve into the Light,* by Sayyid Muḥammad Ridha Husayni Mutlaq, translated by Saleem Bhimji*
39. *The Muslim Legal Will Booklet,* by Saleem Bhimji*
40. *The Pure Life,* by Āyatullāh al-ʿUẓmā as-Sayyid Muḥammad Taqī al-Modarresī, translated by Jaffer Ladak with commentary by Dr. Zainali Panjwani and Jaffer Ladak*
41. *The Third Testimony: Imam ʿAlī in the Adhān,* compiled and translated by Saleem Bhimji*
42. *The Torch of Perpetual Guidance – A Brief Commentary on Ziyārat al-ʿĀshūrāʾ,* by ʿAbbās Azizi, translated by Saleem Bhimji
43. *The Tragedy of Kerbalāʾ,* as narrated by Imam ʿAlī ibn al-Ḥusayn al-Sajjād ◈, recorded by Shaykh al-Ṣadūq, translated by ʿAbdul Zahrāʾ ʿAbdul Ḥusayn*
44. *The Truth Revealed: Volume 1,* by Hamid bin Shabbir, translated

by Mir Baqir Alikhan, Syed Hamid Rizvi, and Kaniz Fatima Alikhan

45. *The Truth Revealed: Volume 2,* by Hamid bin Shabbir, translated by Mir Baqir Alikhan, Syed Hamid Rizvi, and Kaniz Fatima Alikhan*
46. *The Truth Revealed: Volume 3,* by Hamid bin Shabbir, translated by Mir Baqir Alikhan, Syed Hamid Rizvi, and Kaniz Fatima Alikhan
47. *Weapon of the Believer,* by ʿAllāmah Muḥammad Bāqir Majlisī, translated by Saleem Bhimji*
48. *Weekly Spiritual Ascent: Ṣalāt al-Jumuʿah: Philosophy, Practice, and Personal Piety,* compiled and translated by Saleem Bhimji

Other Translations[2]

1. *40 Aḥādīth: Completion of Islam – Ghadīr,* by Mahmud Sharifi •
2. *40 Aḥādīth: Qur'an,* by Sayyid Majid Adili, translated by Arifa Hudda and Saleem Bhimji •
3. *40 Aḥādīth: The Saviour of Humanity – The 12th Imam in the Eyes of the Ahl al-Bayt,* by Nasir Karimi •
4. *40 Aḥādīth: The Spiritual Journey – Ḥajj,* by Mahmud Mahdipur •

---

[2] The following are other translations by Saleem Bhimji available from various publishers:

- Books with a "•" are published by The World Federation of KSIMC – **www.world-federation.org**
- Books with a "••" are published by Islamic Humanitarian Service (IHS) – **www.al-haqq.net**
- Books with a "•••" are published by the Islamic Publishing House (IPH), but are currently out of print – **www.iph.ca**
- Books with a "••••"have been published by various overseas publishers.
- Books with a "•••••" are published by Al-Kisa Foundation – **www.alkisfoundation.org**

5. *A Biography of the Marjaʿ Taqlid of the Shiʿa World: Āyatullāh al-ʿUẓmā Sayyid ʿAlī al-Ḥusaynī al-Sīstānī* ****
6. *A Code of Ethics for Muslim Men and Women,* by Sayyid Masʿud Maʿsumi, translated by Arifa Hudda and Saleem Bhimji **
7. *A Mother's Prayer,* compiled and translated by Saleem Bhimji and Arifa Hudda ** & ***
8. *A Summary of the Rulings of Ṣalātul Jamāʿat,* according to the edicts of Āyatullāh al-ʿUẓmā Sayyid ʿAlī al-Ḥusaynī al-Sīstānī **
9. *Ethical Discourses: Volume 1,* by Āyatullāh al-ʿUẓmā Shaykh Nāṣir Makārim Shīrāzī ***
10. *Ethical Discourses: Volume 2,* by Āyatullāh al-ʿUẓmā Shaykh Nāṣir Makārim Shīrāzī ***
11. *Ethical Discourses: Volume 3,* by Āyatullāh al-ʿUẓmā Shaykh Nāṣir Makārim Shīrāzī ***
12. *Guiding the Youth of the New Generation,* by Āyatullāh Murtaḍā Muṭahharī **
13. *History Behind Masjid Jamkarān along with Selected Supplications to the 12th Imam* **
14. *Introduction to Islam* **
15. *Introduction to the Science of Tafsīr of the Quran,* by Shaykh Jaʿfar Subḥānī **
16. *Islamic Edicts on Family Planning,* by the UNFPA with the Ministry of Health of the Islamic Republic of Iran ****
17. *Istikhāra: Seeking the Best from Allah,* by Muḥammad Bāqir Ḥayderī **
18. *Khums: The Islamic Tax,* by Āyatullāh al-ʿUẓmā Shaykh Nāṣir Makārim Shīrāzī (unpublished)
19. *Meʿrāj: The Night Ascension,* by Mullah Muḥammad Faydh al-Kāshānī **
20. *Message of the Quran: A Translation of Payām-e-Quran – Volume 1 – A Thematic Exegesis of the Noble Quran,* by Āyatullāh al-ʿUẓmā Shaykh Nāṣir Makārim Shīrāzī *

21. *Method of Ṣalāt,* by Muḥammad Qādhī ••••
22. *On the Shore of Contemplation: Authority of the Jurist (Wilāyatul Faqīh)* – compiled by the office of Shaykh Jaʿfar Subḥānī •••
23. *Rules Relating to the Deceased: Condensed Version,* according to the edicts of Āyatullāh al-ʿUẓmā Sayyid ʿAlī al-Ḥusaynī al-Sīstānī ••
24. *Rules Relating to the Deceased: Philosophy and Aḥkām,* according to the edicts of Āyatullāh al-ʿUẓmā Sayyid ʿAlī al-Ḥusaynī al-Sīstānī ••
25. *Simplified Islamic Laws for Youth and Young Adults,* according to the edicts of Āyatullāh al-ʿUẓmā Sayyid ʿAlī al-Ḥusaynī al-Sīstānī ••
26. *Simplified Islamic Laws for Youth and Young Adults,* according to the edicts of the late Āyatullāh al-ʿUẓmā Shaykh Luṭfullāh Ṣāfī Gulpāygānī ••••
27. *The Clear Guidance: The Quran – Volume 1 of...* •••••
28. *The Clear Guidance: The Quran – Volume 2 of...* •••••
29. *The Islamic Moral System: A Commentary of Sūrah al-Ḥujurāt,* by Shaykh Jaʿfar Subḥānī • & ••
30. *The Light of the Family of the Prophet: A Colouring Book with Ḥadīth for Young Muslim Children* ••
31. *The Tasbīḥ of Fāṭima al-Zahrā',* by ʿAbbas Azizi and translated by Arifa Hudda and Saleem Bhimji ••
32. *Ziyārah: History, Philosophy and Etiquette* •••

Upcoming Publications by the IPH

1. *Between Two Worlds: Navigating the Practical Laws of Burial in Islam* according to the edicts of Āyatullāh al-ʿUẓmā Sayyid ʿAlī al-Ḥusaynī al-Sīstānī, translated by Saleem Bhimji
2. *Blessed Desires: Islamic Perspectives on Sexuality and the Soul,* by ʿAlī Ḥoseinzādeh, translated by Saleem Bhimji
3. *Faith on the Move: Praying while Travelling,* according to the

edicts of Āyatullāh al-ʿUẓmā Sayyid ʿAlī al-Ḥusaynī al-Sīstānī, translated by Saleem Bhimji
4. *Guided By Faith: The Islamic Management Model*, by ʿAbbās Raḥīmī, translated by Saleem Bhimji
5. *Knocking on Heaven's Doors*, compiled with translations by Saleem Bhimji
6. *Morals of the Masumeen (Third Edition)*, written by Arifa Hudda
7. *Planting for Paradise: 40 Ḥadīth on Farming and the Eternal Rewards of Stewardship of the Earth*, translated by Saleem Bhimji
8. *Ramaḍān Devotions: A Collection of Supplications for the Nights of Qadr*, compiled with translations by Saleem Bhimji
9. *Sacred Remembrance: Understanding the Exclusive Significance of the Arbaʿīn of Imam al-Ḥusayn*, by the late Āyatullāh al-Sayyid Muḥammad Muḥsin Ḥusaynī Ṭehrānī, translated by Saleem Bhimji
10. *Secrets of the Ḥajj – Second Edition [25th Anniversary Edition]*, by Āyatullāh al-ʿUẓmā Shaykh Ḥusayn Mazāherī, translated by Saleem Bhimji
11. *Supplication for the People of the Frontiers*, by Shaykh Ḥusayn Anṣāriān, translated by Saleem Bhimji
12. *The Arbaʿīn: A Look into the Ziyārat of Arbaʿīn*, by Saleem Bhimji
13. *The Comprehensive Book of Marriage and Divorce Formulas*, by Saleem Bhimji
14. *The Ninth Day: The Complete Collection of Supplications for the Day of ʿArafah*, compiled and translated by Saleem Bhimji
15. *The Young Muslims Daily Devotions Manuals – Volumes I and II*, compiled and translated by Saleem Bhimji
16. *Victor Not Victim: A Biography of Lady Zaynab binte ʿAlī and two hundred Short Stories*, researched and written by Saleem Bhimji

The commentary of the following chapter of the Quran will also be released in the future under our, *Living The Quran Through The Living Quran,* series:

1. Sūrah al-Ṣaff (61)

Supporting Our Projects

عَنْ أَبِي عَبْدِ اللَّهِ عَنْ آبَائِهِ عليهم السلام: قَالَ جَاءَ رَجُلٌ إِلَىٰ رَسُولِ اللَّهِ ﷺ فَقَالَ: يَا رَسُولَ اللَّهِ مَا الْعِلْمُ؟ قَالَ أَلإِنْصَاتُ. قَالَ ثُمَّ مَهْ؟ قَالَ أَلإِسْتِمَاعُ. قَالَ ثُمَّ مَهْ؟ قَالَ أَلْحِفْظُ. قَالَ ثُمَّ مَهْ؟ قَالَ أَلْعَمَلُ بِهِ. قَالَ ثُمَّ مَهْ يَا رَسُولَ اللَّهِ؟ قَالَ: نَشْرُهُ.

Abū ʿAbdillāh [Imam Jaʿfar ibn Muḥammad al-Ṣādiq ﷺ] narrates from his ancestors ﷺ who said the following: "A man once came to the Messenger of Allah ﷺ and said: 'O Messenger of Allah, what is knowledge?' The Prophet replied: **'It is silence.'** The man then asked: 'Then what?' The Prophet said: **'It is listening.'** The man asked again: 'Then what?' The Prophet replied: **'Then it is remembering.'** The man asked: 'Then what?' The Prophet said: **'Then it is to practice (according to what one has learned).'** The man then asked: 'Then what O Messenger of Allah?' The Prophet replied: **'Then it is to disseminate (what one has learned to others).'"**[438]

Established in early 2001, gaining inspiration from the above *ḥadīth* from Prophet Muḥammad ﷺ, the *Islamic Publishing House* (IPH) is North America's premier publisher of high-quality Islamic literature for Muslims of all ages. Our mission is to ensure that the authentic teachings of Islam in all aspects of life as imparted by Prophet Muḥammad ﷺ and his immaculate family, the Ahlul Bayt ﷺ, are made available for everyone – in a clear and easy to understand language.

Over the past 25 years, we have been blessed to publish close to **50** full-length books which have been distributed throughout the world in print and digital format. In addition, we have released

---

438 *Al-Kāfī*, Vol. 1, Pg. 48, Tradition 4.

multiple ePubs and translated hundreds of articles – all thanks to the blessings of Allah ﷻ, the grace of the Prophet ﷺ, and his Ahlul Bayt عليهم السلام, and the continued support from donors all over the world.

Our publications and video content (found on YouTube under the name **Islamic Publishing House**) are all supported by generous individuals for whom we are extremely grateful.

As we continue to produce English publications and original video content, we invite those who have a passion for the spread of the teachings of Islam as preserved by the family of the Prophet Muḥammad ﷺ – namely the Ahlul Bayt عليهم السلام to assist us in promoting these teachings of Islam.

If you would like to donate to any of our ongoing projects, including our many upcoming book publications, video content, or articles, you can contribute in the following ways:

Within Canada: Send an e-transfer to **iph@iph.ca**

International: Send your transfer via PayPal to **saleem1176@rogers.com**

For more information, go to: **www.iph.ca**
Contact us at: **iph@iph.ca**

www.ingramcontent.com/pod-product-compliance
Lightning Source LLC
Chambersburg PA
CBHW071652090426
42738CB00009B/1501

* 9 7 8 1 9 2 7 9 3 0 6 1 8 *